"I did have a favorite Beatle (Pau., strictly for his looks). If pressed, I would name a favorite character on *Friends* (Phoebe, for her self-esteem). But choosing a favorite Satellite Sister is impossible. . . . I identify with Liz because she quit her job on her fortieth birthday and went out in search of something new. With Julie because she's an adventurer, living in Bangkok now. . . . With Monica because she's single and devoted to her 'small but needy' dog. With Sheila because she . . . once let herself get into a teeny bit of trouble with credit card debt. And with Lian because she's completely overcommitted but, when she grabs a free hour, spends it having an all Lancôme beauty make-over."
—Anita Gates, *The New York Times*

"The Dolans believe that the most underexplored love story is the bond between siblings. And their book certainly communicates plenty of affection amid the joys and indignities of life in a large family. . . . Their public radio show is a surprise hit . . . comfy, lively chat, the kind you'd expect from sisters whose lives are quite different . . . and yet who share an effortless, chip-proof familiarity."
—*Time*

"A unique perspective on how to get along in life . . . [with] reminiscences, lists of dos and don'ts, and even a few recipes."
—*Publishers Weekly*

"Our advice? . . . Get on board with these sisters." —*Daily Candy*

Julie, Liz,
Sheila,
Monica &
Lian Dolan

riverhead books

new york

Satellite Sisters'™

UnCommon
Senses

Most Riverhead Books are available at special quantity discounts for bulk purchases for sales promotions, premiums, fund-raising, or educational use. Special books, or book excerpts, can also be created to fit specific needs.

For details, write: Special Markets, The Berkley Publishing Group, 375 Hudson Street, New York, New York 10014.

RIVERHEAD BOOKS
Published by The Berkley Publishing Group
A division of Penguin Putnam Inc.
375 Hudson Street
New York, New York 10014

Satellite Sisters is a trademark of Satellite Sisters, LLC.

Copyright © 2001 by Satellite Sisters, LLC
Book design by Amanda Dewey
Cover design by Charles Björklund
Flower art adapted from an image © Photonica
Author photos © 2001 Anthony Barboza

First Riverhead hardcover edition: November 2001
First Riverhead trade paperback edition: November 2002
Riverhead trade paperback ISBN: 1-57322-954-7

Visit our website at www.penguinputnam.com

The Library of Congress has catalogued the Riverhead
hardcover edition as follows:

Uncommon senses/Satellite Sisters, Julie Dolan . . . et al.
p.   cm.
ISBN 1-57322-208-9
1. American wit and humor.   I. Dolan, Julie.   II. Satellite
Sisters (Radio program)
PN6165.U53   2001   2001048148
814'.608—dc21

Printed in the United States of America

10   9   8   7   6   5   4   3   2   1

To our mother and father

Our grandmother Klarman often said this to our mother
and her three sisters, and our mother often said it to us.

MANY HANDS MAKE LIGHT WORK.

Contents

Introduction

About five years ago, something happened in the universe—a small ripple to most people, but life changing to us. We five Dolan sisters, after a lifetime of growing up, growing apart, and then growing closer again, decided to work together. Five sisters, one gig. But doing what? Though we had a lot in common, our lives were very different. We lived all over the world, had lots of commitments elsewhere, and, frankly, had very few marketable talents. No singing, no dancing, no crafting abilities. We are all excellent swimmers, but no one should have to see all five of us in Speedos. And, really, very few people make a living from swimming. Our only collective skill: talking.

On a "sisters only" weekend at a rundown motel/mud bath in Calistoga, California, Liz made her pitch. She trapped her claustrophobic sisters in Lucy-and-Ethel steam baths and chin-high vats of mud and proposed a radio show. Her sisters were forced to cede to her wishes before the attendant would open the steam bath doors. For Julie, Sheila, Monica, and Lian, it was cave in or call the paramedics. Mudbath Productions was born and Satellite Sisters, the public radio show, got its start.

When we began to develop the radio program, we went in knowing two things for sure: We knew we wanted to conduct conversations that focused on how and why people made decisions in their lives. The practical nuts-and-bolts choices about everything from career moves to childcare issues, from writing a will to what to serve at Thanksgiving. We were interested in whatever it is inside that guides people during a period of transition, good or bad, the simple choices made every day that add up to an overall plan. In other words, the kind of conversations we had with each other.

Which leads to the second thing we knew going in: After spending our childhood trying to differentiate ourselves from each other, we were able to reconnect as adults in a positive, supportive way. People in our lives have always been interested in how we grew into adults, how we remained close despite our differences, and how our common experiences shaped us individually and collectively. We are Satellite Sisters, in blood and spirit, a connection that is uncomplicated and complex at the same time.

What would our show be about? Connection and conversation.

We suspected others out there had Satellite Sister connections, too—friendships that are positive, helpful, fun, and funny, like your real sisters and brothers, your best friends from high school, your walking partners, your great neighbor, your college suitemates, your friend from Mommy and Me. Your Satellite Sister connections are the ones critical for personal enrichment, wise counsel, and everyday survival. With this in mind, we came up with a guiding principle for the show: Not every conversation changes your life, but any conversation can.

So we had a name and a motto, but what *exactly* would we talk about? As a creative exercise, we made some lists about what was important in our lives, how we prioritized, what our biggest influences had been, and how we made decisions. When we compared our individual lists, there was a lot of common ground. We made decisions relying on what we now call the "uncommon senses," many of which we developed growing up in a large family. Did other people make choices using these same senses? The great thing about having a radio show is that we could just ask our guests. So we did.

When we took to the airwaves, guests on the show consistently revealed that they used their uncommon senses to make leaps, navigate transitions, build connections, and be the activists in their own lives. Listeners, too, soon wrote in to share their own stories of which paths they've taken in their lives and why. Or they wrote to tell us about their struggles and solicited our advice. How did we know when something was right or wrong? How did we arrive at this place or that? When did we follow the rules and when did we follow our gut? Those kinds of questions from listeners got us thinking about our imperfect methodology for carving out a life.

Growing up in a big family is great preparation for the big world. All the team-building skills that they try to teach you in grad school, we learned by doing the dishes, sharing rooms, borrowing clothes, bickering over the TV, trading chores, cleaning our rooms, fighting over the front seat, setting the table, and always, always, always traveling in large groups.

As sisters, we shared an approach to life that was rooted in big-family wisdom, and so we refined our developing theory. There are the five senses you are born with, and then there are others you develop over time. We reached consensus surprisingly quickly on what precisely these extrasensory senses are, identifying them as a sense of connection, a sense of self, a sense of humor, a sense of adventure, and a sense of direction.

In our Satellite Sister cosmos, we often use the dinner party as a metaphor. If life is like a dinner party, then a sense of connection guides you to arrive not too early, not too late, and to remember the names of the guests. A sense of self means that you are comfortable in purple even if everyone else is in black. A sense of humor lets you laugh off that blob of artichoke dip that lands on your skirt, courtesy of the guy in the plaid sport coat, and then make a quick toast to the hostess. A sense of adventure encourages you to say "Why not?" when the guy in the plaid coat, who, it turns out, loves experimental theater as much as you, suggests going for a nightcap afterward. And a sense of direction backs you up when you know it's time to go home—alone.

So, pull up a chair, grab a cup of coffee, and settle in. We'll share how we developed our uncommon senses. Where did you learn yours?

MEET THE SATELLITE SISTERS

Before we started Satellite Sisters, we were just the Dolan sisters. We grew up in Fairfield, Connecticut, and spent a lot of time raking leaves, hanging out at Subway, lifeguarding at the beach, and taking the train into and out of New York City. Our mother, Edna Klarman Dolan, made huge meals, cultivated a beautiful garden, worked endless hours as a volunteer, pleaded with us to clean up our rooms, and generally held down the fort. Our father, Jim Dolan, owned a family business in Bridgeport and loved the opera, books, and telling a great story. We also had three brothers who ruled the TV room, took out the garbage, taught us how to drive, and tortured us whenever our parents weren't looking. We were an average family, just bigger.

The family rundown, from oldest child to youngest, looks like this: Jim, Dick, Julie, Liz, Sheila, Monica, Brendan, and Lian. Thirteen years separate the oldest from the youngest.

Julie Dolan is the big sister both chronologically and spiritually. If you're wondering about the right chintz for your couch or what to do with your 401(k), Julie is the one to call. She has been married for more than twenty years to Trem Smith and they have two college-age sons, Nick and Will. Julie and her family have moved eleven times, most recently to Bangkok. Before relocating overseas, Julie worked in MBA admissions at a number of major universities, including UCLA Anderson School of Management. In her twenty years as a working mother, Julie has tried every childcare arrangement ever known and has worked full-time, part-time, telecommuted, and even commuted from the West Coast to the East Coast weekly. She was incredibly tired for two decades. In her new career as a "trailing spouse," Julie studies Thai and yoga and has already managed to overcommit herself to a number of school and community volunteer groups. Julie counts guilt and the desire to please as her biggest motivators.

Liz Dolan is the second oldest sister but the one with the most common sense. Most Dolan family holiday get-togethers wouldn't happen if Liz didn't own a day planner and a cell phone. Other people may talk about taking charge of their lives, but in a pinch, Liz would be happy to do it for you. She climbed to the top of the corporate ladder as Nike's vice president of marketing via her savvy, wit, and hard work, then chucked it all at age forty to get a life. Only then did she discover that she is a workaholic. So far Liz's early retirement has yielded a radio show, a hefty time commitment to several non-profit organizations, and more frequent flyer miles than she cares to admit. Liz is single and splits her time between New York City; Portland, Oregon; and the Red Carpet Room at Denver International Airport. She spends most of her free time watching C-SPAN and dreaming about having a permanent address.

Sheila Dolan may be the middle sister, but she's always been a little off-center, even by her own admission. Sheila is divorced and lives in Greenwich Village, her favorite place on earth, with her college-age daughter, Ruth. Sheila was a teacher in the New York City school system for many years, eventually starting and directing her own public elementary school. She recently left teaching and devotes her time to answering the e-mails from the radio show and standing in line for her tall double-decaf lattés. Sheila holds a BA and two masters degrees which she charged on a now-defunct Visa. Sheila one day hopes to own a cleaning service to satisfy her Irish washerwoman fantasy.

Monica Dolan spent fifteen years as a nurse in hospitals all across the country. This career choice came as a surprise to her sisters, who relied on Monica more for a quick joke than a caring look. But Monica was a born nurse and a born traveler, traits that serve her well in her current job as a medical researcher for a pacemaker company. Monica lives in Portland, Oregon, where she owns a home in constant need of repair, and has a high-needs yellow Lab, Quin. She is single and spends her free time planning her next vacation, mowing her own lawn, and going to the movies.

 **Lian Dolan** is the youngest sister, but she can also be the sassiest. It is payback for years of teasing at the hands of her older brothers and sisters. Lian is married to Berick Treidler and is the mother of two young boys, Brookes and Colin. She is currently juggling a nationally syndicated radio show and the delusion that she is a stay-at-home mom. Lian's work experience includes waitressing, ski instructing, film producing, and screenwriting, all career choices that her family mocked, and yet all skills that came in handy in the writing of this book. Go figure. Lian lives in Pasadena, California, and now that her shot at Rose Queen has come and gone, she'd settle for just riding on a float in the Rose Parade.

We decided our brothers deserved a few moments of their own, at least in this portion of the book.

Jim Dolan is the cool older brother everyone should have. A Paul McCartney look-alike, Jim trailblazed everything from groovy shoes (clogs, Earth Shoes, Dr. Scholl's) to Tiger's Milk bars and turtlenecks. Jim has been married to his college sweetheart Mary McGuire, an attorney, for twenty-five years. They have two teenage daughters, Meghan and Katherine, and live in Connecticut. Jim works in the pharmaceutical business and always has a black bag full of antibiotics and the latest allergy medications, an excellent accessory for family holidays. Who needs a doctor in the family when you have "The Doctor"?

Dick Dolan spent much of his wild youth providing cover for his younger, tamer sisters. There wasn't really any mischief we could get into that compared with fourteen-year-old Dick sneaking off to Woodstock, telling our parents it was "an arts and crafts festival." Dick now leads a quiet life with his wife, Susan Arnold, and their children, Leo and Fiona. Dick started his own computer consulting business servicing state governments. As a result, Dick can not only name all the state capitals, he has lived in most of them. Now retired, Dick devotes himself to masonry (yes, really) and riding the motor-cycle our mother wouldn't let him get when he was eighteen.

Brendan Dolan spent a large portion of his youth either on a sports team or on the couch watching a sports team, so it is fitting he now makes his living in sports marketing. He counts the late Yankee captain Thurman Munson as one of his greatest influences. He lives in Denver with his wife, Laura Leibesman, and their young sons, Sam and Daniel. When he's not watching the Food Network, Brendan keeps himself busy by saving the whale popu-lation, adopting one mammal at a time. Brendan enjoys his boys, his wife, and snacks.

It took more than a village to raise our family. It took a universe that included hundreds of others, including aunts, uncles, cousins, neighbors, family friends, best friends, piano teachers, milkmen, school principals, baby-sitters, coaches, camp counselors, complete

strangers, that mean kid in second grade, and Hugh Downs, many of whom you will meet in this book. We were a big family with a big support system. Their names are important to us, but for you they aren't critical. Just know that, along the way, we have had lots of help in developing our uncommon senses.

Julie, Liz, Sheila, Monica, and Lian Dolan
Bangkok, New York, Portland, and Pasadena
July 2001

a sense of

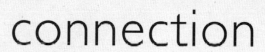

connection

A Sense of Connection

by Julie

We are five real sisters, born of the same parents, raised in the same house, fed the same clam chowder. We shared rooms, took baths, and went to camp and school together. We spent hours outside playing dodgeball, kickball, baseball, football, and capture-the-flag. When it got cold, we moved inside to play school, board games, and make houses out of cardboard boxes, blankets, and stacked furniture.

I am the oldest sister. Liz, Sheila, and Monica follow in quick succession, and Lian is the youngest. We also have two older brothers, Jim and Dick. A younger brother, Brendan, was born among the sisters.

We had one TV, one phone, and one station wagon. If you wanted to watch television, you would have to negotiate with Jim and Dick to watch *The Love Boat* by agreeing to turn to the Yankees game during the commercials. On the phone, you learned to talk quickly and in hushed tones because there was always someone listening or waiting. And if you wanted the station wagon to go shopping in Westport, it meant you had to drop off Brendan and his friends at the movies first.

We wore the same clothes. In the winter, the girls wore matching red coats and red berets; the boys had blue jackets. In spring, we had coordinating Easter dresses. My all-time favorite sister dress was a Marlo Thomas/*That Girl*–like dress—in white with red and blue polka dots. For summer, my mother found six bathing suits—four tank suits for the girls and two Speedo-style racers suits for the boys—all in the same Florence Eisman pattern. Brendan and Lian, as the two youngest of the group, missed out on the initial seasons of many of these outfits but were compensated by having a ten-year supply of the same jackets, dresses, or bathing suits.

You were always someone's younger or older sibling. No matter what you had to do, you could always bring along a brother or sister. My first day of kindergarten was less traumatic because Mrs. Friend asked me if I was Dick's sister. When I went to camp, Liz and Sheila were on the bus with me. Jim drove me to school dances. Monica, Lian, and Sheila helped me look at colleges. Dick moved me three or four times. At my wedding, my brothers and sisters were the ushers and bridesmaids. And, on my first day at a real corporate job, Liz came with me to the employee orientation.

I learned that what happened to others affects me. If Dick got in trouble for carelessly blocking the back door with his discarded hockey bag, my relative standing with my mother was elevated. If Sheila and Monica were fighting about a sweater, I knew that this was not the moment to appeal to my parents about extending my curfew; when Jim and Dick painted me instead of the picnic bench, we were all going to get it.

We honed our sisters' act doing the endless dishes for a family of ten. We didn't think of it as an act then; we were doing what we were told. Night after day after night, we washed, talked, laughed, and did some truly bad renditions of "You Don't Bring Me Flowers." Despite being raised in the era of the Osmonds, the Jacksons, and the Bradys, we harbored no career aspirations in the entertainment field—only the hope that someday our mother would get the dishwasher fixed. In truth, we were more like the Loud family on the original "reality television" series, PBS's *An American Family*: big talkers, bad haircuts, and, well, loud.

Like most family acts, the inevitability of growing up took its toll. We stopped washing dishes together and started living our own lives. We moved out, went to school, got degrees, slept on each other's couches, borrowed money, lent money, got married, got promotions, lost weight, gained weight, stayed single, quit jobs, moved again, had kids, got divorced, found yoga, and stayed friends. It was around this time that we decided to take the plunge and work together.

We discovered that, after years of trying to distinguish ourselves from one another during childhood and adolescence, we wanted to reconnect with each other as adults. We had different lives, and we lived all over the world, but we still needed each other. So we started a public radio show called *Satellite Sisters* to have the kind of conversations on the air that sisters have in real life. We thought that connection might resonate with other people.

Each week, I get up in the middle of the night in Bangkok, down a Coke, and hook up by ISDN line to Liz and Sheila, who are eating lunch in New York, and Lian and Monica, who are drinking their first cups of coffee on the West Coast. Each week we talk, laugh, and sometimes Lian cries. We try to entertain, encourage, empathize with, and enlighten our guests, listeners, and each other.

So far, we've talked about going to a college reunion, clearing up bad credit, finding a lump, tracking a lost dog, having sex after childbirth, breaking the glass ceiling, making the perfect pie, surviving a brain tumor, applying to kindergarten, applying to college, living more simply, writing poetry, getting a new roof, and raising trout.

What surprised us when we started talking on the radio was why people said they were listening. They told us that it really didn't matter what the topic was—they just liked listening to sisters talk. People immediately understood what the show was really about—connecting with family and friends.

We didn't have to explain what a Satellite Sister was. Our listeners knew. They wrote to us to tell us about their three sisters, or their one brother who is like a sister, their mothers and grandmothers, their running group, knitting group, scrapbooking group, their book club, their painting class, their college roommates, their best friends, their cubicle mates, and their cul-de-sac neighbors. Sometimes they wrote to us to say that they didn't have any brothers or sisters and liked listening to us because it allowed them to imagine what having a sister might be like. Others wrote to us about being distant or estranged from their sisters and apologized to us for not being close to their family.

They wrote us about monthly dinner groups, weekly girls-nights-out, spa weekends, and annual weeklong reunions. They told us about how they play music, read books, swim, sail, ski, and ride horses together, bareback and naked. They wrote to us about supporting each other through promotions, firings, childbirth, cancer, divorce, relocations, hysterectomies, widowhood, marriage, and raising teenagers.

Our listeners believe what we believe: that being someone's sister, or brother, or teacher, or friend, is what gives meaning to our lives. Nurturing relationships is what shapes who we are and how we live. We know that you don't have to have shared the same bathroom or traveled in packs of ten to be connected. Those just happen to be our reasons. Most of us are bound together by sharing the small everyday acts of life with the people in our lives who support, accept, sometimes bust, and always encourage us.

A sense of connection is the realization that going through life with other people is a better way to go. My sisters and brothers give me the courage to try things, back me up when I fail, laugh at me, laugh with me, teach me, occasionally cry with me, and show me how to understand people who are different from me. I don't ever want to live with my brothers and sisters again, but I don't want to live my life without them.

Writing a book with my sisters seems like a natural progression from playing dress-up, riding bikes, and styling each other's hair with the one family blow-dryer. It is just another group activity, like going to swim-team practice or to the library. It is not something that I would ever attempt by myself. Like going to kindergarten, camp, or college, writing a book together with my sisters makes it OK.

Like the radio show, we are working together, alone. This time we are sitting at computers thousands and thousands of miles apart, writing to each other about what we remember about growing up and how growing up in a big family has shaped us as adults. It is a collective look back at life in a big family and the uncommon senses we have developed along the way. We aren't radio professionals. We aren't journalists. We aren't experts. Some of us aren't even writers. We are just sisters. And maybe that is enough.

You Are Not Alone

by Lian

From the very first day of my life, I knew that I was not alone. I was part of something bigger. I could look around and see that my life was filled with people, and that was OK. As far as I could tell, all these people had some purpose in my life, big or small. I was the number 8 hitter on Team Dolan. (You see, we were an American League family, complete with a DH rule. Now batting ninth, one of the Morningstar cousins.) I was also one of twenty-seven grandchildren on my mother's side. I was a native of Fairfield, Connecticut, and a citizen of the United States. I was surrounded, and that's what I came to expect. It's not that I don't like to be alone; I just like to know that I am not alone. I like to feel connected.

The sense of connection was congenital. I was born into an intricate web of affiliations that included my seven brothers and sisters, my parents, aunts, uncles, and cousins from my mother's side, and my aunts, uncles, and cousins from my father's side—and beyond the family, to friends, neighbors, and others who helped our big family make it through the week. Work, community, and church connections extended beyond those. And we had an awareness of what was happening out there, in the big world, through newspapers, conversations, TV, and books. We had a lot of people in our lives. We were not alone, and that is the way it should be.

Growing up in the Dolan household involved a lot of rules, both explicit ("Pick your Barbies and Hula-Hoops up off the floor") and implicit ("Don't talk back or else"). What I didn't realize then, but I know now, is that all those rules imposed a code of behavior that would carry us through our whole lives. I'm not suggesting some oppressive militarylike code that might result in eating disorders and a made-for-TV movie starring Shannen Doherty. Rather, I'm talking about a set of guiding principles that would come in handy later in life, which imparted an understanding of what we would need to do to get along in the world as adults.

I would sum up the underlying principle of nearly all household rules as follows: You're not the only person in the whole damn world, so you better get over yourself and pitch in for the good of the group. This may sound cold, but in a big family, it is the simple truth. For better or worse, I was not alone. I was part of something bigger, so I had better learn to make those connections work.

The circles of connection began with my immediate family and then quickly extended to my aunts, uncles, and cousins, even though most of them lived a state away. I realize now how special that was and how much effort and effortlessness it took on the part of my parents. We shared many one-day events with my cousins, from the usual—birthday parties, holidays, graduations—to the more elaborate—watching the Boston Marathon, Bicentennial reenactments, and mandatory *Nutcracker* performances. These events posed huge logistical challenges that the adults pulled off with relative grace time and time again.

We had an extended-stay family policy as well. My mother and her three sisters used to conduct a child exchange over every major school holiday and summer vacation. As kids, we thought nothing of swapping houses, siblings, and parents for a few days or a few weeks. The Lockery and Kirshner cousins lived outside of Boston, across the street from each other. (In fact, they still live across the street.) My Morningstar cousins lived in Westchester County, New York. Our house was centrally located in Connecticut. For February vacation or in August, a couple of Dolans and Morningstars would head up to Boston in exchange for a few Lockerys and Kirshners. Most exchanges involved at least three families and several modes of transportation, including the rest-area-exchange scenario, during which the sisters emptied their wood-paneled station wagons of offspring and refilled them with cousins.

I spent Easter vacations with my Morningstar cousins and felt right at home in my aunt's house. At my house, I had only my brother Brendan, older by three years, as a real playmate, my sisters being at least six years older than me. At the Morningstars, I had cousins Billy, Martha, and Mary. Though I was still the youngest of this group, they did not inflict the relentless torture and teasing that characterized the regime of my brother Brendan. With Mary, Martha, and Billy, I'd re-create *Brady Bunch* episodes in the garage, practice cheerleading cow jumps, and make endless phony phone calls, singing a jingle for Swanky Franks hot dog stand that we had made up into the ears of unsuspecting people. One of the reasons I loved my aunt's house so much was because she allowed her children seemingly unrestricted use of the phone, a privilege rarely granted in our house. I can remember one visit when I was about seven that seemed to stretch on for weeks, with my aunt Eleanor asking every couple of days if I'd like to go home. No, I'm fine here, I'd reply.

Beyond the family, my parents developed a wide network of people to help us get from sunup to sundown—no easy task for a family of ten and a dog. These people ran the gamut, from a series of foreign-born babysitters who spoke just enough English to say "yes" to the job but not enough to leave once they realized it meant watching eight kids, not "ate" kids, to professionals such as our dentist Dr. Ring who gave out great fake jewelry in homage to his name. There was my mother's favorite butcher at Manero's, and the same guy that fixed our same broken washing machine for twenty years, and a man named Knobby who would fill in wherever needed, from dog-sitting to driving carpools. There was even a Mrs. Knobby, who would fill in for her husband in an emergency. My parents never took these people for granted. Every chance she got, my mother would thank them with a basket of blueberry muffins or an arrangement of bittersweet purloined from the median of I-95.

My parents also took their community ties seriously. My father spent lots of time and effort on his college alumni council—going to events and raising money in ways that involved all of us. (In fact, when it was time for me to go to college, I didn't even bother applying to my father's alma mater because I felt as if I had already attended the College of the Holy Cross.) My father also worked for an organization called The International Institute, which seemed to have some far-reaching goals that ranged from relocating Vietnamese refugees to sponsoring cultural-awareness events, before cultural awareness was even a term. I attended the fairs of almost every nationality in town—that's where I learned step dancing and Ukrainian Easter egg making. Our freezer seemed to be stocked with an endless supply of Curacao meatballs.

My mother's list of affiliations was long, stretching from the Cub Scouts to the Historical Society. My mother led history walks and tours of the wetlands for local schoolchildren. She planted thousands of seasonal bulbs in her efforts for the Garden Club. Once, she enlisted me in helping her make 10,000 hors d'oeuvres (yes, ten thousand) for a fund-raiser for a local children's charity. My mother decorated the firehouse at Christmas and the church many weeks of the year. She was also the one to show up with a warm note and a caramel custard in hand whenever a neighbor was ill. (In those days, the cholesterol/heart-attack link was not as well-known. We have no data on how many neighbors my mother might have inadvertently killed with those ten-egg custards.)

We kids were encouraged to connect to the outside world, too—a somewhat risky proposition in the 70s. Don't get me wrong, my parents weren't radicals by any means. But they did have interests that went beyond accepted suburban standards, whatever those were. This was the Age of Aquarius, after all, when the world as they knew it was being turned upside down. The sheer number of children and the age range in our family meant that, especially for the younger ones, we got a little more freedom and a lot more exposure than many of the kids we knew. We read the newspaper, watched the evening news, and took the train by ourselves into New York City, a world away from our quiet town.

We talked about the Vietnam War around the dinner table. I was very young and didn't understand it in political terms; I understood it in terms of the people we knew. Benny Jacobellis, the cute lifeguard at the pool, drew a bad number in the draft and would probably go to Vietnam. My brother Jim suffered from asthma and my brother Dick was deaf in one ear, the result of scarlet fever at age two; they would not be going to Vietnam. One morning, the FBI came to our house to search for Dan Berrigan, the radical Catholic priest whose brother had been a college classmate of my father's. The only thing the agents found in our attic were posters of Davy Jones from *Tiger Beat* magazine, but just knowing that they thought Dan Berrigan might be hiding out in our attic made me think a lot about how we were connected to all kinds of people and issues and events beyond our front door.

Even before our sixteenth birthdays, my parents made us all get jobs. It's one thing to discuss, observe, and analyze the world, but to really connect, there's nothing like getting into the workforce. We could take what we learned at our house about being part of some-thing bigger and apply it to food service or childcare or house painting. We had to learn to get along with bosses, coworkers, cus-tomers—connecting with strangers for the first time, and making those connections all on our own.

I have never questioned being a part of something bigger. I've never wanted to disappear or reinvent myself. I would not be a good candidate for the witness protection program because I could not give up all that I have known. From watching my parents, I learned that developing a sense of connection was critical not just for personal sat-isfaction, but for survival. When I was little, we needed those other people and they seemed to need us. Now I realize that I could not operate as an independent agent out in the big world any more than I could in a big family. I accept and prefer that I am one small cog in a big giant wheel, a wheel that includes family, friends, coworkers, strangers—all kinds of connections. And I've learned that it's the quality of these connections that determines the quality of my life.

Get Over Yourself

by Liz

Some people find out much too late in life that they are not the center of the universe. This must come as a real blow at age twenty-one or forty-one or sixty-one.

Luckily, in a big family you know this from birth. If I had any doubt, it was settled when I was eleven. That's when I found out that we'd been celebrating my birthday on the wrong date for the first decade of my life.

I don't remember being especially shocked. I don't even remember being told. It's just that one year we changed my birth-date from September 12 to September 11. OK. Fine.

A big family means many birth certificates, baptismal records, and immunization reports. That's just the paperwork. There are also many birthdays, anniversaries, holy days of obligation, and other general festivities and command performances. The calendar gets very crowded. If one event slips one day in either direction, no one really notices.

My birthday slipped one day off, then later simply moved back. I've never asked my parents how this might have happened in the first place. It doesn't really matter to me. I went from sharing my birthday with my cousin Joe Morningstar (September 12) to sharing it with my cousin Ted Lockery (September 11). My brother Jim also had a birthday the same week (September 16). Birthday parties in our extended family were often done in batches, so the mid-September party would feature a giant sheet cake that was three-fourths blue and one-fourth pink with birthday wishes for Joe, Ted, Jim, and Liz. Other times we would do "the September girls" as a batch—that would be me (September 11/12) and Sheila (September 30). So as you see, under this system, the specific DOB wasn't that critical.

I still got presents and felt it was my party, but that did not mean that only I got presents or only I was having a party. There is a subtle but essential difference. If you want to learn to get over yourself, sharing your birthday is a good way.

A truly curious reader might ask how the Birthday Boo-boo was uncovered. Good question! That's a little unusual, too. It turns out that in 1968 my parents realized that technically they had two daughters named Lian: one born in 1957 (me) and the other born in 1965 (uh, Lian—the real Lian). Eight kids. Two Lians. This happened because they had originally planned to name me Lian, so on whatever day I was born, that is the name they gave to the nurses at St. Raphael's Hospital in New Haven. Weeks later, but before I was baptized, they caved to severe family pressure coming from both grandmothers and went with the more traditional Elizabeth. Thus, I have always been Elizabeth, except for those first several weeks and on my birth certificate.

Did you know that it only costs a dollar to change your first name legally? That's what we had to do to clear up the confusion. The dollar was completely worth it because that's how we discovered the incorrect birthdate. I think that's a good deal—a new name and a new birthday for a buck!

I have shared my various birthdays with cousins and my name with a sister. It's a good lesson. Nothing is ever completely about you. It's about the connections between you and others.

Are there any lasting scars from all this childhood uncertainty? By all means, yes. My friends will tell you that I simply cannot remember their birthdays. No matter how hard I try, the dates just do not take hold in my brain. I am also really bad at remembering people's names.

Birthdays, names—there are things in life that are much more important, like enjoying a cake that's three-fourths blue and one-fourth pink. Yum.

Me and My Shadow

by Sheila
footnotes by Monica

Everybody needs a best friend. Most of the time, I had one, but when they weren't around, I had Monica.[1] We were a year apart in age and we went through all the trials and tribulations that best friends endure and then some. A best friend goes home to her own house at the end of the school day, but your buddy sister stays with you for the full twenty-four hours. I'm sure there were some nights Monica went to bed wishing we weren't related but, in the light of day, when she needed a certain pair of jeans that I owned, our special relationship was instantly restored.

Monica and I gravitated toward each other, I think, because we were both interested in *things*, while our big sisters Julie and Liz were concerned with *ideas* and *principles*. The only belief the two of us held was that everybody deserved a decent outfit, so on a daily basis you have to grab for whatever clothes you think you need. Not everyone in the family shared this belief, so the two of us often ran into a little trouble fulfilling our credo. I admired Monica's courage in the face of danger, because Lord knows I put her in some tight spots when we were teens.[2]

[1] I was definitely the default best friend bound by age and an uncanny ability to fabricate alibis.
[2] The tight spots started way before we were teens. Like the time at summer camp, when Sheila dragged my innocent cousin Mary and me into her stealing-sodas-from-the-counselor's-cabin "caper." Sheila was a mastermind at this kind of escapade. She had thoroughly cased the counselor's cabin and knew they kept a stash of forbidden Coca-Cola by the back door. We were instructed to hang back from the other campers on the trek home from the required morning lake swim.

Monica was the perfect ally and partner in crime. She kept quiet while I tried to explain my way out of situations, and she understood my pain when I didn't succeed. She came to my aid when I found myself completely defeated after a botched clothes heist. Sometimes, I would make it as far as Julie's closet when Mom would walk in with some fresh laundry and bust me. Times were tough, so I started scavenging through miscellaneous closets, including my brothers' drawers and the musty old attic that harbored some rare clothing items that smelled like mothballs. I taught Monica all I knew about layering (wearing borrowed clothing items under your own), early-morning raids, and footwear.[3]

Monica and I shared the proletariat's view: Life was simply harder for the two of us. We needed to rebel against the forces that controlled us, but mainly, we just needed our stuff. I didn't feel any big-sister superiority over Monica. Maybe that was because I was always getting in trouble and, as a result, I knew I could always count on Monica for getting in trouble with me, because of me, or instead of me. It could have been routine grumbling about doing a chore or babysitting Brendan, but if the two of us were involved, the incident inevitably escalated. We just couldn't let things be. Julie's savoir faire didn't rub off on us, nor did we exhibit any of Liz's good sense. We were a dangerous combination of clumsiness and bad judgment.

It was always "Sheila's in trouble" or "Monica and Sheila are in trouble" or "Monica's in trouble; where's Sheila?" The best part of

Our mission was to hide as many soda cans as we could in our towels, run into the woods, and chug the Cokes. Mary and I were too terrified not to follow her lead—my first living example of peer pressure. Oh, by the way, of course we were totally busted by the head counselor on our second raid.

[3] This is absolutely true. Sheila taught me the fine art of hiding/wearing forbidden garments to school under our winter coats, only to unveil our true outfits at the bus stop.

getting in trouble was having someone there to commiserate with after the fact. It was at those times when my affection for Monica grew even deeper. She was probably thinking, "Better you than me," as she sat at the end of my bed, flipping through *Seventeen* and looking up every few minutes as I railed against humanity, but Monica made me feel like a victor even though I had just been grounded.

Our most epic caper took place when we were in high school. It was 1976, and I was a few weeks away from graduating. Monica and I had transferred to Roger Ludlowe High School together from Catholic school, which "didn't work out" for us. Our bond became even stronger during those two years at Ludlowe, as we learned to survive life at a big school together.[4] That's also when our fighting became more intense, but in those days we didn't know anything about raging hormones. I thought everyone screamed and cried and threw shoes before they left for school in the morning.

In the weeks leading up to the event, Monica and I had been on a fighting jag for weeks. Mom and Dad had had it, and we were running out of steam as well. It's hard to keep up that caustic energy from 7:00 A.M. to 9:00 P.M. Still, even when we were at school in our separate classes, I could sense Monica's fury.

On the morning of that fateful day, Monica and I were finishing our breakfast in the kitchen. Jimmy blew in, grabbed his coat, and headed out the back door for the garage. "Those breakfast dishes better be done when I get back," he called to us over his shoulder.[5]

---

[4]This basically meant retreating to the girls' lav (lavatory) in the basement with our one mutual friend, Polly Wallace, to smoke cigarettes while everyone else was flirting with the football players in the giant lunchroom upstairs. We were labeled "weirdos," which was perfectly fine with Sheila and me.

[5]Jimmy's actual words were "This sh★t better be cleaned up by the time I get home from work"—harsh words from a brother we had never heard swear before.

We stared at each other in disbelief: *This can't be our life.* We were already in trouble because we were fighting. Mom and Dad had left on a trip that day, and before they had gone, they'd let us know that we were pretty much grounded for the rest of the year. Jimmy was in charge, there was a sink full of dishes, so we made a break for it as soon as we heard his car peel out of the driveway—but not before we grabbed some money from our jewelry boxes.

As soon as we had made our getaway, we decided take a walk around the block. I needed a cigarette. (Another bad habit I passed on to my little sister and confidante.) We had to regroup, come up with a plan. We sat on the side of Westway Road and considered our options. Go home, do the dishes, and be grounded. Or go home, don't do the dishes, and get in more trouble from Jimmy. Or blow this one-horse town for the Big Apple and see how they do without us. They'll appreciate us when we're gone! I felt a tingling in my stomach as we hatched the scheme. We counted our change and headed for the train station in Southport. This was big.[6]

The plan was to get on a train and just see what happens. Well, the hour ride from Southport to Grand Central was good for one thing—it killed an hour. It's amazing how slowly time passes when you're on the lam. Though I'd been to Grand Central many times before, everything looked different. There seemed to be more people, more noise, and less fun. This wasn't fun, just going to New York without a plan. The only thing I knew to do was go to Zum Zums, the wacky German coffee shop upstairs where they served hot dogs on round silver plates and you could smoke all you wanted. We took another meeting there.

"What do you want to do?" I asked Monica after a long silence.

"Do?" she said.

Oh God, I knew we were sunk. Neither one of us could think

---

[6]Sheila didn't need to twist my arm this time; I was ready to run.

of anything even mildly exciting to take away the sting of being grounded. Our limited funds were already gone.[7] Still, if we had been more organized, this would have been an outrageous story to tell one day. As it was, no one even knew we were in the city, and so that made it just another stupid idea that I came up with to pass the time and be able to smoke in public. We had no choice; we headed home.

On the way back, we started scheming again. We couldn't help it. Monica came up with the big idea to spend the night at the Church's house. The family lived near the train station and the house was always filled with miscellaneous kids from the neighborhood. Monica's best friend, Susie Church, would cover for us, she said. At this point, we had no idea where Jimmy was and if he even cared that we were missing. If no one knows you have run away, it kind of takes away the drama. We decided not to call home, just ride this thing out to the end. We slept over at the Church's without a hitch.[8] Waking up in a strange house was not the ending I had imagined for our most daring teenage escapade.

The short walk home down Center Street that morning felt a lot longer. I was defeated and scared but didn't want my little sister to see me feeling down. As the two of us had done so many times before, we went over our story. We tried to anticipate what would happen when we walked in the back door. Maybe Jimmy would be sitting there, waiting, and we'd get to tell him the tale of our escape to New York. That would be great. Maybe he had called the Connecticut State Police and they were out looking for us along I-95. That wouldn't be so great. The worst-case scenario was if Mom and Dad had been contacted, but we figured he wouldn't do that

[7]At this point our whole "running away from home" scheme really sucked.
[8]Mrs. Church was our idea of a totally cool mom. The next morning in the kitchen she said, "Don't you think you ought to call your parents or go home? They'll be worried." I think at this point I started to cry.

because he was supposed to be in charge and that would make him look bad.

Like collared convicts, we walked slowly down the back steps leading to the kitchen. Opening the screen door, I felt that familiar twinge of dread coming up through my toes. We tiptoed in and took a look around. No one was waiting for us at the kitchen table. I took a peek outside and didn't see a soul. We stood there for a minute and waited. The coast was clear; we had been successful after all. I turned around to give my partner the high five but she was already headed upstairs to have a look around.

Staring out the kitchen window, I thought about the last twenty-four hours with Monica. She had really pulled through for me. She didn't give up, even when things looked grim back there in Grand Central Station. Coming up with the Church overnight plan—now that was impressive stuff for an eleventh grader. I had taught her well.

I looked in the sink and saw the breakfast dishes from the day before still sitting there, crusted over with cereal and jam. I rolled up my sleeves and turned on the faucet. Welcome home, Thelma and Louise.[9]

---

[9]I thought this life of crime would all end when Sheila went off to college, but she still managed to drag me into her troubles. It took several years and a move four states away to break free.

Find Your People

by Liz

There are the people you are born with and then there are the people you find. They are equally important in your life.

I am very lucky that the people I was issued at birth are good people—my parents, my brothers and sisters, and my extended family of cousins, aunts, uncles, and family friends. This circle of good people reaches all the way out to Norman Kenneally, my parents' pal who drove around every Christmas Eve in an old VW Bug with the top down, dressed as Santa Claus, delivering gifts to friends. These were my original people, and it was a great start on the road to finding people of my own.

Being an adult has taught me that, as important as it is to maintain friendships with your original people, it is also key to find your own. These are your Satellite Sisters, both male and female—the friends you identify the first week of freshman year or during last call at the neighborhood pub. I have found My People in the cubicle next to me, in the apartment upstairs from me, and in my book club. One morning one friend brings another friend running, and it sticks forever. Other times the funny stranger across the table at an industry lunch is just who you need in your life. Don't get me wrong. There aren't loads of Your People out there. That is why it is important to be on the lookout. Your People are hard to find.

Over the years, I have developed a few questions I ask myself in order to determine whether I have found My People:

Do you do things with these people that you would never do alone? For instance, left to my own devices I would never watch an action-adventure movie. With My People, it is: Rent *Lethal Weapon 9*?

Sure! I was hoping to finally catch up with *The Age of Innocence,* but what the hell! This trade goes both ways. I spent Christmas 2000 with My People skiing in Wyoming. Did everyone in the group ski? Not exactly. But were they enthusiastic participants in the whole Grand Teton thing? You bet. The beginning skier even tore his ACL in a fit of enthusiasm for the sport. Is that friendship or what? Another friend ended up in the clinic with a severe case of adult chicken pox. Other than banning all photos, he played along with the rest of the holiday activities very gamely.

It is often mistakenly assumed that Your People are Your People because you have much in common. I beg to differ. Sometimes you bond with Your People through shared interests, but what often makes the relationship interesting are your differences. I learn from My People.

A second question I ask myself: *Do you choose to be with these people or is your socializing purely accidental?* The Chatty Chum at the copy machine serves a purpose in your life, such as filling you in on the latest office scandal or showing you how to operate the "collate and staple" feature. But do you choose to go beyond this? Would you collate after work? We have all learned the hard way that not all relationships can transcend the copy room. Some people actually choose to talk about copies *outside* the office. I was once on a vacation at the beach with some of My People. We were friends from work but our relationship had long since moved beyond cubicular boundaries. Sadly, we bumped into someone else from work. What were the chances? We were a million psychic miles from home. Anyway, in a fit of friendliness, we invited said coworker to meet us for a late-night alfresco dinner by the sea. Unbelievably, with a full moon and a high tide, this Copy Room Chum chattered endlessly about internal office politics. The contrast was stark. My People and I stared wordlessly toward the shoreline. Copy Room Chum bashed on and never seemed to notice that we were *on vacation*! Here's a tip: Never vacation with people you have not test-driven on local dinners and other short outings.

A third qualifying question: *Do you have similar definitions of fun?* I'll admit it—dining in restaurants with lots of fluorescent lighting is not fun for me. It's not about the food, or the people, or the condiments in small packages. It is strictly a lighting issue—the glare, the unflattering shadows, the reflection off the formica. Life is too short. My People may not feel the same way, but they understand this about me. I'll see *Lethal Weapon 9* a third time before I'll dine under those lights. I would rather drive thru and take it home. I love the *pollo* at El Pollo Loco, but the actual restaurant drives me loco.

My People have their own prejudices. One shuns the whole Tom Hanks oeuvre. Forget about ever seeing *Saving Private Ryan* or *Cast Away* with him. Another has an issue with TV shows with laugh tracks. A third would never wear anything less than full-length pants. The whole Capri thing sickens her. I respect this. We all have our standards, however arbitrary they may be. Your People do not force you to violate those standards.

In My People, I seek out funseekers, not funsuckers. Call me shallow if you will but I have more fun with people who believe in having fun than with those who don't. I learned this from my friend Marc, who taught me that laughing out loud is often the best thing you can contribute to any group. My friends Chris and Chris have taught me that fun can be hard work. The time they devote to planning the perfect Fourth of July at the beach has earned my undying loyalty and perfect attendance at any outing they mastermind. They tell me where to report for vacations, and I do.

Question number four: *Do you find entertainment in doing even the most mundane things together?* Don't laugh. This is just as true of friendship as it is of romance. My friend Judy is one of My People. I know that because every time I have spent even an hour in the car with her it has been memorable for me. For example, when she was working in Holland, I planned a short visit. We rented a car and headed south (or so we thought) toward France. An hour later, realizing that we were closer to the North Sea than Gare du Nord, we turned ourselves around, laughing all the way. It was not time wasted. It was time together, no matter which way we were headed.

Another adventure we shared was much closer to home. We were both living in Portland, Oregon. One Sunday we jumped in her car and headed out to Carson Hot Springs in the Columbia River Gorge. Before we reached our destination, we had worked through a major decision about her professional life. Then we soaked. A great day. A great friendship. At the beginning of every Satellite Sisters radio show we say, "Not every conversation changes your life, but any conversation can." With Your People, you feel this most keenly. In a car, in a grocery line, in the dressing room at Loehmann's, Your People can change your life, and you can change theirs.

My business partner, Rosemary, is another person in my life with whom even the most mundane things (such as running our actual business) can be entertaining. Maybe it's because she does all the hard stuff like doing the books and collecting payments from clients, but I know it's more than that. It's not just that she is smart and funny. She is always able to provide Perspective with a capital P. We can attend a business meeting together and come away with two completely different but complementary versions of what happened there. When we put the pieces together, things make sense. You know someone is Your People when you can be in yet another rental car, headed back to yet another airport after yet another business meeting, and be laughing all the way. Thank goodness for people with Perspective.

We all have the camp friend, the French-class friend, the fellow-downtrodden-assistant-to-a-real-jerk friend with whom we have immediately bonded. Those instant Satellite Sisters are the core of Your People. Your need for solidarity drives you together. Other Satellite Sister bonds take time. These are Your People By Choice. All of a sudden you notice that you always choose to sit next to a certain person at a meeting because his asides make your day. Or you realize that the group that was once just your running partners is now planning weekends together, spilling the details of their latest tarot card readings and designing team shirts. Years later, most of you have given up running, changed jobs, and moved to different cities, but you are still planning weekends together, spilling the details of your latest readings and wearing your team shirts. Those are truly Your People.

Perhaps there should be an induction of some kind, sort of a grown-up flying-up ceremony, like moving from Brownies to Girl Scouts, when someone becomes one of Your People, a Satellite Sister for Life. But it's kind of nice just to let it creep up on you—to notice one day that when the Caller ID indicates one of these people, you *always* pick up.

*H*ow to Break Up with a Group

The people you thought were your people turn out not to be. You realize that you are the only one who actually volunteers to do anything in your volunteer organization. Members of your mothers' group become militant antigluten advocates. A professional organization begins to dominate your personal time. You've got to get out. You have to make a break for it, but sometimes it's not that easy. You're in too deep to simply say *adiós*. Here are a few of our tried and tested methods of breaking up:

THE OUTCAST METHOD
The goal of this method is to make yourself a pariah, inviting ouster. Stop paying dues. Show up late or not at all. Repeatedly fail to do assignments until they stop assigning you things. If this fails to incite exclusion, try embezzling the refreshment funds.

THE MEDICAL DIVERSION
Invent some phony medical condition to provide an excuse for resigning. Preferably something with no visible symptoms or one that is highly contagious. Or exaggerate a preexisting condition, like eczema or plantar warts, to the level of a life-threatening situation. Pregnancy, childbirth, and extensive dental work also provide good excuses.

CALENDARIZING
The goal of this method is to create the illusion that you are so difficult to schedule that it just isn't worth

having you on the team, in the club, or on the committee. Provide only a few days a quarter that you can attend meetings, postpone constantly, or allow only fifteen-minute windows for appearances. Eventually, they will stop calling you.

INTERMEDIARY STRATEGY

Akin to calendarizing, the goal is to miss the meetings by shifting blame to an actual or invented intermediary. Use your assistant, baby-sitter, or teenager to cancel for you. Create all sorts of false business travel as an excuse. Or simply accuse a spouse or roommate of not giving you the message.

OBSOLESCENCE

This method is good for those of you ruled by guilt. The goal here is to make yourself obsolete in the organization. Invite many new members to join, groom them to assume your duties, elect them to your offices, and then resign. You're out, but you've found substitute suckers. You're guilt-free.

TRIANGULATION

Perhaps you still enjoy the cause, but just dislike this particular organization. Try joining a competing organization, preferably one that has meetings at the exact same time. If you really want out of the whole cause, join an organization with the opposite viewpoint. Neither group will appreciate your participation, and you're home free.

$\mathcal{O}$rganizations That Suck You Dry

It seems like such a good idea—getting involved with a group of like-minded people, sharing concerns, doing good work, or advancing your career. Perhaps it's an interest group so that you can get out of the house for a while and pursue something creative. But some of these organizations, official or ad hoc, can suck the lifeblood out of you, one meeting at a time. The good news is that there are some warning signs that you are about to commit volunteer hari-kari. Beware of groups, clubs, committees, or organizations that:

- Have bylaws of more than ten pages.

- Require weekend retreats to work on mission and vision statements.

- Have a nonperformance penal code.

- Take attendance at meetings.

- Create lots of extra work but no actual networking.

- Think a fun holiday party involves having everyone bake twelve dozen cookies for a cookie exchange.

- Take a simple book discussion and turn it into a graduate seminar.

- Spend most of the meeting reading the minutes from the last meeting.

- Focus more on what you wear than what you contribute.

- Require selling a constant stream of magazines, wrapping paper, lightbulbs, or nut turtles to your family and friends.

Why I Lived Where I Lived

by Monica

We grew up in a house on Cross Highway in Fairfield, Connecticut, built in 1772. The story goes that during the Revolutionary War, British Army officers occupied our house. It stood at the top of a hill surrounded by stone walls. Most of the houses in Fairfield burned during the war, but ours was spared. Our house had creaking floorboards, banging radiators, and a hundred-year-old furnace. My mother always dismissed the scary nighttime noises as "the house settling." It did not make going to bed any easier.

Upstairs there were three bedrooms in the front of the house that the children shared. The first one next to my parents' bedroom was the official nursery, with a baby crib and a twin bed. Everyone had their turn as an infant in this room. The second bedroom had original wide floorboards and two side-by-side twin beds with wooden railings. You were moved into this room as a toddler. The third children's bedroom was slightly more sophisticated, with matching blue kittycat bedspreads and curtains. There was almost no chance I was ever going to make it into this room in my life-time.

Also on the second floor, a long, narrow hallway led to two smaller bedrooms and a bathroom in the back of the house, where my brothers slept. The hallway was separated from the rest of the house by a door. This was the big attraction for my brothers. For some reason I desperately wanted to have the tiny bedroom in the back all to myself. I was tired of sharing a room with the baby (Lian) and tired of sharing a room with a sister who constantly teased me (Sheila) and tired of sharing a room with a chronic sleepwalker who was always banging into the furniture at night (Liz). My parents decided to draw names out of a hat. This was the Dolan method of handling disputes or handing out rewards. All eligible and interested parties could participate in the drawing for the back bedroom. I won. I wanted independence but it came at a price: I was terrified being so far away from my sisters. I didn't last a single night in that room. To this day I swear there was something living under that bed. That was my first experiment in trying to separate myself from my sisters, and it didn't work out very well.

When it came time for me to go away to college, I automatically ruled out the schools my brothers and sisters had attended. I wanted a school of my own. That seemed to disqualify most of the New England colleges, so I aimed for the Mid-Atlantic states. It seemed a safe bet—my own place, but not too far from home.

I experienced no real trauma when I left home for the first time. My family didn't make a big deal about college good-byes; five of my brothers and sisters had done it already. Liz and Lian drove me down to Washington, D.C., in the family station wagon. On an unbearably hot August day we unloaded my old Camp Quinibeck trunk and my stereo.

After we had hung my groovy Indian print bedspread/tapestry on the wall, we put on Bonnie Raitt's "Success" and boogied in my new home. While all of the other kids had to put up with their dorky parents wandering around campus, I had my two cool sisters with me. My parents visited me only once while I was at school—and that was on graduation day.

Once I secured my first postcollege job and started paying off my student loans, something unexpected happened: I began to reconnect with my brothers and sisters as an adult. We weren't genuine adults, but we had adultlike lives with real jobs and apartments. It started small. Sheila would take the Metroliner down from New York to visit, and to our surprise we had a great time together. No more arguments over boys and clothes, because we each had our own by then. One memorable trip of Sheila's coincided with a legendary D.C. snowstorm—"The Knickerbocker of '82." We holed up inside my house during the three-day blizzard, listening to records and eating frozen pizza.

Around that time, Brendan and Liz were sharing an apartment in New York and had secured a rundown cabin in Connecticut to rent for the summer. I made frequent pilgrimages to the cabin, which had a unique ambiance created by the rusted lawn furniture in the living room, the mushrooms growing out of the kitchen floorboards, and a limited supply of hot water. It also had two essential items for summertime fun: a boom box and a barbecue. Brendan, Liz, and I made a very congenial little group together in that cabin.

Flush with the success of our summer experiment, Liz and I ventured out west to Santa Fe to visit our older brother Dick. The significant age difference between me and Dick meant that I probably said about ten words to him the entire time we were growing up, and I'm sure they were not loving, kind words. Yet there we were as adults, telling stories, laughing, and promising to spend more time together.

After living these separate lives and finding independence, it was time to come back together as a family. I no longer wanted to be far apart from my brothers and sisters. When we reconnected, it was like having an instant circle of grown-up friends, but better because they could lend you money in a jam.

A few years later I decided to move west. All of my college friends had long since left Washington, and nothing was holding me there. Part of the attraction of moving to California was the fact that Lian was in school in Los Angeles and Liz made frequent business trips to L.A. I wanted to live *near* one of my sisters, just not *with* one of my sisters. The three of us would rendezvous some evenings, check out the celebrities by Liz's hotel pool, and basically take advantage of her expense-account life. I lived with complete strangers during the week, but I felt like I had an anchor in California because my sisters were nearby.

The same desire to connect governed my next big move, south of the Mason-Dixon Line to New Orleans. Living in New Orleans had never been part of my original game plan. Julie enticed me with stories of balmy weather, Mardi Gras parades, and chicory coffee and beignets. Over the years, Julie made strong pleas to all of her sisters to move closer to her. I happened to be available. Julie's family helped me to unlock the secrets of the city. Together we went to neighborhood crawfish boils, ate snowballs from the corner store, and commandeered our own parade-viewing corner. There were outings to the Jazz and Heritage Festival with her two toddlers in tow, the Honey Island Swamp tours, and road trips to the Atchafalaya basin.

After a few years in "The Big Easy," I was itching to move again. Then, out of the blue, Liz called. She was quitting her fancy New York job and packing in city life. She was moving to Oregon. Was I up for a road trip? I had to think about it. The last time Liz and I had lived together was in high school. Sure, we had had fun vacations together over the years, but actually living together in a new city was a big commitment. Liz was going with or without me, but the sound of her voice made me believe it would be a lot less scary for her if I came along for the ride.

What I thought would be a six-month look-see in Portland turned out to be fifteen years. Portland is our home now. In the beginning we shared a house on the west side of town. The arrangement worked out well. Liz had no domestic skills, and I had no money. She paid the mortgage, and I was responsible for groceries, lawn care, and making sure the electricity was not shut off. Occasionally I even swept the kitchen floor. People who met us for the first time assumed we had lived together our entire lives. I was always quick to point out that this was not true, but I liked the idea that we were a pair. For the first time since high school, people referred to us as the Dolan sisters. It sounded right.

Some people grow up in a small town and never leave. That kind of loyalty is admirable, but it would never work for us. We are a family of movers. The chronicle of our family peregrinations would make a complicated diagram of where we've lived, when, and in what sibling configuration. It would read like a road map of our sense of connection.

Can't You Just Try to Be Pleasant?

by Julie

The argument would begin shortly after the start of dinner. At this time in our lives, dinner was served at 5 P.M., we had our baths and did homework at 6 P.M., and went to bed at 7 P.M. Dinner was six kids around the kitchen table, Brendan in the high chair, and my mother moving from the stove to the sink and back. My father worked late and ate dinner with my mother after we went to bed.

From the time I was nine until I was thirteen, my brothers, sisters, and I had the same argument at dinner every night. I don't remember any dinner during these years when we didn't argue about this topic. The specifics might change; for example, the debate might be about why Dick and Jimmy's school was better than the girls', or it might be about girls' inferior athletic ability, or how much better boys were in math, or our ignorance of Latin. (Jimmy took Latin at his obviously superior school and liked to underscore his intellectual abilities by peppering casual statements with Latin phrases.) But the heart of the argument was always the same: Boys are better than girls.

As the oldest girl, I would have to assume the role of lead debater, with Liz providing clutch backup. Sheila and Monica could usually be counted on to provide moral support. But it was an endless, useless, and defeating argument, because it would eventually boil down to Dick challenging me to name one famous female artist or female army general or name a girl rock-and-roll band. This was the '60s, so of course my only response was Marie Curie. It didn't matter what category—Marie Curie was always my answer. My feeble response would bring howls of laughter and ridicule by Jimmy and Dick, and I could feel Sheila and Monica's support slipping away with their snickering. At that moment, when I was backed into the corner without a good response as to why there were no women presidents, I would make a crack about Dick's hair or tease Jimmy about his girlfriend, which led to a further deterioration of the discussion, with insults about my face or hair ensuing.

At this point my mother would turn from the stove or sink with the same plea every night, "Can't you just *try* to be pleasant, please?" What she meant was stop bickering/whining/sulking, and say something nice to each other. We didn't really have to achieve pleasantness, but we had to try. Whatever you had to say could be put in positive terms, and if you didn't have something positive to say, better not to say it.

My mother's entreaty forced me to cull through the events of my day and find something pleasant to say. It wasn't always easy to be positive. Sometimes it just meant sitting silently and trying not to look at Dick mouthing the words "pizza face" in my direction.

I know this sounds like suppress and deny, and there was probably a fair amount of that, but it did mean a lifetime of emphasis on the positive. Faced with any situation, you have the choice to be positive—and it is a choice. We all became quite skilled at making positive comments about the scalloped potatoes. And it is funny how, once you start down the road by making pleasantries about potatoes, less hostile thoughts soon come to mind. (Though, if you listened carefully you could hear the argument continue in the subtext of our pleasantries, such as Jimmy remarking, "Girls are really good at making scalloped potatoes.")

Later, in high school, we abandoned the nightly argument for two reasons. One, I actually started to like my brothers. And two, I was self-absorbed enough that I put my needs before those of my gender. I gave up sparring with Jimmy and Dick, in part because I had mastered the art of sulking with dramatic flair. I refined my ability to make nasty comments about my family and family life. My mother continued with her plea: "Can't you just *try* to be pleasant?" It was my responsibility to get over my bad attitude and superiority complex and *try* to be nice to the people in my family. It was as simple as that. Make an effort and be positive.

After years of listening to my mother urge me to make the choice to be pleasant, it is now a habit. When my family moved to Bangkok, it would have been easy to spend my time being critical of another country and culture. If you want to be miserable, there are plenty of things to support your case in Thailand. I made the choice to try to like this strange, new situation and find something positive about it. This approach extends to surrounding yourself with other positive people or people who are at least *trying* to be pleasant. My volunteer group, my international tennis league, and even my bunco group are filled with women who have resolutely decided to try to be pleasant. And you know what? Mom was right; they are.

The Buffer Guest

by Lian

At many events, family or otherwise, there are one or two names on the guest list that make you cringe—the names of people whose presence can send your blood pressure soaring or your fun factor plummeting. The brother-in-law with the inappropriate sense of humor and no family allies. Great Aunt Betty whose fascination with her own digestive system has ruined many a family meal. Or the Annoying Boss whose endless chatter about his golf game is almost as mind-numbing as his third wife's nonstop prattle about her shopping. Your preparty preparations focus more on damage control than decorations. If, when you ask yourself the question "What to serve?," the answer is "Prozac and Bloody Marys," then it's time to call Your People. You need a Buffer Guest.

The Buffer Guest is your go-to relative or friend who helps you through a stressful social situation. A pleasant third party who can neutralize any potentially controversial or uncomfortable event or holiday. A punctual, low-maintenance Satellite Sister who understands the importance of keeping the conversation going, cooing over your food, sucking up to social superiors, and steering unwanted relatives out of your kitchen. A Buffer Guest may be employed for an evening or an entire weekend if need be. As a host in need of a Buffer Guest, it is your duty to inform your intended that this is her role: to buff. And it is a true Satellite Sister who will acknowledge and accept buffing duties.

The idea of the Buffer Guest is age-old, coinciding with the invention of the place card. But it is at this time that we feel the need to honor this Very Important Person and recognize the contribution that the act of "buffing" has made to the sense of connection. Our guess is that the skilled Buffer Guest has saved weddings, jobs, marriages, and possibly even civilizations with a few well-timed bon mots and inquiries about the weather. Hats off to Buffers everywhere.

Buffing is not an easy job and the list of responsibilities is long. First and foremost, the Buffer Guest, or B.G., is responsible for preserving peace and forcing people to behave. The B.G. provides some sort of neutral ground between two potentially combustive guests or one combustive guest and the host (that's you). For example, a B.G. is needed for the real grandfather and the more favored stepgrandfather, who, if left unbuffed, might turn a simple christening into a battle of birthrights. Or for the Negaholic In-Law whose constant comments about your cooking, housekeeping, and personal appearance start to annoy you the minute she pulls into your driveway for a long weekend. In this case, a B.G. would step in and separate you, otherwise known as "the Buffee," from the Negaholic In-Law, or "the Target." The B.G. provides an excuse for everybody to be on their best behavior, neutralizing the Target's nasty comments and deflecting his/her barbs for use at a later event.

The B.G. is also responsible for elevating the conversation and providing some verbal diversion. Let's go back to that Great-aunt Betty with the GI problems. A successful B.G. will come to the party armed with several good stories and be prepared to monopolize the conversation. Fresh tales from someone outside the family for the afternoon's entertainment! What a relief! Aunt Betty won't be able to get a word in edgewise. For once, Thanksgiving will proceed without the mention of the word "spleen." And, for once, the family is truly thankful.

A B.G. is also critical in the case of the Humorless Date of a Good Friend who fails to see the difference between "conversation" and "debate," sucking the fun out of every party. The B.G. must be prepared to steer the conversation away from anything remotely concerned with euthanasia, the NEA budget, or other dangerous lines of conversation into something suitable for a dinner party, such as show tunes. A brilliant B.G. might lead a Cole Porter sing-along to confound the Humorless Date.

It is also the job of the B.G. to protect the host or hostess from the Target of the buff, like The Annoying Boss or The Negative In-Law. There is no point in engaging a B.G. if the Target has unlimited access to the Buffee. This is particularly true in a long weekend situation where there are many hours to fill and many events to endure. In this case, the B.G. might want to bring props, like small dogs or children, slide shows, novelty items, or photo albums. Sporting and gaming equipment is appropriate as well.

Furthermore, the B.G. should consider removing the Target from the premises as much as possible—a postbreakfast walk or a predinner drive, or perhaps even both. A thoughtful B.G. understands that buffing is a 24/7 responsibility; even the smallest window of opportunity could allow the Target to upset the delicate balance of civility. Listen up, B.G.—it helps no one to take an afternoon off to go to the museum alone. Invite the Target. It's your duty to protect the Buffee at all times.

In our opinion, the successful Buffer Guest is as important as the Thanksgiving turkey. Without one, everyone sits around the empty table, stares at the host, and dredges up old indignities to fill the silence. With a Buffer Guest on hand, everyone eats up, behaves, and saves the complaints for the ride home. A buffing triumph!

Buffing is hard work and should be recognized as such. We hope someday buffing will be recognized with its own Nobel Peace Prize and awards dinner—a fun, chatty affair, where no one complains about the food or how long it takes the valet to retrieve a car. But for now, Buffer Guests everywhere will just have to be satisfied with a lovely parting gift and a promise to return the favor.

Congratulations, Graduate

by Julie

Our family has celebrated sixty-three graduation and prize-day events, from twenty-one different nursery schools, elementary schools, middle schools, high schools, colleges, and graduate schools, spanning forty years, from 1957 to 1997. This number does not include other minor academic award ceremonies and/or sports banquets. The graduation events ranged from one-hour celebrations to weekend events. The ceremonies were held in backyards under trees, in all-purpose rooms, in cafeterias, in football stadiums, on basketball courts, in theaters, on front lawns, and in school quads. As we watched one of our siblings move on, we sat on cafeteria benches, folded metal or wooden chairs, plastic lawn chairs, bleachers, brick walls, and blankets on the grass. Sometimes we had to stand. We went to early-morning processions, noontime

stadium ceremonies, late-afternoon teas, and evening chapel events. We attended graduations in blistering heat and in the rain. Graduation parking was always a problem.

Family representation varied from the solo student to a full family showing. There was no correlation between the academic degree attained and the number of family members present. Lian got a bigger showing for her Oldfield Elementary School graduation ceremony than for her college graduation.

There was no expectation that your entire family would show up. It wasn't that siblings didn't care. Well, maybe that was part of it, but mainly, there were just too many events.

You were merely looking for some sibling representation. The combination of attendees varied greatly, depending on work and school schedules. It was always a surprise to see who would show up. It may have included the youngest kids who were still living at home or an older sibling who happened to be home between jobs. In any given June, it was safe to say that if you were home or within driving distance, you could be assured of an invitation to at least one graduation or prize-day ceremony.

My parents were graduation experts. They approached these ceremonies in a professional manner. Joy and enthusiasm, yes. Tears, no. There wasn't time. There were outfits to coordinate, station wagons to load, and picnics to be staged. Most times we traveled in multiple cars to these events. An advance team was sent to secure good seating—in the shade, near the door to catch a breeze, or in the back for easy exit. It wasn't necessary to be in the front row because we rarely had a camera to document the occasion. After a ceremony, my parents usually had postgraduation production notes about how to

"tighten up" the event for next year. We had plenty of time to
review the day's event as we sat stuck in the traditional postgraduation traffic jam. They were particularly fond of the one-hour graduation ceremony. In their minds, if managed correctly, any number
of students could graduate from any type of institution in sixty minutes. Over time, they also developed a clear sense of what should
and should not be included in a graduation speech. Keeping in
mind their one-hour target, there really wasn't enough time to get
into thoughtful discussion of social, political, or cultural trends facing the new graduates. Short and snappy was the way to go. I am
not sure whether my parents ever shared their comments with
school administrators, but I know that once my father wrote a letter
to the editor of our local newspaper questioning whether 70s-style
leisure suits were appropriate graduation attire for school officials.

Given the high volume of graduation festivities, certain aspects
became standardized over time. If we were having a graduation,
you could count on the following four elements being present:

WHITE SHEET CAKE

We always had a Devore's Bakery white sheet cake decorated with the words "Congratulations Graduate" and a
frosting diploma. The diploma was always done in blue and
brown. I am not sure why blue and brown became the official color combination of all our graduations; none of the
twenty-one institutions we attended had blue and brown as
its school colors. I suspect that the Devore's Bakery cake
decorator attended a school where blue and brown were the
school colors.

GRADUATION OWL

This was a twelve-inch-high Hallmark paper decoration
that unfolded accordion-style to become an owl in a cap

and gown. I think Hallmark intended it for one-time use only. We had the owl for at least fifteen years. Near the end of its life and our family graduation cycle, the owl's head bent from being packed and unpacked so many times. When my oldest son graduated from high school, I asked my mother about the whereabouts of the owl, thinking it might be a nice bit of tradition to introduce to my own family. No one seems to know what happened to the owl.

MEXICAN WEDDING DRESS

While this doesn't seem like it would be a standard graduation prop, in the seventies and eighties, female students were required to wear white or pastel colors to graduation events. A white Mexican wedding dress fit the bill. It was cool enough for the girls to want to wear it and it met the schools' graduation dress code requirements. No Qiana dresses with spaghetti straps for us. With five girls and multiple events, by the time Lian, the youngest, was ready to graduate, she had a range of Mexican wedding dresses to choose from.

CHICKEN SALAD

We had many memorable graduation parties, picnics, dinners, and lunches. We ate steak dinners, Italian dinners, cucumber sandwiches, spicy meatballs, and Kentucky Fried Chicken. We drank tea, punch, and sometimes champagne to celebrate our academic progress. Over time, however, chicken salad emerged as the food of choice. It is hard to remember a graduation, in fact, when we didn't have some kind of chicken salad. Curried chicken salad; chicken salad with grapes; chicken salad with homemade mayonnaise, celery, and walnuts; and just plain chicken salad. There were two main reasons for this trend: First, the graduations were usually in May or June, which is perfect weather for chicken salad. And second, my mother makes great chicken salad.

Graduation Chicken Salad

3 pounds cooked chicken breasts
½ cup sour cream
½ cup Hellmann's mayonnaise
2 celery ribs, diced
½ cup shelled walnuts
1 tablespoon fresh tarragon
salt and pepper to taste

Shred chicken into large chunks and transfer to a bowl. Whisk sour cream and mayonnaise together in a small bowl and pour over chicken mixture. Add celery, walnuts, tarragon, salt, and pepper to taste, and toss well. Refrigerate, covered, for at least 4 hours. Yield: 4–6 servings.

In a few weeks, my second son and last child will be graduating from high school. It will only be the fourth such graduation event for my family, and the last high school ceremony. In deference to my parents' vast experience, I am relying on their basic outline to get me through the weekend, but I am adapting their plan slightly to accommodate my Bangkok locale. I'll serve chicken satay rather than chicken salad, a white cake with the correct school colors, and I have jerry-rigged a *garuda* with a graduation cap in lieu of the paper owl.

I find myself far more emotional about this academic ceremony than my parents ever were, probably because my family's three graduations pale in comparison to their sixty-three. I have not developed the graduation Teflon suit that made my parents such pros. When a letter from school marked, "Graduation Information Enclosed" arrived this week, my eyes welled up with tears. It wasn't the first time I had gotten emotional about my son's impending departure. I cried the first day of classes of his senior year because I knew it was the beginning of the end of this period in our lives. I cried when he was accepted to college. I could see how excited he was to be leaving. He was ready; I wasn't. I cried in the spring when he brought home his graduation invitations. It couldn't be time for invitations—I wasn't done yet. I cried when I attended a meeting about graduation for parents of seniors. The school activities director outlined the graduation day schedule. I didn't want to hear the details.

I know I am going to cry again on graduation day, but I am trying to prepare myself for it by focusing on the positive aspects of the day. Here's my list of what I am looking forward to:

1. *Celebrating accomplishments.* I realize the event is nominally for my son, but my husband and I feel it is a victory for us as parents. Graduation is the moment when you get to step back and notice that the small, blond boy who wore a yellow ducky suit is now a tall, sandy-haired person with broad shoulders and a deep voice. It is no small feat to have a child alive and well and standing on a stage at eighteen years of age. Together, we have survived the physical threats of growing up: fevers, ear infections, the flu, chicken pox, a broken arm, stomach viruses, strep throat, and orthodonture. We navigated our way through late-night rock concerts, learning to drive, R-rated movies, messy rooms, suspicious-looking friends, and a foray into homemade beer making. We have also survived multiplication

tables, U.S. state capitals, spelling bees, the eighth-grade science project that required collection of fifty different species of insects (wings intact), ninth-grade Spanish, and calculus. The high-school superintendent will hand the diploma to my son, but my husband and I know that it is really meant for the three of us.

2. I can stare. I won't be applying my parents' one-hour rule. Who cares if the speeches are drawn out? For one, maybe two, hours, I can sit in a chair and look at my child without hearing, "Why are you staring at me?" or "What are you looking at?" I know I am supposed to be listening to the various speakers, but I plan to enjoy the simple act of looking at my child. There are very few moments, particularly in the last five years, when I've been able to have a really good, long look at him. And when he leaves for college, I know those opportunities will be even fewer.

3. I can cry. A high school graduation ceremony is a free-crying zone. I won't be embarrassing anyone if I weep a little. I am confident that there will be other parents, friends, and grandparents taking advantage of the occasion. It is one of the few events when I can shed a tear without my son saying, "Mom, what are you crying about?"

4. He will be dressed up. (I think this requires no further elaboration.)

5. I can yell and scream. When the school official calls out his name and he crosses the stage, it is perfectly acceptable to yell and cheer for your child. My husband and I have cheered for him a thousand times before at soccer games, baseball tournaments, Family Fun Day races, Easter Egg hunts, school plays, swim meets, award ceremonies, and sports banquets. But how many more occasions will there be? How many more times will I be able to stand up, whoop, and yell for our child? So excuse me if I yell a little harder and louder this time.

6. *He will be happy.* After all, that is all I ever wanted for my son—for him to be happy. I know he will have other happy moments in his life, but I won't always be there for them. I also know that he will experience pain and unhappiness that I won't be able to shield him from. But on graduation day, in a gym in Bangkok, Thailand, my son will be happy, and I will be there to see it.

Graduation Chicken Satay

From *Keo's Thai Cuisine Revised,* Ten Speed Press, Berkeley, California, 1986, 1999 Bangkok Thai Cuisine Inc.

1 pound boneless chicken breast
3 tablespoons vegetable oil
1 stalk lemongrass
3 cloves garlic
½ teaspoon seeded and finely chopped
   red chile peppers
1 tablespoon curry powder
1 teaspoon sugar
1 teaspoon fish sauce

Cut chicken into thin 2-inch strips. In a food processor or blender combine oil, lemongrass, garlic, chile peppers, curry powder, sugar, and fish sauce. Blend until smooth. Pour over chicken and let marinate for at least two hours. Thread marinated chicken onto skewers and grill until cooked. Serve with satay sauce and cucumber sauce. Yield: 4–6 servings.

SATAY SAUCE

¼ cup vegetable oil

2 cloves garlic, minced

1 onion, chopped

½ teaspoon ground dried red
   chile peppers

3 kaffir lime leaves

½ teaspoon curry powder

1 tablespoon chopped fresh lemongrass

1 cup coconut milk

½ cup milk

1 2-inch cinnamon stick

3 bay leaves

2 teaspoons tamarind paste

1 tablespoon fish sauce

3 tablespoons dark brown sugar

3 tablespoons lemon juice

1 cup chunky peanut butter

Heat oil in skillet and sauté garlic, onion, chile peppers, kaffir lime leaves, curry powder, and lemongrass for 2 to 3 minutes at medium-high heat. Stir in coconut milk, milk, cinnamon stick, bay leaves, tamarind paste, fish sauce, brown sugar, lemon juice, and peanut butter; mix well. Reduce heat and cook, stirring frequently, until sauce thickens, about 30 minutes. Be careful the sauce does not stick to the bottom of the pan. Satay sauce is an excellent dip for vegetables as well.

CUCUMBER SAUCE

1 cucumber

5 tablespoons sugar

1 cup boiling water

½ cup of white vinegar
1 teaspoon salt
3 red chile peppers, seeded and finely chopped
3 shallots, finely chopped

Thinly slice and then quarter cucumber; arrange in bowl. Dissolve sugar in boiling water; stir in white vinegar and salt. Pour sauce over cucumber slices. Sprinkle with shallots and chile peppers. Chill and garnish with 6 to 8 sprigs of Chinese parsley.

Just Like a Real Grandmother

by Monica

Growing up, we never had a chance to know our grandparents. The only things I remember about my only living grandmother was that she lived in a dark house with lots of heavy drapes and she wore a mink stole. I don't think we were allowed to make noise in that house. My mother's father, Papa, lived with the cousins in Massachusetts. I always thought he belonged to their family and not ours. They affectionately referred to Papa as "funny Grampa." I suppose that was in contrast to their other stern Grandfather.

What the Dolan children did have was Mrs. Rahrig. My friends would ask, "Is that lady your grandmother?" and I'd say, "She's kind of like my grandmother."

Mrs. Rahrig was the baby nurse who came to stay with us to help my mother take care of a new baby. She spent a lot of time at our house. Mrs. Rahrig's arrival was the sign that a new baby was coming home. A four-year-old's logic works like this: Let's see,

Mom isn't here and Mrs. Rahrig just showed up in her starched uniform carrying a suitcase. *Hmmm.* We must be getting a new brother or sister. My parents did not provide much in the way of disclosure in those days.

Mrs. Rahrig would get to work right away, helping us make a cake and a banner to hang in the front hall to greet my parents and the new baby as they arrived home from the hospital. My mother said Mrs. Rahrig was magic at soothing crying infants. My mother could never duplicate the way she wrapped those babies up in a blanket to comfort them. In fact, everything Mrs. Rahrig did was with a firm but loving hand.

Mrs. Rahrig was a no-nonsense retired nurse who had no children of her own. Every morning, she would make us form an assembly line and proceed to braid our hair so tightly it made our scalps hurt. Then, she would scrub our faces and behind our ears with a washcloth. Finally, she would double knot our shoelaces. After all the protesting, she kissed our faces. Just like a real grandmother.

Mrs. Rahrig had many talents. She could sew, knit, crochet, and bake things from scratch, just like a real grandmother. When we were older, she always took care of us during my parents' annual two-week vacation. On those visits, she arrived with a tray of her famous butterfly cupcakes and a sewing machine. Our sewing projects were disasters and we never learned how get the butterfly wings perfectly straight on the top of those cupcakes, but by the end of the visit, we were demons at Scrabble, crazy eights, and canasta, thanks to her.

One year, Mrs. Rahrig didn't come to take care of us. My mother said it was because her eyesight was failing and she was officially retiring at the age of seventy-five. I think it's because we had turned into sassy adolescents, misbehaved too often, and she was terrified of Tor, our big black Lab.

We saw Mrs. Rahrig every year until she passed away. We would visit her at her home at Christmastime. We'd give her the same present every year, a beautiful silk scarf that the girls were allowed to pick out. She would show us her latest sewing projects, tell us about her nieces and nephews, and hand out a few small gifts to Lian and Brendan because they were the youngest, her babies. Then, we would move into her dining room and sit around her doily-covered dining-room table, drinking tea and eating the world's best butter cookies. At the end of our Christmas visit, we would stand by the back door in her spotless kitchen. She would kiss all of our faces, then go into a secret closet and pull out a big tray of butterfly cupcakes for us to take home. Just like a real grand-mother.

Good Sense and Tidings and Joy

by Lian

One of the more memorable holidays I've spent with my own little family was Christmas 1997. By mid-November, I had a long list of holiday ambitions, despite the fact that I was seven months pregnant. This was to be my son Brookes's last Christmas as an only child, and I wanted to make it special. So, armed with a stack of inspirational magazines, I mapped out a December that would be unachievable even for Martha and her minions.

Host the *Nutcracker*-themed party for playgroup? Sure, I'm your girl. Make cookies for the neighbors and have Junior distribute them in his Santa suit? You bet! Harvest our persimmon tree (yes, I said *harvest*), bake eight persimmon puddings, and send them to my siblings? No problem. And while we're at it, let's send out the as-yet-not-taken photo cards of our adorable two-year-old, decorate the house like the Pottery Barn catalog, and insist on having Christmas Eve dinner at our house. Why? Because it's all here in the magazines, complete with photos, instructions, schedules, and templates, whatever they are.

Apparently, Mother Nature does not appreciate the importance of a marzipan nativity, because on Thanksgiving weekend, I went into preterm labor, thirty weeks into my pregnancy. At the emergency room, my doctor was able to stop the immediate threat of delivering early, but small contractions continued to be a problem. Instead of visions of sugarplums, I was faced with the very real vision of a premature baby in the Neonatal Intensive Care Unit if I didn't stay horizontal for eight weeks until the baby was deemed "full term." Complete bed rest, a T-Pump drip of an anti-contraction drug, and round-the-clock monitoring made crafting, baking, shopping, and frankly, sleeping, impossible. No cards, no party, no cookies, and no persimmon pudding.

Just one of my best Christmases ever.

My to-do list went from seventy-two items to one: deliver a healthy baby. The first step I had to take was to let go of all the plans that surround the holidays and completely refocus on my unborn baby. This is a lot harder than it sounds. When friends ask, "What did you do?" I say, "I called in My People."

I was completely dependent upon My People to take over my life. And My People delivered, in spades. My mother and sisters flew to the rescue in shifts. Julie came in first, then my mother, then Monica, who canceled a ski vacation to nurse me. They took over all childcare duties for my two-year-old and provided much-needed moral support to me. My mother, of course, brought a holiday wreath with her. My mother-in-law filled in during the gap days and provided food and holiday baked goods. My sister-in-law

Jamie flew down from Oakland to spend the day with Brookes. Liz couldn't be there in person, but she sent a big package of fresh maternity loungewear. Good wishes came from every corner of the family.

It was like a two-month party all about me, except it wasn't a party at all, because I was scared.

The combination of the stress of the situation, the anticontraction drugs that cause sleeplessness and heart palpitations, and the reality of complete bed rest did not make me the most fun holiday gal. Brookes was better behaved than I was. Still, My People showed up.

More came to the rescue. My friends from playgroup delivered dinner every night for two weeks. My friend Alyssa sent several pairs of beautiful earrings, and my friend Danielle brought more holiday baked goods. The women from the home nursing association made special trips out to my house to help me change my IV and brought gifts for my son. A friend's sister who also had been through bed rest sent a giant envelope of information. Neighbors dropped off soup and lasagna. And on Christmas Eve, Connie from next door arrived unannounced, bearing an entire pork tenderloin dinner and, I think, a halo over her head.

Each week as I lay in bed, my baby got bigger and stronger inside of me. My son and I made paper chains, cloved oranges, and cranberry garlands. My husband burned his candle at both ends and the middle, being my emotional support, my son's pal, and Santa Claus. On Christmas morning, the load around the tree was significantly sparser than I had envisioned, but my son didn't care. The lone gift, a coveted hook-and-ladder truck, is still a favorite toy. We finished the day with a frozen chicken potpie, not Beef Wellington as I had originally planned, and a single glass of champagne.

And the best gift? A healthy baby boy born on Groundhog Day. After all that, Colin was born two weeks *late*.

I learned two great lessons over those long weeks in bed. The first was about good karma. The people who brought me soup and good wishes and put up with my moods gave me a great gift. Now, I feel I have a never-ending debt to repay. Mother has always believed in the healing power of food, and now so do I. A pan of lasagna did not keep my baby out of the NICU, but it did make a difference to me. So now, when I hear about a sick friend or a new baby or a death in the family, I am there on the front steps, pan in hand. I bring lasagna roll-ups because they are less hassle to make than lasagna and they freeze well. But the thought is the same. Good karma begets good karma, and I have a lifetime to pay it back.

Second lesson: It's easy to get lost in the holiday hubbub. The calendar from Halloween to Thanksgiving to Hanukkah to Christmas to Kwanza to New Year's has become one big to-do list for many people. What starts as a desire to create lasting memories dissolves into a frenzy of plans, parties, and pressure. I only realized this when I was forced to lie down. Sometimes, frenzy *is* fun. But people are more memorable. If my son had gotten a pile of presents that year, would the look on his face when he saw that shiny, red fire engine have been the same? Would I have noticed his joy if I had been too busy pulling the perfect Christmas frittata out of the oven?

Now I have a holiday policy. Each year, I make my list and check it twice, and then I cross half of it off. Joy shouldn't be an assignment, and I don't get bonus points for turning the holidays into a festival of stress. These days, I also don't buy as many gifts. I try to appreciate the ones I already have.

Dear Friends:

OUR POSITIONS ON HOLIDAY LETTERS

Lian: Sisters, I thought I might share with you some excerpts from the holiday letter I'm sending out this year, and then I wanted to get your positions on holiday letters.

Liz: You're sending out a holiday letter?

Lian: Here's a little bit of mine, OK? See what you think of it....

"Where did the time go? We spent the whole year remodeling our house and barely noticed as the days turned into weeks turned into months. We re-created the days of Laura Ingalls Wilder as our little family of four camped out in our living room, eating microwave SpaghettiOs and stringing popcorn for amusement. What special memories! My husband and I found only strength in our differences during the process. Contractor Mike brought the project in on time and under budget. He became a treasured member of the family, and we look forward to sharing a holiday meal with him, his family, and all of our dedicated subcontractors, especially Sal, the carpenter. Of course, the children thrived. Brookes, our five-year-old, seems well on his way to a career in cartography, completing a scale version of the Los Angeles freeway system in toilet paper and Play-Doh. And Colin has surprised us all by turning that positive two-year-old energy into all things equestrian. He took the blue ribbon in the peewee dressage event and we were very proud. It will be no time at all before he's challenging the rest of us in our nightly game of Scrabble in Greek. . . ."

What do you think? Should I send this one out? I have to say, my position is this: I love those holiday letters. I don't care if they're over the top, under the level—I read the holiday letters of people I don't even know. I go to my mother-in-law's house—I read the holiday letters she gets. I love them. I'm all for them. Liz, what is your position?

Liz: Well, Lian, I love getting them, but I would never write one—that's where I draw the line. But the reason I love getting them is I have a terrible time remembering the names of my friends' kids, or their partners, or, you know, where they might be living lately. I kind of lose track of the details. So it's nice to get this little annual refresher course on their lives. So the next time you talk to them on the phone you can say, "Oh, how is little Sally?" which is good. But I would never write one of these letters because, if anyone wants to know what I'm up to, they should just listen to the show.

Lian: OK. Sheila, what is your position on holiday letters?

Sheila: I'm threatening to prepare a little Calvin Trillin poem this year. You know, about Ruth being off in college and the resurgence of my love life. I mean, what do you think?

Julie: Rhyming holiday letters are so nice.

Sheila: Well that's what I fantasize about. So, it would be my special gift to you.

Lian: OK, Julie, how about you?

Julie: Well, I think these letters have to break new ground. I mean, I'm sick of reading about Joey making the traveling soccer team. But I did have a friend who was going through a messy divorce and devoted his holiday letter to ragging on his soon-to-be ex-wife. That was good.

Sheila: Oh, that's terrible.

Liz: Nice holiday spirit.

Julie: I also got one from a family that listed all the colleges that their son did not get into. Again, breaking new ground, so I would want to encourage people to just really move out there with these holiday letters.

Lian: Monica?

Monica: Liz, I'm with you. I love holiday cards, I love the pictures, I love the postcards from friends, I love those letters—but there's no way I'd ever write one. I just think coming from a single woman, one of those holiday letters would be so pretentious. It's the same reason I don't send a picture of Quin, my dog, and me—it would just be crazy. But, you know, Julie, I had a similar experience. I got one of those holiday letters a couple years ago from a former neighbor, and it chronicled this extremely rocky year in his marriage. I wasn't even really very good friends with this man. So—I was just thinking there was a lot more detail in that holiday letter than I wanted to know. But the message at the end was hold fast to the people you love—so it had a very nice holiday message at the end. Still, it was a little over the top. So that's my position: I'm not going to write one, but you can send me yours.

Mother's Day

by Lian

Let's face it, I'm not the best mother. I'm terrible at arts and crafts. I don't feel like sacrificing my Saturdays to soccer. And refined sugar is fine by me. I lose my patience too often. I'm quick to blame. I miss my life before children more than once in a while. I can't relate to new parents who declare in that dreamy way, "I don't remember what my life was like without them."

I do. Life was so easy. I was thin, we had spare cash, and my husband and I could conduct a conversation uninterrupted. How could I forget that?

I do try to be a better mother, though. Every day, I wake up and think, "Today's the day." Today's the day I get through toothbrushing time without yelling. Today's the day I put a special note in Brookes's lunchbox. Today's the day I let them go at their speed and not mine. But almost always, at the end of that day, I have renewed my vow to be a better mother—tomorrow.

It's not as if the women around me haven't tried to teach me a few things about being a mother. I owe them a great deal for making it this far on my journey.

From my own mother, I have learned that a good plate of hors d'oeuvres can turn any bad day into a good one, that pulling weeds does wonders for the soul, and that the rituals of our lives add meaning and purpose.

From my aunt Eleanor, who raised nine children on her own after being widowed one June morning, I have learned that real courage is something that happens every day, in the smallest ways.

From my aunt Patty and my aunt Virginia and my aunt Nancy, whose warmth and laughter are the glue for many of my childhood memories, I have learned that next to motherhood, sisterhood is the most powerful bond.

From my sister Julie and my sister-in-law Mary, I have learned that you can love your children and your husband and also love your work.

From my sister Sheila, I have learned that sometimes as a mother you are both the teacher and the student.

From my sisters Liz and Monica, I have learned that there are many ways besides giving birth to be a part of a child's life.

From my sisters-in-law Laura, Jamie, and Susan, I have learned that a child can never have too many aunties.

From my mother-in-law Judy, I have learned that the greatest gift I can give my sons is self-determination.

From my baby-sitter Lorena, I have learned that children understand love in any language.

And from the women we have had on our radio show, I have also learned a great deal.

Kristin Armstrong, who gave birth to a son through in-vitro fertilization after her husband Lance's cancer treatment, taught me that it doesn't matter where the baby comes from, but it does matter what the child becomes.

Sally Bjornsen, who stepped into motherhood and marriage at the same time, taught me that the only job harder than being a mother is being a stepmother.

Leslie Richards, who scaled back her medical practice after

three daughters and lots of missed school events, taught me that it is more important to do things *with* my children, than *for* my children.

Kerry Kennedy Cuomo, who continues a family tradition of public service, taught me that teaching conviction is much easier than being complacent.

Ryan Newman, who gave birth to twins twelve weeks early and now faces a lifetime of uphill battles, taught me that it is possible to rise to the occasion with grace and humor even when you are challenged daily.

And Ellen Gallinsky, who studies the effect of work and family balance while trying to work and balance her own family, taught me that it is never too late to be the mother I want to be.

And so I learn a little every day. And to all of them, everyday, I say, Happy Mother's Day.

Dinner Table Learning

by Liz

In our house, dinner was a big event. After the plates were on the table but before grace was said, there was always one thing left to do: Take the phone off the hook.

The white family phone with the emergency stickers on it hung on the wall in the kitchen. Throughout dinner, the handset would swing slightly from its cord, and if you walked by it you could hear the faint, fast beeping a phone makes when it is mistakenly left off the hook. In our house, it was no mistake.

We were not a big phone family anyway. Ten people on one line does not allow for a lot of chat, but dinnertime and phone time never overlapped. The phone came off the hook during dinner because dinner was about conversation with each other—conversation in the loosest sense of the word. The ratio of thoughtful story-telling and thoughtful discussion to teasing/tattling/talking over one another was pretty even. The dinner hour could be quite a ride.

I always counted on "the little kids," Brendan and Lian, to create a diversion or provide the light relief. My older brothers would pick on "the girls," usually Julie because she was the closest to their age, and my parents would attempt to maintain some order and civility. They also managed to teach us a few things about the world, our community, and the importance of not putting our elbows on the table. Somehow these lessons seeped in between the laughter and loud disagreements.

In this Balkanized setting in which the boys, the girls, the little kids, and the parents all had competing interests, we were forced to find common ground. After all, the phone was off the hook and we could not leave the table until officially excused. My mother would ask, "Can't you just try to be pleasant?" and we would nod, knowing that as hard as that was, the alternative was worse.

At my family's dinner table, I learned that even people who grow up in the same house, take the same bus to school, make castles of leaves in the same backyard, and dance to the same Sly & The Family Stone records in the kitchen can be very different. Julie's willingness to take on the boys was high. Sheila's sensitivity to when my parents were about to reach their limit was low. Someone would be full of stories of the day (Lian), while others just wanted to stay out of the line of fire (Monica). My own goal was to try to contribute to the emotional equilibrium of the group in order to avoid any yelling or tears. For this peacemaking role, I was voted Child of the Week for three consecutive weeks once, but that's another story altogether.

These were volatile years, not only in our lives but also in our culture. I entered the fifth grade in 1968 and left for college in 1975. The years in between provided plenty of lively debate material for our family of ten. In 1968, my parent's children were sixteen, fourteen, thirteen, eleven, ten, nine, six, and three. There were small issues, like haircuts or the lack thereof, and big issues, like war, women's rights, and Watergate. It is a wonder my parents even wanted to eat dinner as a family. In their place, I might have been tempted to lay some cold cuts and condiments on the kitchen table and call it a day. I had friends in big families whose parents took that approach. Our nightly dinner was a daily act of faith on my parents' part.

Every family absorbed the shockwaves of assassinations and antiwar activities in its own way. We talked about Vatican II, the Chicago 7, and the Catonsville 9. The news did not just happen on the news. A moratorium march came right down the Post Road in Fairfield, Connecticut, and I can recall walking down from Tomlinson Junior High School to join it, then getting home in time to set the table for dinner. Our family dramas included characters like Spiro Agnew and The Who. The clash of culture and counterculture played itself out every night in very personal ways.

In polling my brothers and sisters now, we all have different lists of the most epic dinner-table debates we can recall. Topics that come to mind include Joe Cocker, Shakespeare, and why the name Jason was suddenly so popular. The Joe Cocker discussion was part of the ongoing rock-and-roll debate, with the kids pushing the limits on what we listened to and what concerts we would be allowed to attend, and our parents trying to get us to appreciate *Bobby Short Loves Cole Porter* and the Clancy Brothers. This reached a crescendo one summer when my brothers went to a Joe Cocker concert in Port Chester, New York, and never made it home. The Shakespeare conversation was part of the ongoing girls-against-boys dinner-table debate series. I can still hear this question ringing in my ears: "If women are just as smart as men, why isn't there a female Shakespeare?" And the Jason conversation? It is hard to imagine the controversy this inspired, but I suppose any ten people can disagree about anything if they try. That's a key dinner table lesson.

The same ten people can also find things to agree on if they try, and that's another important lesson. We agreed on the Yankees, but even the Yankees were off limits when my mother's father, Papa, was visiting. He practically lived at Fenway Park. We'd always see him at holidays and during the World Series, when he would drive his Studebaker down from Boston to watch the games on our color TV. But still, most baseball discussions were pretty safe.

At the dinner table, with the phone off the hook, we discovered our similarities and our differences.

When we put the phone back on the hook as we cleared the table, there were no saved messages or indicators of missed calls. In the world before answering machines and voicemail, none of those options ever occurred to us, and we were none the worse for it.

There were simply calls that did not happen because we were having dinner together. As my mother always said, "If it was important, they'll call back."

It is ironic to me that I spend so much of my adult life on the phone. Work calls, calls to set up social plans, e-mail over phone lines, or endless conference calls instead of face-to-face meetings are the stuff of my day. I seem to be making up for every phone call I did not make growing up. Before the age of eighteen, I think I made four phone calls. Maybe five.

The phone was like jumper cables or a fire extinguisher— equipment you used in an emergency but not part of your daily life. I remember my mother saying that she had only called my father at the office five times—three times she was going into labor and twice kids were in the emergency room. My mother spoke to her twin sister every morning on the phone, but other than that, we had no chatty phone role models.

When is it we would have spoken on the phone? We were at school all day long, then outside playing between school and dinner. During dinner the phone was off the hook, and after dinner we did our homework and went to bed.

Who would we have called? Most of our social plans were either with our school friends—who, we were reminded, we would see the next day at school—or with our cousins who lived half an hour away in New York. That call would have been long distance, an exotic concept to us.

There was also the issue of where to call from. The main family phone did not lend itself to long chats spilling secrets to best friends. It was on the wall in the intersection of the kitchen, the family room, and the back hall—a high-traffic area ruled by the din of the dishwasher and the television and the general hubbub of siblings looking for their bookbags and gymbags, the brother who just hit them, or the sister who stole their sweater. There was no chair in this area. I suspect this was not an accident. My parents had a phone in their room, but that was not for our use. When I was a teenager, an extension was added that allowed for a little more privacy, but it also made us vulnerable to the dreaded pickup—the parent or sibling who would burst into your conversation from the kitchen phone to tell you to hurry up and get off or just generally humiliate you by making strange animal noises. Sometimes, you would just hear the heavy breathing of a brother gathering intelligence on your personal life. Under this system, there is little incentive or opportunity for an intimate phone conversation.

So we learned to talk to each other at the dinner table instead of talking to others on the phone. As an adult now, I often think about how rarely we take the phone off the hook and focus exclusively on the people we are with. It seems we are always willing to let ourselves be interrupted. In our "always connected" world, we are, in fact, continually disconnecting. We leave the table to answer the phone. We take cell-phone calls during lunch with our friends. We click off one conversation because our call waiting indicates that someone else wants to get through. We confuse online "chat" with actual conversation. We page, e-mail, beep, voice mail, or Instant Message people about urgent issues like picking up the dry cleaning, but when do we get to the big stuff like Joe Cocker, Shakespeare, or why the name Jason is still so popular?

At our dinner table, we learned many things about each other, ourselves, and the world. If a little under-the-table kicking went along with those lessons, there was plenty of milk coming out our noses, too. It was worth it.

The How of It

by Sheila

I've always been an asker. When you grow up with lots of siblings around, you learn to go to them first before bothering Mom or Dad. Siblings are usually helpful but abrupt. Busy brothers and sisters give you the short version of whatever it is you need, whether it's algebra or driving instruction. My brother Dick would stop me before I reached the end of the driveway and simply point to the garage. "Take it in," he'd say, and my driving lesson would be over. Though I was never surprised, I was always a little hurt. He said it had something to do with the way I worked the clutch. There was one notable exception when I knew I had to go to

Mom. There was a delicate subject my brothers most certainly could not assist me with. It concerned the birds and the bees. We had seen a movie in school that afternoon, and I needed further clarification. Mom would not only know the answers, she would give me the long version, which is what I wanted.

In fact, Mom knew exactly what I was asking for, but she gently handed me off to Julie, who, she said, had "the book." The book was a tattered, incomprehensible text accompanied by diagrams, which were, frankly, frightening. I studied the book carefully. Still, I was very confused. So I consulted my friends, who gladly gave me their books. Though their diagrams were more palatable, I realized this was not the kind of subject matter I could hope to grasp overnight. I appreciated the help though, and I guess that's the most you can hope for when you go to your friends. The process of asking and sharing information helped me overcome my fear, even if I still wasn't sure what, exactly, I was afraid of. But I understood that, at a certain point, you're on your own. You need to go out and experience life, make mistakes, and be ready to pass on what you learned in the process.

Before I separated from my husband in 1995, I asked a lot of people what they thought I should do. But I was asking the wrong question. I knew in my heart what I should do, and I had known for some time. What I didn't know was how to go about doing it. It was impossible for me to imagine how I would physically separate from a man I had lived with for fourteen years. Where would I go? How was I supposed to organize a move in the middle of the school year? How does one leave a home, a marriage? Still, I kept asking, and in the hundreds of hours of talking to friends and family, we never talked about how. I don't think that is something we are comfortable asking or accustomed to receiving. Instead, they listened to me, sympathized, commiserated, and encouraged me not to be so hard on myself. This was especially true of my female friends. I felt as if I'd placed myself in the center of a giant blanket, with my friends and family poised along the perimeter, pulling up gently on the edges, trying to keep me from hitting the ground. I know now that no amount of people could have kept me aloft, but they did try, and for that I am grateful. I was carried as long as I needed to be, and in my case it was roughly three years after my divorce before I could stand on my own again.

Which brings me back to the book. Life is really all about the *how* you do something, isn't it? We all basically know *what* it is we want to do, but the *how* always seems to elude us. At fourteen, I knew that I wanted to find Prince Charming and run away with him on his great, white horse. Not impossible, I thought. At eighteen, I wanted to write poetry by the sea and live in a house made of stone and wood. Tricky, but doable. By twenty-one, I would have settled for my own car to get away on weekends. I even dared to think that Dick's yellow mustang that I ran into the ground during our driving lessons could be my weekend escape vehicle. I was becoming slightly more realistic, and yet, in every instance, I never thought to ask how.

At thirty-eight, newly separated, I wanted to open my own bank account. After fourteen years of never seeing our bank statements and never knowing how money was saved and managed, I was now going to have a checkbook with my name on it. My friends all agreed that this was a positive first step in the direction toward becoming financially independent. They encouraged me and wished me the best. No one had any idea that I didn't know how to do this.

As I walked to my local branch, I felt empowered. In the waiting area, I went over my papers. A small check to open the account, my lease (did I need that?), a piece of school letterhead from my job (was that necessary?), and some old ATM receipts from the account I had shared with my husband. I walked over to the desk, smiled, and said that I wanted to open an account. After reviewing the options, I announced that I wanted a basic checking account. I wanted the basic checks, no flowers, and I wanted it as soon as possible. *We're in business now,* I thought. The bank officer smiled and asked for identification. "Identification? What kind of identification?" I asked, tensing up. He said a driver's license.

"Oh, I don't have a license," I started to explain. "It expired, and my husband, I mean, my ex, my old husband, well, he used to do all the driving." The bank officer just looked at me.

"How about a birth certificate?" he asked.

"Well, that isn't possible, because I didn't get all of my stuff out of my old apartment, and I know it's there somewhere, but I'm between apartments right now, and . . ."

"What's your name?" the bank officer asked.

"My name, well, that's complicated, because my name is really Sheila Dolan, but none of my identification has that name on it because—"

At this point the bank officer interrupted me and asked, "Exactly what kind of identification do you have?"

I took out my wallet. I held up my red plastic public library card, which had expired. "Here," I said. "This is all I have," and I burst into tears. Now, the bank officer was not prepared for this and, frankly, neither was I. I didn't know opening a bank account could be a life-altering experience, but it was becoming clear to me that this was no run-of-the-mill financial transaction. The bank officer let me cry little longer, and then he looked at me carefully. He told me that I needed to go back into my old apartment and get my birth certificate. "Come back to the bank with the birth certificate on Wednesday. Ask for me. You don't need any of these other papers," he said calmly. I apologized as I grabbed a handful of tissues from my purse. He waited as I collected myself. I thanked him and got up to leave.

First thing the next morning, I did exactly what the bank officer had told me to do. I suddenly felt as if everything was going to be all right because I had instructions on how to make it through the next few minutes of my life. As a newly separated woman with a child, that was the only time increment I could handle. Occasionally, I go back to my old branch just to see the officer's face, and it makes me smile to think how far I have come since that day.

Sometimes, it's our Satellite Sisters who help get us through life, providing an emotional springboard to launch from and a cushion to land on when we touch down. Other times, it only takes one person, like the bank officer, to be there in your hour of need. He didn't care about why I ended up with only a library card after fourteen years of marriage. He only cared about the how of it—how I was going to open a checking account. I have always been the type of person inclined toward the long version but, as I learned that day, there are occasions when the kindest version is also the shortest.

Calling All Satellite Sisters

by Lian

What exactly is a Satellite Sister? A Satellite Sister is a sounding board for your wacky career plans, a guaranteed chitchat partner at cocktail parties, someone who's seen you in your glasses, someone to put on the emergency form at your child's school. A Satellite Sister brings information, perspective, and balance to your life when you are lacking all three. A Satellite Sister is the person who gets you through, makes you laugh, and, every once in a while, changes your mind.

In our opinion, self-sufficiency is an overrated, particularly American attribute. Interdependence gets a bad rap in this country, and we'd like to change that attitude. We're all for relying on Your People to make life more satisfying, interesting, and fun. We're not advocating helplessness here—our "no whiners" rule still stands. But there's nothing wrong with mixing a little commiseration in with camaraderie. Everyone needs someone to see them through life's travails, from an unfortunate haircut to an unfortunate marriage. People need people, as the song says. And everyone needs a Satellite Sister.

Satellite Sisters come in individuals, pairs, or large groups. They can be male, female, single, married, straight, gay, or undecided. Some are old; some are young; some are just your age. They are your actual sisters—or brothers, or parents—or they are not related to you. They are your college roommates, your best friends from third grade, or your training partners for the New York City Marathon. Whether they live next door or across the country, they are always there for you. Your Satellite Sisters are the people who get you though life, one cup of coffee at a time.

There are many benefits to having Satellite Sisters, not the least of which is having somebody with whom to dish Oscar night fashions. Here are a few easily identifiable duties of a true Satellite Sister:

THE BUCK UP

Probably the most important job of your Satellite Sister is to get you through the tough moments—from a bad breakup to a bad mammogram. Your Satellite Sister will appear with just the right attitude and a bottle of wine, ready to listen. She will provide support, empathy, and constructive advice. She will not provide a constant stream of I-told-you-so's or examples from her own life that have nothing to do with your current situation. A Satellite Sister knows when to talk and when not to talk.

THE BUST

That said about bucking up, a Satellite Sister also knows when to bust you—to point out the folly in your plans, to remind you of your humble origins, or to alert you to the fact that, despite how cute the ski instructor is, you can't ski. It is your Satellite Sister's responsibility to bring you down a notch when need be. And for this, you are grateful. You have been saved from buying a convertible in the middle of a Minnesota winter, appearing in public in a midriff-baring top, and taking a job with an Internet startup that folded in three months.

THE CAMOUFLAGE

Sometimes, you just need to lie low for a while, and your Satellite Sister is there to provide cover. Perhaps you're transitioning from grad school to a real job, or from married to single, or from redhead to your natural brown. Your Satellite Sister can provide you with a couch, a hot meal, or a kicky hat. There are times when you just want to play second fiddle and put your troubles on the old back burner. What better way to avoid your own relationship problems than by counseling your Satellite Sister through hers? Think about how much easier it is to endure being a bridesmaid again if you let your wilder, much drunker Satellite Sister do the chicken dance while you watch from the sidelines. Your Satellite Sister takes center stage when you just want to fade into the background.

THE FUN FACTOR

There are lots of perfectly nice people in the world with whom you can have a thoughtful, life-changing conversation. But it's your Satellite Sister who makes you laugh so hard that Coke comes out your nose. And so it should be. Good, old-fashioned hilarity is a key responsibility for your Satellite Sister. Even if it's been years since you've been in the same room, your Satellite Sister can still crack you up with her rendition of Bon Jovi's "Livin' on a Prayer" or her impressions of your high-school field-hockey coach. Support, respect, empathy—all good things. But nothing beats big laughs.

THE NO-FLY ZONE

Every relationship has boundaries, and your Satellite Sister respects that notion. She's set some of her own. Having a Satellite Sister does not mean that you are required to spill your guts on everything from your fertility treatments to your greatest financial fears—although you could if you really wanted to. Being a Satellite Sister means recognizing the acceptable areas of conversation. Some Satellite Sisters have specialties, and that's perfectly fine, even preferred. Think about the possibility of having a Sex Satellite Sister and a Health-and-Fitness Satellite Sister and a Child-Rearing Satellite Sister. We call it Satellite Sister segmentation.

THE BETTER HALF

All right, so maybe it's not technically 50 percent, but your Satellite Sister does have the responsibility of being some of the things that you aren't. She's a flirt; you specialize in quiet disdain. She subscribes to *People*; you only read it at the dentist. She volunteers for Big Sisters; you wish you had the time. You share a lot of common ground, but you are not mirror images. For instance, it is inspiring to have a Satellite Sister who is a clog-wearing, cross-country-skiing, grows-her-own-herbs kind of gal, especially if you live in the big city, wear nothing but black, and think vegetables grow on salad bars. She sends you dried lavender on your birthday; you send her a big box of really expensive bath products. The great thing is, you both love your gifts. Your Satellite Sister brings along some of the attributes you lack and, chances are, will never develop. And you do the same for her. That's what Satellite Sisters are for.

It is hard to imagine life without Satellite Sisters. Who else could truly appreciate your story of going to the interview with toilet paper stuck to your shoe? Who else would you call when you thought you were pregnant or you found out you weren't? Who else would *not* plan a surprise fortieth birthday party for you, but suggest to your significant other a trip for two to Paris instead? Let's face it: If it weren't for Satellite Sisters, you'd spend a lot more time talking to yourself.

What exactly is a Satellite Sister? You know. We don't have to tell you. Go ahead—call your Satellite Sister.

*W*hen to Call Your Satellite Sister

When you discover that the guy in the cubicle next to you is making $15,000 more for the same job.

When a one-hour layover becomes a five-hour layover.

When you've got the 8:00 A.M. presentation/sitter no-show/vomiting child combination.

When you're about to use this month's rent money as the down payment for next summer's vacation house.

When you need to recast your skills as a waitress on your resume into something akin to financial analyst.

When your ex-husband's lawyer asks you out on a date right after you sign the divorce papers.

When you find a lump.

When you find out the lump is benign.

When you find out the lump is not benign.

When your big life issue is cocktail dress vs. pantsuit.

When your smartass e-mail response to one person gets sent company-wide.

When your son gets tossed out of preschool for biting.

When you have some unexplained breakout or other dermatological situation.

When you just want to relive some JFK Jr. or Princess Diana moments.

Things You Would Never Say to Your Satellite Sister

Sometimes you're cruising along in a new friendship, thinking that maybe you are headed for Satellite Sisterdom, and then out it pops. Some completely unsupportive, knife-in-the-back remark that reveals the true nature of your new friend. Or maybe it's just a small, guilt-inducing comment that forewarns of a high-maintenance relationship ahead. Rethink Sisterdom if you hear any comments like:

"Have you ever thought about breast enhancement?"

"You've got to be my bridesmaid. You're the only woman I know who's still single."

"It's more complicated for me. I'm in a much higher tax bracket."

"Let's go out. My husband's out of town, and I'm desperate."

"I didn't know redheads could wear red."

"I wouldn't know about that. My son isn't as hyper as yours."

"What a surprise. You haven't called me in forever."

"It's easy for you. You're single. You don't have a family."

"You know what? I can't. I have a pedicure scheduled."

"You look so much better. You must have lost fifty pounds."

"I told you that would happen, but you didn't listen."

"You remind me so much of my cat."

$\mathcal{S}$atellite Sister Qualification Questions

It should be fairly easy to spot the Satellite Sisters in your life. In fact, you're probably getting together for a game of canasta later on. But just in case you have doubts about a potential Satellite Sister, we've developed a set of qualification questions. There are no wrong answers, just dull ones. Funny, smart, like-minded—those are good qualities to look for in responses. Try a few of these out on your potential Satellite Sister:

What would you rather win—an Oscar or a Nobel Prize?

What job are you not qualified for?

Did you ever abuse "hold" or "layaway" privileges?

In what fashion trend do you most regret taking part?

Do you lie to your doctor?

If you really wanted to shake up the Supreme Court, who would you nominate?

If you could change any part of you with plastic surgery, what part would it be?

What great book do you claim to have read but never really have?

In what Olympic event would you want to bring home the gold?

What's the worst job you've ever had?

Are you intimidated by your hairdresser?

Where were you when you heard about the death of Princess Diana?

What is your personal theme song?

a sense of

self

A Sense of Self

by Liz

Which one are you?

This is a question that only children never hear. Or members of neat, nuclear arrangements. "Which one are you?" is a question that members of big families hear all the time. Teachers, doctors, coaches, and milkmen ask. And as you grow, you learn to have an answer. It is good training.

While I cannot claim to have experienced any deep existential crises in my childhood, I do believe that constantly being asked by friends and strangers who I am made me think about it more than, say, your average five-year-old.

So, which one am I? At five, I was the fourth child, the second girl, the first blonde (Jim, Dick, and Julie all being redheads). I was already the older sister to Sheila and Monica, and would later be the same to Brendan and Lian. I was to be one of eight.

At seven, I was the teacher's pet in Miss Sorchiotti's second grade, a member of the Horses reading group with Lynn Miranda, and roommate to Sheila in the blue kittycat room. Color-coding our bedrooms made it much easier for baby-sitters—blue room, yellow room, red room. We each had our places and partners.

During my youth, I shared bedrooms at various points with Julie, Sheila, Monica, and Brendan. When I was eight and Brendan was two, his crib was right next to my bed so I could hold his hand when he woke up frightened in the middle of the night. The blue kittycat room (named for the wallpaper and matching bedspreads) was always my favorite, except that Sheila made me get up every night and make sure there were no monsters in the closet. After all, I was one year older than she was, so it was my responsibility. This was fine except that we both knew there were alligators under our beds, so I had to get to the closet and back without being eaten. This required a running leap from the middle of the room onto my bed, a dangerous and loud maneuver. My parents also kept a chair right next to my bed to keep me from climbing out because at seven, I was also a sleepwalker.

By nine, the answer to "Which one are you?" began to include clues about which one I was not. I was not the one who plays the flute (Julie). I was not the one who hates green noodles (Monica). I was not the baby (Lian).

Growing up in a big family, you are surrounded by people who are a lot like you. You share rooms and friends with them. You take the same bus to school and learn to swim or ski or sing together. Your voices sound alike. People say that you have the same hair or the same eyes or the same freckles. In our case, you also wear the same blue-and-white dresses to Easter Mass or polka-dot bathing suits to the beach. Your group identity is clear and constant. Which one are you? You must be one of the Dolans.

Despite what some may think, group identity can be very liberating. It allows you to focus on the things that are unique to you.

In most ways you are like other people but, in a few key ways, you are completely different. Being in a big family forces you to develop those special traits early. After all, who will you say you are if someone asks?

In a big family, being different is a survival technique. How else would you get any attention at the dinner table? It is important to have your own story, your own joke, or your own point of view. Nobody is going to turn to you and ask your opinion. Just jump right in.

At the same time, however, you also learn that you don't have to be 100 percent different. You only need to pick a few key characteristics and work on them. Be the bookish one, or the sassy one, or the best Scrabble player, or the troublemaker. Much later in my professional career as a marketer, I learned that this is called product differentiation. As a kid, it was called getting a word in edgewise. You need a skill or a weakness or an attitude that is yours alone.

We were the same, but very different, and our childhood together was an exploration of how much the same and how different. For instance, we were all on the same swim team, but Julie was a breaststroker, Sheila's specialty was butterfly, Monica was a freestyler, and I preferred backstroke. In fact, the four Dolan girls were our own medley relay. Thinking back, it is kind of a corny metaphor for our lives—one team, different contributions. But it is not an accident that we picked different strokes. Which one are you? I am the first leg of the relay, the backstroker. Being different allowed us to hold our own inside the family. Later in life, it would be how we held our own in the world. We had learned how to pitch in without simply blending in. Everyone made a specific contribution.

While members of smaller families grew up being told that everything they did was fascinating and unique, we knew this was simply not true. There were plenty of others like us at the table or in the next bed. Our parents would always react with interest when one of us recounted a new book read or a milestone achieved, but a sibling could always be counted on to belittle it or top it. No one is fascinating and unique in every way, but everyone is in a few ways. We learned early to work on those features in ourselves and appreciate them in each other.

Julie staked out drama. Sheila wrote poetry. Monica played the vibes. They were really good at those things, so I avoided them.

School was one of my best things. I loved the books, the spelling bees, even the bus, but all of my brothers and sisters generally liked school, too, so this was not enough to forge an identity on. The real breakout moment for me came in the fifth grade when Miss Agostino introduced the poetry contest—a public-speaking competition in which all of the fifth graders picked a favorite poem and performed it for the school. My two older brothers had won public-speaking contests at their school and tried to coach me in selecting my material, but I made my own choice. My father's advice was to just find something I loved.

I went with what I thought was an obscure but edgy Ogden Nash howler about Christopher Columbus. The combination of history and humor seemed well suited to my talents and personality, but everyone knew that Pam Handy had a lock on first place. Smart, popular, and cute, with a tear-jerking performance of that "Little Boy Blue" number included in every anthology of poetry ever printed, the rest of us were long shots at best. Miraculously, I won. Perhaps the Academy wanted to reward the riskier material; I don't know. But that's the day I learned that I was the public speaker and the lover of smart, funny writing. I also learned that I could trust my own judgment. Which one are you? I am the one who won the poetry contest.

The truth is, you have time to refine your sense of self in a big family precisely because no one is paying close attention. There is simply too much going on for anyone to notice that one month you are thinking of being a veterinarian and the next month you know you will devote yourself to uncovering ancient civilizations. In college I had a different major every year: European history, semiotics, French, and comparative literature. Not only did I never have to explain this to my parents, I am certain if you asked them today that they could not tell you exactly what I earned my degree in. Why is this good? Because if life teaches you anything, it is that your major in college does not matter at all. My parents already knew this, so why bug me about it? This was true throughout our childhood. The lack of scrutiny allowed for some low-risk adolescent experiments that paid off in adulthood. We each eliminated some poor choices early on, before anyone noticed.

Perhaps modern child psychologists would say that dressing kids alike suppresses their sense of individuality. For most of us, most of the time, this was not true. I only feel sorry for Lian because, as the youngest, she kept growing out of one blue-and-white striped dress and into another one in the next size. There were some basic things our parents made all of us do. We all had to make our beds. We all had to behave at dinner every night. We all had to have summer jobs as soon as we were of baby-sitting age. We all had to take Latin in high school. There were a few other rules, but that's the gist. There was still plenty of room to not do things. All my sisters played musical instruments. Not me. Some were Girl Scouts. I hated it. Tennis, anyone? No thanks. Looking back at those years, I am amazed at the level of personal choices we were actually allowed to make. Having the freedom to opt in or out of any of those activities further honed my individual identity and my relationship to the group.

If there were challenges to forming an identity of one's own, it was because our lives were so closely interwoven that it could be hard to have anything that was exclusively yours. Your own room? Not likely. When Lian finally got her own room, it was little more than a landing, with a staircase that came right up into it—not quite the private lair that eleven-year-olds dream of. Does it count as your own room if everyone has to pass through it to get down-stairs? Your own clothes? Not really. We shared freely and stole freely from each other. Your own friends? For those of us who were really close in age like me, Sheila, and Monica, all one year apart, even our social lives overlapped. Sheila and I used to fight about whether our cousin Beth Morningstar was her best friend or mine since Beth was six months younger than me and six months older than Sheila.

So, which one am I? I am the Dolan who is a sister and a spokesman. I am a lover of good books and great jokes. I am a small-business owner and a big-business veteran. I work in New York, but live in Oregon—a lazy person who has run two marathons and a frequent flyer who loves nothing better than stay-ing home. My family members are my friends, and I have friends who are like family. I am both the one in the middle of the big family and a single person who lives alone. Formerly the first blonde, I have now chosen to be a redhead.

Carry Your Own Skis

by Lian

When my mother was forty, she took up skiing. Or, more cor-rectly, she and her twin sister took up skiing. They got on a bus, went to ski camp for a week, and learned to ski. After that, they'd get in the car and head up to Ladies Day at Powder Hill as often as they could to practice their stem christies. Don't let the name fool you, Powder Hill (which later became the more Everest-like "Powder Ridge") was no pushover bunny slope.

This was in the mid-sixties, when skiing was work—decades before valet parking, fondue lunches, and gear that actually keeps you dry, warm, and safe. My mother and my aunt took up the kind of skiing that entailed wooden skis, tie boots, and rope tows that could jerk your arm out of its socket. This was the kind of skiing where skiers, not the Sno-Cats, groomed the hill in the morning. Ticket buyers were expected to sidestep up and down slopes and herringbone the lift lines. The typical A-frame lodge had a big fireplace, a couple of bathrooms, rows of picnic tables, and maybe some hot chocolate for sale. At the end of the day, there were no hot toddies by a roaring fire in furry boots or glasses of wine in the hot tub of a slopeside condo. Instead, my mother and her sister faced the inevitability of a station wagon with a dead battery and the long, dark drive back home in wet clothes.

Why did they learn to ski? It wasn't to spend some quality time outdoors together away from their responsibilities at home. They learned to ski so that they could take their collective children skiing, all seventeen of us. My mother's eight children and my aunt's nine. And learn to ski we did, eagerly. There was, however, one rule my mother had about skiing: Carry your own skis.

My mother didn't teach us to ski until we could carry our own skis from the car to the lodge in the morning and—this is key— from the lodge back to the car at the end of the day. Even cold, wet, and tired, we had to get our skis, poles, and boots back to that station wagon on our own. No falling behind. No dragging. And no whining. My mother had the responsibility for her gear, the giant lunch, the car, and the occasional trip to the ER for broken legs. We were in charge of our own gear and meeting at the end of the day. These were the conditions to be allowed to accompany siblings and cousins to the slopes. Carry your own skis or sit in the lodge all day.

No one wanted to get left in the lodge. A cold, wet day on the ice-blue slopes of New England, freezing in leather boots and the generation of ski clothes before microfibers was far preferable to being left out of all that fun. Miss the lunches of soggy tuna fish sandwiches and Hershey's minis? No way! Sit in the lodge instead of sideslipping your way down a sheet of ice disguised as a trail or tramping through three feet of snow to get the pole you dropped under the chair lift? Not me! Forgo that last run of the day in near darkness, cold and alone and crying because your siblings have skied on ahead without you? Who'd want to miss all that fun? Sitting in the lodge all day just wasn't an option once we reached ski age. We were expected to participate. We learned to carry our own skis.

The lesson was simple, really. Be responsible for yourself and your stuff or you miss out. No one wanted to miss out. Getting across the icy parking lot and back seemed a small price to pay for the potential of great fun. And even if you dropped your poles or the bindings cut into your hands or you fell on your ass, that was part of the experience. The "carry your own skis" mentality filtered into almost every area of our life as we were growing up.

Doing homework, getting to practice, applying to college—be responsible for yourself and your stuff or you miss out.

I began to notice the people who hadn't learned to carry their own skis when I was as young as eleven. I didn't have a name for this concept yet, but I had the notion that maybe other kids operated by a different set of rules. They thought that somewhere, somebody was going to take care of things for them. I remember the girls at summer camp who never signed up to pack out or pack in for a camping trip, expecting that someone else would provide food or do all the cleanup for them. But me? I would sign up to make the PB&Js and to clean up the mess. I'd load the canoes onto the truck and take 'em off again. And the tent? I'd put it up and I'd take it down. I didn't know any different. As a result, I was invited to go on a lot of camping trips. The lodge and back, baby—that was my attitude.

In high school, the kids who didn't carry their own skis called their parents to bring in assignments they'd forgotten or to ask for a ride home instead of walking or taking the late bus. In college, the no-ski carriers all had pink T-shirts—a sure sign that they had never done laundry before—and they complained about how much work they had. Isn't that what college was about—doing your own laundry and finishing your work? Then you could get to the fun stuff.

The real world is riddled with people who have never learned to carry their own skis—the blame-shifters, the no-RSVPers, the coworkers who never participate in those painful group birthdays except if it's their own. I admit it: I don't really get these people.

I like the folks who clear the dishes, even when they're the guests. Or the committee members who show up on time, assignment completed and ready to pitch in on the next event. Or the neighbor who drives the carpool even though her kids are sick. I get these people. These people have learned to carry their own skis.

In early adulthood, carrying my own skis meant getting a job, paying off my student loans, and working hard for the company that was providing my paycheck. If I did those things, then I could enjoy the other areas of my life. Dull, yes, but freeing, too. When I wasn't responsible for myself or my stuff, I felt lousy. Sometimes I could get to the lodge, but I just couldn't get back to the station wagon at the end of the day. It was an unfamiliar feeling to let someone down by missing a deadline at work or not showing up for an early-morning run. I even felt bad for the people at American Express when my expense reports got a little behind my bills. On days like that, the parking lot seemed bigger and icier than I had anticipated.

Now I have a life that includes a husband, two children, a dog, a house, friends, schools, and a radio show that involves lots of other people, including four sisters. The "stuff" of my life may seem much heavier than two skis, two boots, and two poles, but it isn't really—just a little bit trickier to carry. I have to do more balancing and let go of the commitments that I'd probably drop anyway. If I commit to more than I can handle, I miss out. That's when I think of Powder Hill.

The funny thing is, some of the worst moments of my childhood were spent on skis or in pursuit of skiing. The truth is, I didn't really like skiing as a kid. And I wasn't a very good skier. Most days, skiing for me was about freezing rain and constantly trying to catch up to my older, faster, more talented siblings. The hard falls on the hard ice. I can still feel the damp long underwear and the wet wool during the endless ride home. But whether I liked to ski or not didn't really matter. I was expected to learn to ski, and I did. And I also learned that in life you need to be responsible for yourself and your stuff or you miss out. The lodge and back, baby.

How to Carry Your Skis in Everyday Life

- Add paper to the office copy machine.
- Take the dirty diapers home.
- Bring the serving utensils for your potluck dish.
- Find a sub.
- Do your action items.
- Have your checkbook and ID ready.
- Return books you've borrowed from friends.
- Get directions instead of winging it.
- Eat whatever the hostess is serving.
- Call your parents just to check in.
- Bring in the garbage can for a neighbor.
- Show up early when traveling with others.
- Start the next pot of coffee.
- Return your shopping cart.
- Pick up after your dog.

Signs That You Have Not Learned to Carry Your Own Skis

Suspicious about a new friend or coworker and their ski-carrying ability? A person who has never learned to carry his or her own skis will exhibit some of the following behaviors:

- Shows up late for a group night out with no cash and no ID.

- Monopolizes the only common-area phone.

- Never sits on the hump.

- Wears all white to the community clean-up day.

- Waits for the closest spot in the parking lot, backing up a line of traffic.

- Checks luggage when everyone else in the group has rolling carry-ons.

- Never schleps toys to the park for their child but borrows yours.

- Fails to bring the laptop for the group presentation.

- Parks in the handicap spot "just for a minute."

- Responds "I don't care" when an officemate is rounding up lunch orders for the deli.

- Arrives late to the meeting, then talks the whole time.

- Keeps everyone in the group waiting in the lobby while checking his or her e-mail.

- Brings six liters of Diet Slice when assigned beverage detail.

Things Don't Always Divide Evenly into Eight

by Julie

It started with a single pork chop. There were six of us at the long pine kitchen table and there was only one leftover pork chop. Sautéed pork chops, mashed potatoes, and green beans was one of my mother's classic midweek dinners. It was my favorite meal. My mother would brown the pork chops and then pour a can of Hunt's tomato sauce over the top and let them simmer. It was the ideal combination of salty, fatty, and tomato-y tastes.

I was still hungry, but so were Dick and Liz. It is pointless to try to divide a pork chop into three pieces. You can't eat a third of a pork chop; it just doesn't work. Somebody was going to get to eat the whole thing and the other two would be out of luck.

I had several good reasons why I should get the pork chop. I asked first, I don't usually ask for seconds on pork chops, and I set the table. Dick and Liz had their reasons, too. Dick used the "growing boy" argument that goes something like because he was a boy, and boys played sports and needed to be big and strong, they deserved more food. Buttressing this argument was the fact that Dickie was the oldest at the table and nobody would protest if he got the chop. Dick didn't even have to make this second point; we all knew it. Liz had the strategic advantage—she was sitting closest to the stove where the pork chop was, so it would be easy for my mother to reach over and put it on her plate.

My mother was neither fair nor unfair when it came to the distribution of goods and services. I now think that she purposely pretended not to hear our arguments about the remaining pork chop or who got to sit in the big chair in the den or why Dick and Jimmy got to stay up later than I did. Rather than enter into the fray, she let us work it out. I think she was also trying to send the message that just because you missed out on the remaining pork chop, that didn't mean you weren't loved or that you didn't deserve it. It just meant that there was only one pork chop and your life would go on without it. On that night, I don't remember how my mother resolved the final pork chop debate. I know I didn't get it.

Growing up, there were a lot of situations like that. Somebody else might have drunk the last bottle of Pal or my father had only two tickets to the Rangers game. Usually, my parents tried to prevent such altercations by buying eight of pairs of skates or six bikes. We had plenty of bats, dolls, gloves, and balls. With eight kids, though, not everybody gets their own room or their own sled. We had one dog and one blow-dryer. Despite my parents best efforts to make things even at birthdays and Christmas, sometimes there was only one pork chop left.

While I knew things didn't always divide evenly, others didn't. When I would visit my friend Sarah Adams and her sister, Carolyn, her mother would cut the last brownie into two pieces or three pieces. I was amazed at the precision that Mrs. Adams used to cut a brownie. I remember thinking that if the same brownie had been at my house, it would have been long gone.

In my own family, I adopted many of my mother's practices, including turning a deaf ear when my sons bicker. I always adhered to her advice to buy two of the same thing or don't buy it all. My husband and I try to treat each of our sons as individuals, which sometimes means giving more to one than the other. I hope my sons have come to understand what I learned around the kitchen table—that things don't always divide evenly, and that's OK.

As an adult, I have seen many people go through pain because they learned this lesson later in life. In the workplace, I have seen a lot of bad behavior when the topics of budgets and allocation of resources are raised. Certainly, many of these discussions are based on rational business practices. But sometimes the bad behavior is just because somebody else got the new copier or a better parking space. At the source of the bad behavior is the expectation that you should always get an equal portion of whatever is being served.

The pork-chop lesson has served me well in life. I still fight for what I deserve, but I don't begin with the expectation that what I deserve is exactly one-half, one-third, or one-eighth of the pie. I also know that not everything can be divided up evenly. I know that even if you miss out now, maybe next time around the pork chop will be yours.

Bell-Bottoms

by Sheila

The world changed when I bought my first pair of bell-bottoms. My life depended on purchasing a slightly faded pair of blue flared pants with a twenty-six-inch waist. I had been plotting this acquisition for weeks. By seventh grade, I had already earned the reputation in my family for being a self-obsessed clothes worshiper. I eventually stopped talking to my family because it was too hard to plan outfits in my head and speak at the same time. My brothers and sisters mistook my silence as antisocial. One afternoon, while slinking around the boys' rooms looking for old shirts, I nearly scared my little brother Brendan to death. Brendan was nine at the time and looked like he had just seen a ghost. "You're weird, you know that?" he blurted out. I loved that kind of attention.

My sisters' aggravation with my sense of style became clear at my thirteenth birthday party, which I organized myself. My party plan involved locking five of my closest friends in my room all afternoon for a teenage angst session. Marcia Cameron gave me a stuffed signing owl, which all my friends signed in pen. They wrote "Love ya Sheila" and other warm sentiments that made me feel wonderfully appreciated. The next morning, I woke up and went to look at my signing owl. That's when I saw it. The words: "Miss Grooviness" scrawled in ink across my new owl. My sisters had defaced my owl!

They began taunting me with their horrible little name for me. I pretended I didn't hear them when they whispered my name in the car so Mom couldn't hear. They'd mouth the words "Miss Grooviness" and then say it out loud when I ignored them. They accused me of living in my own world and, you know, they were right. I did live in my own world and it was called my teenage fashion fantasy.

As I sat in my color-coordinated bedroom imagining James Taylor walking up the front steps, ringing the bell, and asking my mother if I was at home, I knew it would be because I wore bell-bottoms. He would only go out with me if I did. I already had the perfect shirt, which was a blue-and-white shirred Indian print with short sleeves and a tassel in the front. I carefully planted the seed with Mom that I would be making a small purchase in the way of pants, which I absolutely needed. If I could justify the need and spring it on her while she was busy making dinner, Mom was often susceptible to the stories I made up concerning clothes. After I secured the money, I would need to find transportation. I talked my best friend, Martha, into asking her mother, who was great when it came to rides, to give us a lift. The deal was set. We were to be dropped off on Saturday in front of the Landlubbers store. It meant crossing the Fairfield line into Westport, which was my mecca for fashion, the Forbidden City of Cool.

Westport was a tiny one-way street that started with Landlubbers and ended at The Remarkable Bookshop. A rambling old pink house that had been converted into a bookstore, The Remarkable Bookshop was the first store I ever set foot in where you could actually sit on the floor and read. You just couldn't do that in any Fairfield store. Between these two landmarks, there were tantalizing little shops for food, candles, shoes, and records. Oh sure, there were also sporting goods and hardware stores for regular folks, but once I made up my mind to be James Taylor's girl, I didn't have any use for that kind of stuff.

On any given day in Westport, you could spot Paul Newman, Sandy Dennis, or Erica Jong walking down Main Street in black sunglasses, nonchalantly doing the weekly shopping. I wanted to be a part of the Bohemian life of this tiny town and, clearly, wearing bell-bottoms was a prerequisite.

Martha and I went over the plan in the back of her mother's Wagoneer. We would get the pants first and then eat lunch at a small place called Soup's On. We would stuff our faces with cheesy onion soup and french fries, but only after we squeezed ourselves into the smallest pair of jeans we could fit into. We didn't want to be full from lunch when we tried on our first pairs of bell-bottom jeans.

As we approached downtown Westport, my eyes widened with anticipation. We passed the Fine Arts movie theatre, the Westport YMCA, the triangular park that was nicknamed Needle Park (completely off limits to us), and then, right next to Needle Park, was our first stop, Landlubbers. As we entered the unassuming store with its handmade wooden sign on that Saturday in 1972, I changed from the Sheila Dolan my family knew to another girl entirely—my true self. As I stared at the endless racks of blue bell-bottoms cramming the narrow, incense-filled space, I heard someone from the back call out, "Can I help you girls?" The owner approached us slowly and, as I stood there checking out this aging hippie with his long black hair, huge mustache, and weird grin (was it the incense?), I knew Martha and I were not in Kansas anymore. He was wearing Landlubbers, a Jerry Garcia T-shirt, and silver jewelry. "So, what can I get you girls?" he asked us serenely. We had arrived.

In addition to the hundreds of pairs of bell-bottoms in every length and waist size, Landlubbers also sold the famous rainbow belt. A multicolored stretch fabric with a simple clasp, the rainbow belt was the perfect accessory for bell-bottoms. As I stood in front of the long, white-framed mirror and stared at my new self, I couldn't believe that I was minutes away from purchasing my first pair of real bell-bottoms. The pants weren't like any other pair I owned or any pair my sisters owned. They were going to be all mine.

Julie wore slacks and corduroys, but never bell-bottoms. Liz resisted the whole blue-jean trend. My new pants would make my brothers Jim and Dick finally notice me and wonder if I wasn't their favorite sister after all. Up until that time, my brothers were just two guys I passed on the stairs, who would look at me with a kind of wonder and apprehension. Who is that sister and where did she come from? How come she's hiding our Joe Cocker album under her bathrobe? They would understand my need for bell-bottoms, though, because they were both trendsetters too. Jim was one of the first guys in our town to own earth shoes, or the "ugliest shoes in the world," as our Dad liked to refer to them. He also returned home one Thanksgiving wearing patchouli oil, which really shook things up. I sampled the musty brown perfume on many occasions. Dick was not as daring, but liked to associate with guys who went out on a fashion limb. He once wore a dashiki, or was friends with a man who did. My brothers could help me make the transition from bell-bottoms to bigger fashion statements if they would just stop thinking of me as "one of the girls."

The bell-bottoms would also make my little sister Monica respect me and wonder how she ended up with a sister so cool. I needed to start exerting some authority over Monica. She didn't quite understand my role as the middle sister, and frankly neither did I. Was she supposed to listen to me, or did Julie and Liz override any power I might have? I looked to clothes as the way to influence and inspire. In high school, we would enter into a four-year battle over separates, but no one could have predicted that at the time.

Most important, my bell-bottoms would make you-know-who drive down from Massachusetts so we could start getting to know each other. We would probably go to Westport on our first date.

At fourteen, I thought that I could build a personality based on my album covers. Joni Mitchell, Carole King, and Laura Nyro were the female triumvirate. They wore a lot of scarves and, of course, bell-bottoms. On the male side, I had Jackson Browne, Cat Stevens, and my man, James. They were the reasons I went shopping. My true self was buried somewhere beneath the years of matching clothes and sensible shoes. I was determined to uncover who Sheila really was, and so I thought that I would start from the outside and work my way in. Bell-bottoms were at least 70 percent of my identity. I was still working on the last 30 percent with the help of my record collection. If I started to feel totally uncool inside, which was often, I'd just give my rainbow belt a little tug and try to pull myself together.

I'll never be able to repay my mother for falling for the lost-pants story or Martha's mother for believing us when we told her we wanted to go to the library that day. And I'll always be indebted to Martha for being my partner in this life-changing enterprise, even though at age fourteen, she stood five-feet-eight-inches tall and had the same waist measurement as me. It was a new dawn as I rode home with my sense of self folded inside the tie-dye-colored plastic bag. You can only imagine my dismay when I showed up at the school dance the next weekend and every other eighth-grade girl was wearing brand new bell-bottoms, an Indian shirt, and the rainbow belt.

I still fuss over my clothes and I think I always will. It's not that I look fabulous, because, really, I don't. My "look" hasn't changed that much since 1972. Give me a pair of pants that fit, a pretty shirt, and a scarf or belt that makes me feel special, and I'm set to go. It's simple stuff, but it makes a big difference in my day because it still makes me feel like I know who I am.

J.T. never did show up and I didn't die without him. But Miss Grooviness is alive and well and living in New York City, and she's planning her next purchase as we speak. It's probably going to be something in pink.

*F*ashion Forward Moments

In every sister's fashion annals, one item of clothing stands out as a fashion moment that defined a little piece of her sense of self.

LIZ

All-purpose black jumpsuit that became after-work uniform for the early New York career-girl era in the early 80s. Sleek, slimming, and indispensable in the days of limited disposable income. Dress it up; dress it down.

JULIE

Red maxi coat inspired by Paul Revere and the Raiders. Double-breasted with a zip-off bottom. Very 1972. First in all-girls high school to embrace the maxi. Needed to wear platform shoes so the hem wouldn't drag on the ground.

SHEILA

A mauve corduroy cape with a hood, lined with a romantic Laura Ashley floral. The year was 1975; the feeling was *The French Lieutenant's Woman* in the suburbs. Perfect for wearing to the beach on a foggy winter morn to smoke a cigarette.

MONICA

A purple, orange, and green polyester belted tunic-and-pants combo circa 1970. Highlighted by a prominent fashion zipper and gold buttons. Marcia Brady meets

Judy Jetson. Worn, of course, with black clogs. A much-coveted item by all the sisters.

LIAN

Sasson baggy jeans, 1981. Purchased at Lord & Taylor under Liz's guidance. Created a stir in the high school hallways as onlookers crowded around to see the trendy rebuttal to skintight Calvins. Nice with red, slouchy boots.

Uniforms

by Liz

I have always kind of liked wearing a uniform. In my life, these have come in different forms. As kids, my mother dressed all the girls alike for special occasions, such as Christmas, or when we were going to busy public places, such as the beach or a ticker-tape parade for the astronauts in New York. It made it easier for her to keep track of her group. For instance, when Sheila wandered away from the rest of the family at the 1964 World's Fair, a helpful adult figured, "She must be with the other red coats," and brought her back to the fold. I think we were waiting in line to see the *Pieta* the whole time, having just enjoyed a snack at the waffle stand in "Belgium." The line of little red coats made us easy to spot.

I also wore a uniform on our swim team at the Fairfield YMCA, though I am glad no photos exist of those pre-Lycra, baggy, striped nylon suits. I have shunned stripes ever since. And for my summer at Camp Quinibeck in Vermont, we were issued the classic white T-shirt/blue shorts combo, this look being much more flattering than the swimming attire.

I was grateful when the intense wardrobe pressure of the seventh and eighth grades at Tomlinson Junior High School was relieved in high school. It may be incredibly uncool to admit to liking a Catholic school uniform, but I was grateful not to have to think about different looks for different days of the week. A white shirt and blue-checked wool skirt was fine with me. I had other things I could worry about and work on: hair, weight, shoes, friends, school—the list of concerns was endless.

I liked people knowing what team I was on, whether it was the

Dolans, the YMCA, or Sacred Heart. Everyone needs to be part of a group; the more, the better, in my opinion.

Here's my policy on uniforms—it's the same as my policy on learning a sense of self in a big family: You don't need to be 100 percent different from others to be unique. You need to be 10 percent different. It is good to accept that you are 90 percent the same as other people. Even recent human genome research reinforces this. There simply aren't as many genes as we thought, yet people can still be very different. Small differences mean a lot.

Continuing the uniform metaphor, I would put it this way: The key to life is to accessorize. Your skirt and shirt might be standard issue, but there's still lots of room to make your own statement. High-school girls have done amazing things with socks. The course of history has been changed by as little as a beret with a rhinestone pin.

Accessorize! You can be part of a family or group or team and still differentiate yourself from others by how you tell a story or the way you appreciate someone else's well-told tale. A good laugh is an excellent accessory! So is a commitment to Meals-On-Wheels in your community or a training program preparing you to kayak through the Boundary Waters. All these things that are unique to you enhance the group as well. The best accessories are the things that not only improve your life but are also positive for those around you. Your senses of humor, adventure, and direction are more important than your skirt.

All this dressing alike also makes occasions when you are not part of the group very special. I could describe for you in detail the orange smocked dress I am wearing in my second-grade school picture. I recall vividly the red velvet party dress I got in the fifth grade. I even remember the trip to the store with my mother to pick it out. I know that in the seventh grade I saved up all my baby-sitting money and took the bus to the Sport Mart in down-town Westport to buy a pair of ski pants that were pale blue with pink hearts. What was I thinking? I was thinking no one else in the whole family would have these. (I am sure now that they were grateful for that.)

As an adult, I have shunned uniforms in general but continue to enjoy the benefits of team affiliation. My running group had spe-cial T-shirts printed for ourselves with our team name, The Rum-bledolls, but that was it. It was every woman for herself on tights, jackets, hats, and the other things you need to run through an Ore-gon winter. The team name was taken from a song by Patty Scialfa. We picked her as our role model for her talent and her soul, and it didn't hurt that she is also Mrs. Bruce Springsteen.

My sisters and I no longer dress alike. In fact, there are certain styles and colors that I purposely shun because they are owned by one of my sisters. Julie owns the sweater set. Lian owns turquoise. I would never wear either. On our radio show, we've heard from lots of groups of friends who meet annually and devise their own cos-tumes and rituals. Some have uniforms, like the group of sisters we met at a sisters' convention in Sisters, Oregon, who had matching sweatshirts with their birth order on them. At the time, we thought this was a little over-the-top, but many listeners since have shared similar tales with us. Others do away with clothes altogether. The Galloping Mermaids, a bunch of friends who meet for a week of camping each summer, told us of their annual naked bareback ride on the beach. You know what? I'll bet these women are perfectly normal in the rest of their lives, and this is part of their 10 percent time. A bunch of naked friends on horses is a really good accessory.

Here She Is, Florence Nightingale

by Monica

When we began doing the radio show, people would often ask us to describe the other sisters in a few words. What they were really looking for was a handy label to affix to each of us. Liz is the smart one or Lian is the funny one—these were easy answers that sprung to mind. For some reason everyone kept pinning the label "nurturer" on me. I was surprised the other sisters saw me that way. Maybe the label "nurturer" was the obvious choice because I am a nurse but, in truth, it's a word I would use to describe all of us.

Growing up, we were expected to help take care of our brothers and sisters. Every day, my mother would say, "Girls, I need your help now." And, every day, we would pitch in. Often, this meant taking the baby outside in the stroller so our mother could make dinner for the rest of the family. I would ask, "Where do you want me to take her?"

"Just wheel her around the driveway," my mother would reply.

Sometimes, helping out was as easy as helping a younger sister put on her coat and hat so no one missed the school bus. But more often, it meant doing things you didn't want to do.

On Brendan's first day of nursery school, my mother brought him into the classroom, intending to leave him in the comfort of Miss Buckley's little red schoolhouse. Brendan started crying and clinging to my mother's leg, begging her to stay. She didn't have time for that nonsense. With the other six children waiting in the car, her solution was to make me get out of the car, miss school, and stay with him all day in the classroom. Frankly, it was humiliating. I was in the second grade. I hope when Brendan tells his own children about his first day in nursery school, I'm mentioned somewhere in the credits.

I did not grow up longing to become a nurse. There weren't any nurse Halloween costumes or toy doctor kits or Cherry Ames books in our house. Based on the games of pretend that went on in our house, I was going to become a schoolteacher or a cashier.

Our basement on Cross Highway was the girls' playhouse. Basically, it was divided into three areas. The first was a make-believe apartment where we had an old, worn-out sofa and a broken rotisserie oven. The second area was set up as our classroom, complete with a chalkboard and a desk and chair for the student. My mother had even gotten us some teaching textbooks with lesson plans, but we didn't focus on the teaching. Mostly we were just fascinated with the chalk and eraser. The third area was a pretend retail establishment, with a checkout counter, toy cash register, and monopoly money.

There was no area for a hospital or doctor's office—nothing to spark some inner desire to help others, despite the fact that my mother had herself been a nurse.

I'll admit I was a little jealous of Julie when she became a candy striper in junior high school. Julie wore a cherry-red-and-white striped pinafore, cardigan sweater, and white shoes. My brothers used to tease her and say she looked like she should be behind the counter at Baskin-Robbins. Julie was sweet and kind, but I really think her interest in healthcare was all about the uniform.

Liz, on the other hand, could never be a nurse. The mere mention of needles and shots makes her green and woozy. For that reason, my mother always kept smelling salts in the house. One Saturday when my father was attempting his once-a-decade tricky home-improvement project, he cut his hand deeply, panicked, and asked Liz to look up the doctor's number in the phone book. She passed out cold on the floor. I was just nine years old but I took charge, helping my dad with the bandage, reviving Liz, and calling the doctor. Was that the moment I had my calling?

I don't really know why I decided to become a nurse. I arrived at it by default. I knew I wanted to have a job when I finished school, and becoming a nurse seemed like an easy way to get into college. My high-school friends and my own family were pretty shocked when I announced I was going to nursing school.

During freshman orientation, I was totally intimidated by the other students who had all been hospital volunteers and candy stripers. I hadn't even taken a Red Cross baby-sitting course in high school. In fact, I have very little patience for people.

I didn't really know nursing was right for me until I got my first job as a nursing assistant at George Washington University Hospital. GW was where the renegades in our class went to work. The preppy girls got jobs at Georgetown. All I know is that I loved that job from the first day. I loved taking the bus to work. I loved my timecard. I loved my white polyester dress and my nursing shoes.

I also knew I worked well with a group, having had years of training as a Dolan. The nurses liked having me on their shift because I was a hard worker, cheerful, and could tell a good joke. Besides, I really needed the money so I was willing to work all shifts all the time.

I quickly realized that the nursing classes at school were too theoretical. Nursing is a practical job—you need to learn how to talk with patients and bathe them and feed them and get their IVs running and transfuse blood. I saw that hospital nursing is about hard physical work and being part of a team. It means being responsible for your work, finishing on time, and leaving things ready for the next shift. But mainly, it's about small, reassuring moments with the patients, such as shaving them or soaking their feet in a pan of hot, soapy water. They didn't teach any of that in school.

All summer, I worked the day shift every Saturday and Sunday from 7:00 in the morning to 3:30 in the afternoon. Frequently I would work a double shift from 7 A.M. until midnight, then come back the next morning and do it again. I was nineteen years old. I absolutely loved going to work. My People were there.

At midnight I would take the number 32 bus home, up Wisconsin Avenue. Every night, as I paid my fare, the bus driver would say to me, "Well, here she is. Florence Nightingale!" Taking the bus alone at midnight in Washington, D.C., then walking six blocks to your house was a crazy idea, but I loved hearing the bus driver call me Florence Nightingale and I loved telling him about my night at the hospital. Every night as I got off at my stop, the bus driver would say, "Keep on givin' all that good nursing to the people."

Those words have made me smile a million times over the past twenty years.

People find their sense of self in different places. Maybe it's through their athletic or intellectual accomplishments. Maybe it's in discovering their roles as mothers or sisters. I was lucky to have stumbled onto finding a sense of self through my job.

Strengths and Weaknesses

by Julie

When you grow up in a group, you figure out pretty quickly that you are better at some things than your brothers and sisters. And conversely that there are things that your brothers and sisters are better at than you are. The former observation is easy to grasp. The latter comes as a shock. For both lessons, you have to decide what you are going to do with the information.

There are two very distinct points in my childhood when I realized that my brothers and sisters had talents and abilities that I didn't have. One was when Sheila won the President's Physical Fitness Award, and the other was when Liz got herself a berth on the TV game show *Concentration*.

When Sheila won the President's Physical Fitness Award, I was shocked. Sheila had already managed to establish herself as a disinterested renegade as early as the fourth grade. Despite the fact that she was on the swim team, I didn't really think of her as athletic or interested in sports. She seemed to spend a lot more time after school laying out her clothes for the next day (including accessories) than joining in the ongoing backyard kickball game. No doubt she was the best at the butterfly stroke among all the Dolans. She had a natural grace and rhythm. While all I got were stomach cramps and mouthfuls of water when I attempted butterfly, Sheila moved easily through the water. Her abilities on the Powder Hill ski slope were the same. While she seemed much more interested in her ski outfit and ditching the group, she still managed to outski Liz, Monica, and me.

Sheila was coordinated, but that didn't make her a presidential athlete in my mind. We had all been tested as part of the Fairfield Board of Education physical fitness program, but Sheila was the only one in the family to win the award. There was Sheila, on the stage of the Timothy Dwight Elementary School all-purpose room, receiving a diploma with the seal of the president of the United States. At first I told myself I hadn't qualified because I was older and had to compete in a tougher division, but the competition was tough in all of the divisions, and Sheila managed to qualify. At some point, I had to concede that Sheila was a better athlete—better at running, the butterfly stroke, and skiing—than I was.

Similarly, I had a vague sense that Liz was smart. When we watched *Concentration* or *Jeopardy,* Liz knew all the answers. If you needed to know the capital of Wisconsin, you would ask Liz. If you needed to know something about Japan or how to spell Mississippi, Liz was your go-to girl.

Liz entered a contest for "Kids Week" on the national television game show *Concentration.* She wrote the letter, proofed it, and mailed it all by herself. She didn't ask anyone for help. To our surprise, she was chosen to take the *Concentration*-qualifying quiz. And naturally she passed the test with flying colors.

It was unbelievably exciting to watch her on TV. My mother took us out of school for the day so that we could go to New York and sit in the studio audience to cheer her on. We hooted and hollered from one of the back rows, flailing our arms wildly every time the cameras panned the audience.

There was Liz in her blue-checked dress, standing behind the podium, talking to Hugh Downs. She didn't even seem nervous! It was as if she always talked to Hugh. Liz led off the game and immediately started to make a string of matches. She was racking up gift after gift on the electronic scoreboard behind her—first a sewing machine, then a cocker spaniel! When Liz made the match for the cocker spaniel, I thought I was going to faint from excitement.

She was making match after match, but suddenly she hit a string of "Forfeit One Gift" matches. It all happened so quickly. I wasn't even sure what the word "forfeit" meant, but one by one prizes were being taken away from Liz's side and given to her outclassed opponent.

At the end of the day, we left disappointed because we all knew that Liz had been the superior player, even if she didn't end up winning the game. Liz had made more matches. We knew, everyone in the studio audience knew, even Hugh Downs knew, that Liz was the better of the two players. Though she only came home with the consolation prize, a World Book Encyclopedia set, my sister had been on a television game show and that in itself was quite an accomplishment.

Sitting in the audience watching Sheila and Liz, I felt I was part of something. I was a Dolan watching Dolans receive presidential awards and almost winning a cocker spaniel on television. I basked in the reflected glory. My sisters' achievements made me feel good about myself because, well, they were my sisters.

In a big family, you learn pretty much instinctively that everyone has strengths and weaknesses. Eventually, regardless of age,

certain family members stand out either because of their talents or because of a lack thereof. In some ways, it is very liberating to realize that you don't have to be the best at everything—that there are others to play that role. The pressure is off; there are other people to cover for you. If you are not the most athletic, no problem, someone else will fill that role. Not the funniest? Don't worry, just bring Monica along.

The sooner you come to grips with the fact that everyone has their strengths and weaknesses, the easier life is. You learn your place in the world. It allows you to concentrate on the things you are good at and not spend excessive time worrying that your butterfly stroke is pathetic. Someone else has that covered.

Yes, there were things that I could do very well, some even better than my brothers and sisters, but there were other things that I had to accept as the talents of my siblings. Instead of trying to compete with your siblings, at some point you just have to stand back and applaud. The same is true in my adult life. It is easy to applaud Cathy Freeman because I won't be running any races with her, or Bill Gates because I don't plan to start a software company. It is harder to admire the PC whiz in the next cubicle or your neighbor's green thumb. I think if you can stop and smell the roses—even if they are in your neighbor's garden—you might enjoy life a little more.

The Most Influential Albums of Our Formative Years

JULIE

Carole King, *Tapestry.* No surprise here. Like many Smith classmates, wanted to be Carole King upon graduation.

LIZ

Anything by CSNY or by C, S, N, or Y individually, especially Neil Young's *After the Gold Rush.*

SHEILA

Joni Mitchell, *Blue.* The perfect album for smoking or journal writing or both simultaneously.

MONICA

Joni Mitchell, *Blue.* But for completely different reasons than Sheila. Tops the personal "most listened to album ever" list.

LIAN

Elvis Costello, *My Aim Is True.* Began a lifetime of loving music that happens off the pop charts.

Thunderbird

by Lian

Pequot Elementary was a small, brick school just around the corner from our house in Southport. It was a traditional kindergarten-through-sixth-grade school with one class in each grade, the kind of school where students still went home for lunch and then returned in the afternoon. Schoolmates were neighbors, a rare phenomenon these days. My sister Monica was in sixth grade when I entered kindergarten. Improbably, it was the only time I was ever in the same school as any of my siblings. On the first day of school, my mother said good-bye to us at the front door, and Monica and I walked down the street together to Pequot Elementary.

When we reached the door of the classroom, I could hear the wails of many, including my best friend Sarah Ostheimer. These were the days before daycare and preschool, so for most of my new classmates this was their first away-from-home experience. It never occurred to me to cry. I was finally in school, a place I knew I would love. And my sister would be somewhere in the building. I'd be just fine.

I loved Pequot. It was cozy and warm, with cloakrooms and a big field, and all the teachers, not just mine, knew my name. In my short career there, I had many triumphs, including standout performances as Rudolph in the holiday spectacular and a seal in the first-grade circus. I couldn't color as well as Cathie Walton, but I racked up more weeks as line leader than anyone else. I loved walking down the street to school and I loved walking home again at the end of the day.

Sadly, the little school closed at the end of my first-grade year. The baby boom was over, and schools all across town were being converted to senior centers. Pequot became the home of the Board of Education because it was the most charming. The children from my class were divvied up between two different elementary schools, depending upon which side of the Post Road they lived on. I was to take the bus to Oldfied Elementary with about six of my classmates, including Sarah. The rest of the kids went to Mill Hill, the cooler school. None of my siblings had ever been or would ever go to Oldfield. I was a traiblazer in a red-and-white kilt and brown-flap oxfords.

I'll never forget my first day of second grade at Oldfield. The Pequot kids didn't have classroom assignments yet. The principal hurried us off our bus and made us wait on the blacktop. One by one, she called out names and put people into classes. I was assigned to Miss Ericson's class. All of my former Pequot classmates were assigned to the other second-grade class. I stood alone on one side of the basketball court, watching the clump of kids I knew— including my best friend Sarah—head off to the other classroom. My teacher, the wonderful but painfully skinny Miss Ericson, looked down at my troubled little face and said, "I guess you're all alone. That must mean they think you're very brave."

I knew then as I know now that the times when my sense of self is tested most are the times when I am all alone. It is easy to be yourself with family and friends. You have context; you have a role to play. But it is much more important to be yourself when you are not among familiar faces. Those are the moments that truly define your sense of self.

That first day of second grade, I may have been surrounded by people, but not My People. My former classmates, my best friend—they had each other. But I just had me. I didn't need to be brave so much as decisive. Who was I going to be in this new place without the context of my family and friends? The talker? The shy one? The girl who hates arts and crafts? It was my choice. I decided to go with my strengths: All the stuff I had learned at home as the youngest would work well in a classroom setting. I was a good helper, a good listener, and a good jump-roper. I did just fine in second grade.

Obviously, everyone has to make their own way eventually. I am sure I learned this no sooner than someone from a small family. In fact, coming from a big family could have been a liability in this case—because we did so many things in groups, it could be a little unnerving to be alone. But most of the time, coming from a big family gave me a great deal of confidence in new situations. I rarely got intimidated but, at the same time, I knew my place. It was a good combination.

At home, I was the smallest and the least experienced. I had a role to play, and for a long time it was fairly insignificant. My older brothers and sisters ruled everything from dinner-table conversation to the coveted front seat of the station wagon. I took everything in, but nobody expected me to contribute much until I reached my teen years. I did some cute impersonations of my sisters' friends, I could tap dance, and I was always willing to set the table. That was enough to get by on for many years. During this time, I was absorbing the possibilities of who I could be like. I favored Dick's wicked sense of humor, Julie's willingness to help, and Liz's grasp of current events. But I knew eventually it would all come down to me.

It happened when I was twelve at summer camp in Maine. The girls' camp that my sisters and cousins had attended went out of business—like Pequot Elementary School, a victim of the end of the baby boom. So I boarded the bus bound for Camp Wyonegonic by myself, with a trunkful of green clothes and a good attitude. Though forest green is not really my color, camp was definitely made for me. I loved sleeping in a cabin with no electricity, learning to canoe, singing at mealtime, and even shampooing in the lake. I worked well in groups, respected the rules, and pitched in on every activity. As much as I adored my family, I loved getting away from them, too. For seven weeks every summer, I could just be me, not anyone's sister or cousin.

One of the most anticipated events of the summer was the "play day" with our brother camp down the lake, Camp Winona. This special day of adolescent torture was filled with gaming and sporting, followed by a cookout and a dance at night—just the right combination of competition and burgeoning sexual tension to give a preteen girl like me a stomachache.

I was the leader of one of the two teams in intermediate camp, the Thunderbirds. Our team and one of the boys' teams would hook up and compete against the other two boys' and girls' teams. For some girls, it was all about having the right color Izod shirt to go with the rainbow belt, but I was one of the girls who thought it was important to win. I had signed up to compete in swimming, archery, and canoeing, my best event. When it came time for the canoe race, I was paired up with a scrawny boy from Winona. I wasn't scrawny. I had Shane Gould shoulders from swimming and the strength to stern the canoe. We stood on the shore as the other teams loaded up. There was no question who would be in the back of the boat, steering: me. I wanted to win for the Thunderbirds. He agreed. We got in the canoe.

As we approached the starting line, I heard laughing and comments from the shore. I looked around and realized that out of ten canoes in the water, I was the only girl in the back of the boat. I was alone again. My partner recognized our predicament, too. We could have changed positions; we had the time and good reason. I was suddenly self-conscious. I felt betrayed by my fellow Thunderbirds, who were just as capable as I was but had acquiesced to their skinny, eleven-year-old partners. I didn't want to come in last, but now I had to consider the possibility. The boy in the front of my canoe asked if I wanted to change places. Was this my test?

I think it was. Here was a chance to choose who I wanted to be and what was important to me. I was a Dolan, and along with that came a lot of family attributes, both good and bad, that I could draw on. But that was really just raw material: It was up to me to mold that into something uniquely mine. I watched my brothers and sisters use this same raw material to turn themselves into unique individuals. And now it was my turn.

On that day in the canoe, I chose Dick's sense of athletic confidence, Liz's sense of independence, and Sheila's sense of rebellion. Then, I threw in some of my disdain for selling out and a dose of conviction for doing the right thing. The result was a twelve-year-old with a sense of self that isn't much different than the one I have today in my thirties, just a little more raw. I knew my place. It was in the back of that canoe. I was a stronger paddler than that boy.

"No," I said, "you stay put. I'm fine right here."

The Immutable Laws of Liz

by Liz

In an effort to embrace midlife, I decided to identify the things that were causing me stress and attempt to fix or remove them. Why not take advantage of everything I've learned up until now and make some changes? Here's the problem: I isolated the number-one cause of stress in my life and decided it's me. Right. Not a boss or a family member or an IRS agent. I cause most of the stress in my life by not recognizing that there are things about me that will never change. Instead, I delude myself into thinking that I will become a new person this year. A neater, more organized Liz is always about to emerge. The New Millennium Liz won't throw her clothes on the floor, write her appointments on a scrap of paper, and then shove it into her pocket, or forget to pay the phone bill. The New Millennium Liz is going to get a system and get a grip.

Well, it's time to face facts. I am a forty-four-year-old woman who has had the same general characteristics since I was zero. Emerging from the womb, I was messy and I barely made the deadline. What else is new?

So, my strategy for the new millennium is to face the facts. I need to accept The Immutable Laws of Liz. Those laws fall into two categories: Things That Will Always Be True and Things That Will Never Be True. By accepting these truths about myself, I can remove 90 percent of the stress in my life. That other 10 percent includes big stains on new shirts, airline delays, and other laws of nature and family dynamics over which I have no control.

THREE THINGS THAT WILL NEVER BE TRUE

1. I will never have all the buttons on all my garments. I don't know why sewing a button on a shirt and hemming a pair of pants seems so much harder to me than, say, running the NYC Marathon or starting a business, but they do. Time to roll up those buttonless sleeves and get on with my life. Staples and Scotch tape have their purposes. My mother would always say, "A galloping horse would never notice." I think this is what she meant.

2. I will never be a single-digit size. I am at peace with this. I would love it, however, if I could just stay in the same general double-digit-size range for a year at a time.

3. I will never get birthday cards out on time. The multiple steps involved in card-shopping, finding the address on a scrap of paper, buying a stamp, and mailing it, all in time to beat the clock, are just too much. Instead, I try to call. By now I have set expectations so low with my family that any contact at all around a birthday is a pleasant surprise.

THREE THINGS THAT WILL ALWAYS BE TRUE

1. I will always be early. Growing up, we arrived at 11:15 mass every Sunday at 11:00. I cannot shake this youthful training. I must learn to enjoy all the extra time I spend in airports, movie theater lobbies, and, of course, in doctors' offices. Even if a miracle happens and a doctor is actually on time, what do you think the chances are that they will be early? About the same as the chance that I will have all the buttons on my shirt.

2. I will always be the one in any meeting to ask, "Could we move on to the next item on the agenda?" It's not just that I am impatient. It's that I know the people in the room who want to keep talking about this are not going to follow through anyway. They just like being in meetings because no work gets done.

3. I will always drive my car until the tank gets to dead empty. I hate getting gas. Why stop for gasoline when I can keep driving to my appointment and get there even earlier? This element of living on the edge also applies to work deadlines. Waiting until the last minute is my version of flirting with danger. I believe this deadline pressure actually enhances my productivity. Running out of gas, however, does not.

The advantage of aging is that we see more clearly the patterns in our lives—things that may make no sense but are just true no matter what. I must accept The Immutable Laws of Liz in order to allow peace into my life. Fight these laws and I am doomed to repeat the useless to-do lists of years past. Where are those to-do lists now? In the lint tray of my dryer.

Little Mother

by Julie

The teasing started at breakfast with a comment or two before I left to catch the school bus. It would resume in the late afternoon in the kitchen over Hawaiian Punch and would build to a crescendo by dinner. I hated when Jim and Dick called me "Pizza Face," an unsubtle reference to my latest facial blemish. "Zit head" was another favorite of theirs that exploited the same general insecurity. The generic "Loser," when expertly delivered by my brothers with a singsong tone and a squinting of the eyes, could also drive me away in a huff. Jim began taking Latin in junior high and spiced up his usual repertoire of taunts with more classical sounding verbal abuse that tripped haltingly off his tongue as he stumbled over the conjugations. To simplify matters and still maintain his linguistic superiority, he would call me Julius Caesaras, pronounced *Jew-lee-us Kai-sa-rus,* a term that really didn't mean anything at all but achieved some kind of derogatory status through constant repetition and my own overly dramatic reaction to it. Even Brendan, the baby, would laugh when Jim mocked me with this name. It was humiliating to have a two-year-old laugh at you. Of all the names they used to tease me with, however, "Little Mother" bothered me the least.

Not only did I not mind, I actually enjoyed it when they called me Little Mother. This was my secret desire: I wanted to be more like my mother. She had shoes that matched her pocketbooks, and when she dressed up to go out at night she smelled of Chanel No. 5. She kept her jewelry in a silver box on her dresser and would let me try on her rings and bracelets. She never got mad at me when I woke her up in the middle of the night with an earache. She would give me a couple of orange-flavored aspirin, put me back to bed, and give me her softest sweater to rest my ear on. She enrolled in French cooking classes and made towers of meringue balls and beef covered with jelly. She was my brothers' Cub Scout den mother and wore a blue uniform with pins on it. She let my brothers and their friends paint birdhouses on the kitchen table. She would go into the wetlands near our house and come back with large bunches of what looked like weeds and fashion them into beautiful dried-flower bouquets. She let me make Jell-O anytime I wanted. And even after having eight kids, she looked better in hotpants than any of the girls.

My mother always had a plan for the day and packed a corresponding lunch. I never saw her sit down. She cooked our dinners in the morning and set the breakfast table at night. If you drifted into the kitchen at any hour, my mother was always in the process of packing, organizing, wiping, straightening, stacking, grouping, and unpacking children and things. On days when we stayed home, she organized long afternoon walks up the lane to look at the cows or sent us out the back door with bags of stale bread to feed the ducks.

I was happy to be the Little Mother. As the oldest girl, I felt like I was in charge of the other girls. It was my responsibility to organize the games or set the rules for our make-believe clubs and schools. If we were planning a backyard show, I was the director and choreographer. If we made a new clubhouse out of the abandoned brick barbecue grill hidden behind the two fir trees, I was the one who set the membership rules.

I was the one in charge of breaking up the squabbles between Sheila and Monica before Mom found out. I was the principle spokesperson for the girls when we finally got up the nerve to address the issue of household-chore inequity with our parents. I was the one who argued with Jimmy and Dick that watching *The Partridge Family* was just as legitimate a television viewing choice as a Yankees or Rangers game.

Later, I was the sister who became the baby-sitter/chauffeur-in-residence. I was the one who would nag the group to get up off the couches in the den and clean up the kitchen before Mom and Dad got home. It didn't matter if we had just reenacted *The Lord of the Flies*, as long as the kitchen was cleaned up by the time they walked in the back door.

Sometimes Sheila and Liz would rebel and say, "You're not our *mother*, you can't tell us what to *do*." Their insubordination was infuriating. I really felt as though I was in charge. I think the source of my bossiness came from knowing that, as the oldest girl, I had wisdom and perspective that my younger brothers and sisters didn't have.

It was also my role to break ground. I was the first to get a shag haircut, to get my period, and to own mod clothing. I was the first girl to break free of matching outfits, and the first to take a bath by myself. (Until I was eleven, my mother would bathe two or three of us together in the tub. I didn't mind taking a bath with my sisters as long as I got the end of the tub farthest from the faucet. For some reason the faucet stayed very hot, and if you were sitting near it and you weren't careful, you could burn your back.) I was the first to go on a date—I think. I can't be sure of this. Sheila led a fairly secretive romantic life, even as early as sixth grade. I was the first to drive and the first to go college. I was the first of the girls to get married and the first to have a baby.

Being first meant making a lot of mistakes. I am sure my sisters made some mental notes to refrain from inviting out-of-town boys to Christmas dances after my date showed up three hours early, *with his parents*, when I still had pink spongy curlers in my hair. Sheila learned from my experience that if your curfew was midnight, Mom would be standing in her nightgown and raincoat in the driveway when you came home at 1 A.M. My sisters also probably picked up on the fact that it's not a good idea to smoke a cigarette, hold a can of Tab between your legs, fiddle with the car radio, and drive at the same time, as evidenced by my collision with a parked car.

Perhaps the choices I made freed my sisters and brothers to be more adventurous in their own lives. Maybe the parental pressure to pursue more traditional routes was lessened for them because Jim as the oldest boy and I as the oldest girl had already been down those roads. While I felt compelled to sport a future-leader-of-America wardrobe à la Tricia Nixon, Monica was free to wear groovy purple, yellow, and green knit pantsuits. My sisters, who were my bridesmaids, thanked me after my very traditional wedding because they knew that my mother had gotten double-skirted reception tables out of her system and they could freely plan to elope to Las Vegas. It was as if I had unconsciously set up a diversionary tactic for our parents' approval/disapproval system. I'll go right, so you can go left.

My Little Mother tendencies found a home in my adult psyche. I couldn't wait to have my own kids. While many of my friends were just beginning to make headway in their careers, I plunged into motherhood. I was never happier than the day I became a real mother for the first time.

I also tended to find jobs that let me live out my mothering bent. I ended up working in organizations where the principal task was to organize others, essentially telling other people what to do—not that different from organizing a good game of school in the cellar with Liz, Sheila, and Monica.

My husband says I worry too much. I worry about my family, friends, neighbors, and coworkers. He tells me that some things are not my responsibility, but I want to make things right for the people around me. I want to help even when nobody asks for it.

While I am still the oldest girl in the family, I am no longer the first. Now I watch as my brothers and sisters run marathons, start businesses, volunteer in foreign countries, and change careers. I think I am more likely to seek their advice than give them advice of my own. Still, sometimes I just can't help myself—I offer Lian unsolicited parenting advice or give Liz suggestions about how she could reduce the stress in her life. Their responses are usually the adult version of what they'd say so many years ago: "You're not my mother; you can't tell me what to do."

OK, I admit it. I still like to be in charge, set up the rules, and give unsolicited advice. I am not afraid to be first, even if it means making mistakes. A lot of times people don't appreciate my mothering, but I can't help myself. Go ahead, call me Little Mother—I don't mind.

Red Sweatpants

by Lian

It all started when my husband threw out the red sweatpants. Literally threw them out. I had worn them through nine months of pregnancy and thought they were still working fine as my baby approached six months. Apparently my husband thought otherwise. I found them in the garbage, irretrievable even by my low standards. When I questioned him, he pleaded, "Can't you find something else to wear?"

"No," I wanted to scream, "I'm a new mother and I don't know what my style is anymore!"

When I worked, dressing was easy. I knew who I was and what I needed to communicate through my clothes. I devised a streamlined, working-girl uniform. As a video producer, I didn't have to dress up, but I did have to look in charge, of the moment. Jeans, an excellent T-shirt, and a decent blazer usually sent the right message. Every once in a while, I'd swap the jeans for a black skirt. My entire wardrobe fit easily on the floor of my closet. But once I had children and decided to stay at home, the bottom fell out of that closet, and the results weren't pretty.

Like many new mothers, I took refuge in sweatpants and well-stretched maternity clothes. Some days I'd wake up for a 5 A.M. feeding, throw on yesterday's red sweats, and, before I knew it, twelve hours had passed and I still hadn't showered—in fact, I'd gone grocery shopping and run a full day's worth of errands in this smashing ensemble. Not surprisingly, a fresh application of lipstick at the dinner hour didn't fool my husband.

There are lots of reasons why new motherhood dislodges your

fashion sensibility. First off, your body has changed and continues to mutate for many months after giving birth. You may get right back to your prebaby weight, but it's not the same body. Even your feet get bigger, which seems like an Eighth Amendment violation of cruel and unusual punishment. Second, your job description has changed, and therefore the uniform must change. I believe there are still states in which nursing in a blazer can land you in jail for indecent exposure. And we all know that bodily fluids and "dry clean only" don't mix. Third, you're broke. If you go back to work, your entire salary is now going toward day care, pump rental, and professional spit-up removal. If you stay at home, you just can't clip enough coupons to make up for the salary loss. And finally, you're tired—too tired to care, too tired to shop, too tired to spell self-improvement, let alone enact it. And there's always the nagging thought that it really doesn't matter what you look like because now you're somebody's mother.

Lately, though, how I look has started to matter again. Not in a slave-to-fashion way, but as a means of communicating who I am. After two children and six years of motherhood, I've regained a sense of myself, of what I'm doing. I'm ready to reclaim that part of me that I checked at the door of the labor-and-delivery room years ago. I'm not as hip as I was in my twenties, but I'm a long way from the red-sweatpants-wearing time of early parenthood. My rediscovered sense of style is a reflection of my growing confidence in the job that I have chosen: mother.

Neo-Traditional Thanksgiving

by Sheila

So you are busy stockpiling cans and yams and paper products, are you? Have you ordered the twenty-pound turkey from the butcher or booked your flight home? You know, these aren't the only choices available. There are other traditions you might follow. For instance, you might decide to honor your seventeen-year-old daughter (who is vegetarian), her boyfriend (who recycles everything), your boyfriend (who is Japanese), and yourself (a chronic dieter from Connecticut) by planning a Vegetarian/Asian/New England/Lean Cuisine feast for four. In which case, here are some tips you might follow.

Assuming you live in New York City, the first thing you'll need is a second kitchen. That way your boyfriend can roll the sushi while you sauté the spinach. Then again, seeing as it's probably tight when two people are just breathing in that kitchen, you might have to send everyone out. After all, it's Thanksgiving and you want to preserve some decorum, so out, everyone, out of the kitchen! And don't forget to wash the spinach thoroughly.

Now that everyone has gone into the one room that functions as living room/bedroom/dining room/office, you can all sit down and talk. Thankfully, this Thanksgiving everyone you're having over likes one another. You and your boyfriend, your daughter and her boyfriend, the young folks and the less-young folks—it's a virtual festival of liking. Remember, Thanksgiving can be a long day, so a lot of liking can really keep things moving until it's time to eat.

After mingling and liking comes dinner. Hooray! But where?

How about that area with the small desk against the wall, also known as the office? Of course you will have transformed the desk into an East/West tableau for the holiday—a wonderful choice. I love the way you're going to use every plate you ever owned and just keep passing them around. No one will notice that the Pottery Barn soup bowls you bought for your college boyfriend in '79 are juxtaposed with the Williams-Sonoma clearance items you bought after the divorce. Stripes and checks, plastic and porcelain are great together, so enjoy!

You know what comes next—video and pie! Trust your instincts and keep it simple—no need for mince or fancy tarts. Apple pie is fine by me (a slice of tradition never hurts). Sleepily situate yourselves in the living area. Ask your daughter to put in her video from Europe—as if she won't volunteer first. Give your tummyful of yellowtail an understanding rub, and tell whoever's closest to hit the lights. I can just hear your daughter's boyfriend now, as the video starts to play, saying, "Hey, don't throw out that centerpiece, it can be crushed and used as mulch." Now that will be a holiday to remember. Enjoy it, and enjoy those who mean the most to you.

Sheila's Thanksgiving Menu

APPETIZERS

Hand-rolled sushi
Olives, nuts, and pickles
Cheese and crackers
Green tea punch and cranberry spritzers

MAIN COURSE

Salmon fillet with lemon and herbs
Seasoned vinegar rice with nori
Sautéed spinach in sesame oil with pine nuts
Stuffed eggplant
Broiled tomatoes with garlic cloves
Watercress and endive salad
Miso soup

DESSERT

Apple pie
Coffee and tea
Nashi pears

The Trailing Spouse

by Julie

There it was in the company manual, an entire section on the "trailing spouse." It just didn't sit right. Something about the word "trailing" sounded so pathetic, as if I were some aimless soul being dragged off to a foreign land.

"Trailing spouse" didn't describe anything about my married life. My husband and I always worked together to make sure that the kids were picked up, dinner was made, and job demands were met. We both decided to move to Bangkok, even though it would mean taking time off from my career to follow his. To have my husband's employer assign me this new title felt just plain weird.

Still, my first week in Bangkok was exhilarating. While it had been an emotionally exhausting experience to pack up the house, see our oldest son off to college, ship the family dogs to Colorado, say goodbye to family and friends, and fly twenty-three hours to my new home, it seemed like we were going on an extended vacation. It was the first unstructured time I had had in years. I was stunned by so much change all at once, but I was happy to be free of the weekly commute from San Francisco to Los Angeles, daily household chores (we were in a sparsely furnished apartment and eating out frequently), and my constant state of guilt for not living up to my PTA fund-raising responsibilities. I finally had the mental space to take a nap or read a book in the middle of the afternoon. I had a new life, but actually I had no life.

The myth of my extended vacation in Thailand came to a halt the first morning that my husband and son went to work and school. At 6 A.M. one Monday morning, they both marched out the front door. For my husband, working in Bangkok was not that different than working in the United States. He worked for the same company with the same logo and the same e-mail system. And for my son, although his classmates were very different and the cafeteria served Som Tam soup, school still involved calculus and PE class. He still lived the life of a high school student. In some ways, I was envious of their ready-made lives. I wanted to have somewhere to go in the morning and people to talk to.

When the door closed behind them that first morning, I thought, *Now what?* How was I going to build a life here in Bangkok? I had no knowledge of Thai, no firm grasp of where I was in the city of Bangkok, and couldn't distinguish a five-Baht from a ten-Baht coin. I knew no one. I spent most of my day not speaking. This had never happened to me before. I have always been able to strike up conversation as a means of making myself more comfortable in new situations. Without Thai, I became a desperately smiling mute.

I was overwhelmed by loneliness. One day early on, I sucked it up, put on my bathing suit and flip-flops, and went to the swimming pool in our apartment building. I didn't really want to swim, but I thought I might meet someone. After swimming a few laps, I stood by the side of the pool, as insecure as a seventh grader, nodding and smiling at a group of women comfortably chatting in the shallow end. At that moment, I have never wanted to talk to anyone so much in my whole life.

Chrissy from New York, whose husband works for the Mars company and who has three kids (it is standard practice in expatriate communities to identify yourself by your husband's employer—something I will never get used to), probably sensed my loneliness from fifty yards off and came over. She asked if I was new to Bangkok. I tried to control myself as I replied because I was afraid all the emotion of the past few weeks would come tumbling out with my answer. I was just so relived to be talking to someone. I was having a hard time organizing my thoughts; I wanted to say so many things, and Chrissy had only asked one question. We really didn't talk about much of anything; mostly we talked about her kids, who were bickering over who was going to ride the one family bicycle. Chrissy was trying to establish some turn-taking system. I am sure our chat didn't mean much to Chrissy, but to me, that small conversation was a turning point—it was a first step toward finding a way to connect to my new home.

When my husband goes to work and my son is at school, I am the one who lives in Bangkok. I have to figure out where to buy a screwdriver or if the foul-smelling durian fruit in the market is edible. I am also chiefly responsible for determining if our family is going to be happy here. My role is to interpret this strange new place for my family. After multiple moves, I am convinced that attitude is everything. You'll have a negative experience with a negative attitude. You have to try to like it.

When my son staggers home after cross-country practice, it is my job to help him focus on the amazing python he saw on his run, rather than the ninety-five-degree heat and humidity. Or when my husband innocently asks why the washer and dryer are not hooked up, it is my job not to explode with frustration but to laugh as I recount the saga of the power outage, broken water pipe, and subsequent flooding and retiling of our kitchen floor.

I am the one who has to try to maintain stability in the midst of instability. We don't know for sure how long we will stay in Thailand or where we will go next. Because we aren't certain where we are going, it makes appreciating where we are even more important.

I guess I have always been the emotional center of my family. In Bangkok, it is up to me to see the differences not as hardships but as adventures. It is up to me to set an example and to learn Thai and to discover everything that is great about this place. So even though my husband's company may label me as the one "trailing," I know that for my family I am leading the way.

Rub It Up

by Sheila

On a hot June morning, in the middle of an enormous concrete playground, with more than one hundred kids in my charge, I was hit on the right side of my head by a flying soccer ball. What are the odds? The seventh grader who did it looked at me, half laughing, half scared, and knowing that this freakish accident could have real consequences. I was the principal after all, even though I felt a lot more like a child on that particular day. As the tears flowed down my cheeks that morning, I looked for a place to hide in the big empty schoolyard, but found none. The last time I'd cried in front of children was when I'd finished reading *Charlotte's Web* to my first-grade class, and I had sworn I'd never let my guard down again. The principal is not supposed to cry, and soccer balls are not supposed to land anywhere but on the ground. I was hurt and humiliated, but I was relieved somehow that this had happened so early in the day. You see, I had had a bad week—my divorce was being finalized. Nothing was more wrenching than the pain of seeing fourteen years dissolve on a piece of cheap, white paper. I cried because I got hit and it hurt, and my whole life hurt. I cried because I felt like I couldn't control anything in my life, and so the random soccer ball landing full force on my head felt like just another blow among the many I had received that week.

First there came the call that a meeting time had been set. I would have to sign the papers in person, in front of a lawyer. Going anywhere other than to my job felt like an impossible task. That same week I received a threatening letter and phone call at work about some money I owed a credit card company—a lot of money.

So I was considering staying at work and just dealing with it. Not only was I used to the pain, I also felt comfortable working under duress. The whole year of my separation, I went to work with a pain in my heart so deep that taking care of children was the only thing that kept me from succumbing to it. Teaching is a full-time responsibility that doesn't allow you a moment to reflect on your needs as a person. The routines and the needs of the children kept me from focusing on my life. I was the one who administered first aid; I was the one who made people feel better. I'm sure the children were shocked to see that I had feelings too.

A concerned parent at the school took me to the emergency room at St. Vincent's Hospital that morning after I saw the school nurse. While I sat in the emergency room I imagined that something truly terrible was wrong with me and I started to panic. What would happen to my daughter? This couldn't happen now, especially now when she needed me most. I looked over at the parent and said, "I think I'm going to faint." That's what I used to do in church and other places where I had to sit and wait for a long time. He didn't flinch, but gave me his hand and said, "It's going to be OK." He had no idea how those simple words, true or not, made me feel. They were like the magic words my mother used to say when we ran into the house with cuts and scrapes as kids. "Rub it up," she'd say. What she meant was, *I know you got hurt, and I'm sorry, but it's going to be all right. Everything is going to be fine.*

"Rub it up" is the mantra that replaces the chant, "It hurts, it hurts, it hurts." That week, I had been walking through quicksand, dreading the signing of the divorce papers, cursing the creditors, and trying to show up for my life. I hadn't considered that things might actually turn out all right. "Rub it up" buys you a little time to think about something besides the pain. It also means that you have it within your power to make yourself feel better.

The X rays showed that my head was fine and I could go home.

I hadn't taken a day off in years and didn't know what to do with the rest of the afternoon. I was supposed to rest, which was a foreign concept to me. I took a cab the ten blocks home and remember buying some ginger ale at the store. Another one of my mother's prescriptions was ginger ale for the injured or sick. I went into my dark, tiny apartment and stared at the bed for a few minutes. I got set up with the soda, some crackers, and a magazine. I climbed into my bed slowly and leaned back on the pillows. I started to cry again, from the pain of letting go. I needed to rest and I needed to feel again. Most of all, I needed to rub it up, because everything was going to be all right.

a sense of

humor

A Sense of Humor

by Lian

When I think back to my childhood, certain images come rushing toward me—giant night-time games of flashlight tag with friends and cousins, playing dress-up in the attic with my mother's old clothes, shooting a plastic arrow at my brother Brendan's head with my bow-and-arrow set that I earned selling Burpee seeds. I see the pictures of my child-hood. But even more clearly than the pictures, I hear the sounds. And the sounds are always laughter.

There are other sounds I hear, too—teasing and retorts, fighting and yelling, Bruce Springsteen and the Clancy Brothers—but laughter drowns them out. We laughed on the bus to school, in the snow forts we built outside, sitting around in the family room, and in our beds at night. We laughed loudest at the dinner table and hardest at church, where we weren't supposed to laugh at all. As the youngest, I watched as my sisters and brothers went off to school or to new cities or to get married, and what I missed most was the laughter, and what I loved most was the laughter when they came home.

I can't remember exactly what was so funny—or even if it was that funny—but I do remember that it was important that everybody try to be funny. We weren't big joke tellers or practical jokers. Ours was not a house of impressionists or physical comedians. But we all developed into storytellers by necessity. With so many voices in the house, we couldn't get away with average conversation, so we learned to observe life in a certain way and be on the lookout for things that made us smile. To set ourselves apart from one another, we had to translate our own day-to-day world into something unusual. Humor was the tool.

As the youngest, I felt this most particularly. Sitting around a dinner table with seven older siblings, it was imperative to tell a great story or no one was going to listen. The expectations were high that the story be entertaining, and the "I care" factor very low. By that I mean nobody really cared about what went on in my day—who I played with at recess, the name of my music teacher, what I learned in ballet. Those sorts of small concerns were for people from small families, where people cared.

If I had a social studies project due that day, it was no big deal. Probably half the crowd had had a social studies project due that day, too. Or, in my case, everyone sitting at the table had done the exact same social studies project—a diorama depicting some aspect of our ethnic heritage—at some point in his or her life. I had to come up with some new angle on the diorama or I was dead. No one would listen and I would never get my moment at the table.

I had to work on my material. What *about* the diorama of the Blarney Stone could I highlight? Its resemblance to a baked potato? That I had dropped it getting off the bus and stuck it back together with paste and toilet paper? Or the fact that 90 percent of the kids in my 90 percent Irish fourth-grade class had also chosen the Blarney Stone as the symbol of their Irish pride? What was so funny about my Blarney Stone?

So I listened and I learned about what was funny from my family. Steadily, we developed a collective sense of humor that defined us as Dolans and gave us great confidence when we went out in search of a larger audience. I learned that observational humor is funny; whining is not. Making fun of yourself, funny; making fun of your mother, not funny. I absorbed how to pace a story and turn a phrase; where hyperbole, embellishments, and colorful fibs worked; what details to keep in and what could be edited out. And, of course, I learned the value of a great punchline.

My father is a wonderful storyteller, a link in the chain of Irish men with a way with words. My mother is the ultimate straight man whose constant refrain is, "Oh, you think everything's funny." Well, it was to us. We laughed at each other's expense, sure. The family heckling about bad haircuts, loser boyfriends, and cheap Christmas gifts continues today. And there were favorite targets outside the family that made us choke with laughter. The milkman who delivered milk twice a week for fifteen years and every time asked, "How's the big family this morning?" A certain baby-sitter who tied us, crying and screaming, to the refrigerator and called it "the refrigerator game." Or the neighbor who had a few too many cocktails, wished us all good night, and walked straight into our coat closet. He stayed in there for a minute, too, just in case it really was the way home.

But mainly, we laughed at ourselves—our bad food-service jobs or baby-sitting mishaps; low grades, poor athletic performances, or missed cheerleading opportunities; and the usual crimes and punishments of the teen years. Any story of personal humiliation, funny. Any story of personal triumph, not funny.

I actually used to rehearse in the bathroom before going to the dinner table. I realize now that I was working on my material—a key concept in developing a sense of humor. Back then, I was looking for an edge, so as not to be swallowed up at the table by my brothers and sisters. I would stand in front of the mirror and shape up that story of the arts-and-crafts project gone horribly wrong. A precisely folded origami swan, not funny. An origami swan that looked like a pregnant beaver, funny. Or I'd spend time on a boffo punchline to my "took the class gerbil home and it dies on me" tale. I couldn't just show up and talk about a dead gerbil, though that alone is funny.

If I wanted my moment at the table, my gerbil couldn't just die—he had to die spectacularly. My gerbil, Gerbie, blind and three-legged, had to die of a heart attack while running on the gerbil wheel. Not just any heart attack: a heart attack brought on by the sudden threatening appearance of our barking dog, Tor. That was a more exciting end to the class pet than the truth, which was that he was old, blind, and three-legged. "Gerbie," I could tell my siblings, "was, in fact, barked to death."

It was a luxury, really, to be the creator, editor, and performer of my own material. It was up to me to pick and choose the parts of my day to share with my family. I controlled the flow of information and the content. The delivery system was all mine to determine. And in our family, the delivery system that got you the most attention was a well-told story. So that's what I would rehearse in front of the mirror. I could leave out the garden-variety awkwardness of junior high or the standard angst of the teen years, and then reconstruct my life to be more entertaining than it really was. I didn't fabricate things. I only worked on the truth. Highlighted the hilarity, downplayed the downers. Because nobody wanted to hear the truth—that would be dull and tedious. But my family would listen to an entertaining, snappier version of the truth. That was dinner table–worthy. Failing to get a lead in the school play, not funny. Failing to get a lead in the play because of an unsightly blemish and an unfortunate misstep during the audition, funny.

These days, having a radio show about the real happenings of my life forces me to rehearse the one about making meatballs for one hundred twenty-seven preschoolers or the encounter with the suck-up saleswoman. But even before I had a public forum, I worked on my material. Voicemail messages, sales transactions, opening lines for interviews? I practice. Parties, book club meetings, or family holidays? I like to arrive armed with a few good stories, like the one about the tarot-card reader correctly predicting my marriage to a man I had not, as yet, dated. Or the one about my complete breakdown after a large earthquake and my insistence on eating canned food for a week, even though we had open and fully operational supermarkets stocked with all sorts of produce and fresh items. Or the one about the wedding toast gone awry in which the groomsmen dropped their drawers and mooned the bride. This was good raw material that just needed a little shaping to elicit belly laughs.

Let's face it. Like most people, my life is not inherently fascinating to others. I'm no Jane Goodall. Working with chimpanzees, interesting. Picking up dry cleaning, not that interesting. Neither is refinancing your house, colonoscopies, or a new diet. But these things can be sources of humor if you work on the material. Take out the unnecessary details, compress the timeline, eliminate the unsavory subplots, and add a touch of deprecation—that's the beginning of a good story.

The benefits of working on my material are twofold. One, it helps me put my life into perspective. And two, I don't drag other people down with me. The much-anticipated vacation to the beach that became one long ER visit, including three cases of the flu and one of strep throat, becomes much less tragic when I can tell the story of my eighteen-month-old strapped into the Tube de

Hannibal for a chest X ray. The postpartum funk I sank into after baby number two is much livelier in my shortened, complete-with-accents cocktail party version.

I find this to be true of my friends as well. I don't have to hear the blow-by-blow heart-attack story of my friend Michael to know how serious it was or how scared he felt. In Michael's suitable-for-public-consumption version, along with the heart attack comes a few laughs and a great "white light" moment in the operating room.

Or I think about my father, a master at this technique, signing mortgage papers on a house several years ago. The house was in Florida ('cause that's the law) and the signing day was Halloween. Many workplaces encourage employees to dress in costume. This is a business practice I don't understand. Unless your workplace is Ringling Bros. and Barnum & Bailey Circus, please come to the office in your regular clothes. Anyway, my father is at this bank, signing the papers for a hefty mortgage, and the loan officer is dressed as Raggedy Ann. Red wig, white face, big black shoes. You can imagine the scene. Mr. Dolan, please sign here to borrow hundreds of thousands of dollars. And I, Raggedy Ann, will witness your signature.

I laughed out loud when I heard that story. A bank officer dressed as a bank officer, not funny. A bank officer dressed as giant rag doll, very, very funny. And about once a week, I smile when I think of my father doing business with Raggedy Ann. Postpartum depression, dead gerbils, home mortgages—it's all what you make of it. And I think people have the obligation to make the best of it. Work on your material a little so the rest of us can see a slice of your life, but not a cross section. Save the gory details for your Satellite Sister; most people just want the highlights.

It sounds so obvious to say that a sense of humor is important. Sentiments like that are the stuff of bumper stickers and inspirational stories in *Reader's Digest*. "Have a sense of humor about life!" Thanks, that's a big help. Will do. But it's one of those clichés that is true. Using your sense of humor as a guide makes life more of everything—enjoyable, uplifting, and, most of all, tolerable.

In many ways, humor is not a sense at all, but a filter through which to view the world. Life is full of moments of wonder, confusion, panic, joy, humility, and self-doubt. You can choose to observe these moments through a magnifying glass of introspection or through the flip shades of humor. The magnifying glass gives you a picture of reality that can be unrelenting and, ultimately, counterproductive—too much of the real thing to provide any perspective.

If you choose to see things through the flip shades of humor, you can adjust the view and make it better. Of course, not everything in life is a laugh riot, nor should it be. Illness, divorce, a teenager in trouble—these sorts of situations need to be talked about with somebody close, with honesty and openness, not worrying about the audience response. Not every moment of my life needs to be fodder for a dinner party or a book club or a radio show. But, ultimately, I find that even the most difficult transitions can be made more tolerable with a little editing and a good punchline.

A sense of humor can turn the serious into the bearable, the humiliating into the humbling, the mundane into the unique. A sense of humor allows you to take the moments of your life, from the brightest to the darkest, and make them funny.

One Saturday morning, I was spending some rare time alone in my house. My husband and two small children were out, the dog was asleep under the avocado tree, and I was doing a yoga tape in the TV room. The voice on the tape told me to be a cobra reaching for the sun. In reality, I must have looked like a sway-backed chicken reaching for the last bit of grain in the trough.

"Focus," the voice on the tape said. And I was really trying to quiet the running to-do list in my head when the doorbell rang. Not an unusual occurrence, as my front door seems to emit some siren call that only solicitors can hear. Choco-nut turtles, frozen pizza dough, wrapping paper, and magazines, magazines, magazines all find their way to my front door and, depending on my mood, into the house.

On that day, a rocket scientist rang the bell. Really, I could tell he was one. Nervous gaze, short-sleeved button-down shirt, and thick glasses. We live near the Jet Propulsion Lab, so I have experience with these types. "Yes?" I inquired.

"I'm a scientist at JPL and I'm going door-to-door to sell my novel, *Mars Attack!*" the solicitor said without a trace of irony. "Would you like to see a copy?"

Despite the fact that I am fairly familiar with the novel format, I took the copied-at-the-office-in-my-spare-time book and thumbed through it.

Now, I could have been annoyed at the guy for disturbing my peace and quiet, turning up at my door uninvited, hawking wares. I could have been turned off when he described the science-fiction plot—my least favorite genre of writing, as if the title *Mars Attack!* didn't already give it away. Or I could have been insulted when he told me the price was a whopping $22.50 for a plastic-bound, mimeographed copy. But I wasn't any of these things. I was thinking about my material.

I reached for my wallet and bought his book.

I bought the book because selling anything door-to-door isn't easy. I bought the book because the writer had put his heart into that work and no one would publish it, so he did it himself. But truthfully, I bought the book because a struggling writer trying to sell his book, not funny. A rocket scientist selling novels door to door, funny.

And for $22.50, I got a great story for the next family get-together.

We are not together every night anymore, my brothers and sisters. But we save up our material for special events. We save up the little things we've seen or heard, the observations we've made, and we shape them into a story so that we can all revel in the comforting, connecting sounds of laughter.

𝒯hings That Are Always Funny

When looking for the perfect story to tell at a dinner party, neighborhood get-together, or wake, here's a list of good starting points. Any story that involves one or more of the following setups is always a winner:

- Personal humiliation at the hands of hotel employees, gas station attendants, or bathing suit saleswomen.

- Brushes with the law.

- Wedding disasters, especially inappropriate toasts and drunk bridesmaids, but only if the wedding is not your own.

- Travel mishaps that involve misdirected luggage, language barriers, or emergency room visits. Or preferably, all three.

- Your dress getting caught in the top of your pantyhose. Or the male version: shirttail through the fly. Can't lose with either one.

- Unexplained facial blemishes that coincide with job interviews, TV appearances, or first dates.

- Road trips.

- Small kitchen fires and other dinner party disasters.

- Your family fights, but only to people who are not your family.

- Your old boyfriend, but not to your new boyfriend.

- Bad haircuts and other fashion faux pas (your own).

- Wild animals trapped in your house.

- Dog imitations.

*J*okes That Just Aren't Funny

No, we haven't lost our sense of humor. No, we don't take everything too seriously. No, we're not interested in hearing the punchline. These kinds of jokes just aren't funny:

- Ex-wife jokes.
- Ex-husband jokes.
- Mother-in-law jokes.
- Jokes about bodily functions.

- Jokes about body parts.
- Private jokes in a public forum.
- Ethnic jokes.
- "My wife the compulsive shopper" jokes.
- The one about the priest, the rabbi, and the drunk.
- Cat jokes.

You Can't Make This Stuff Up

by Julie

I think some of my friends think I'm funnier than I actually am. I never consider myself funny, but I realize I benefited from living with funny people. Growing up, I got a lot of mileage repeating to my friends the funny stories that my brothers and sisters told at the dinner table. But it was my father who introduced me to an eternal spring of comedy.

As far as funny goes, my father was always the leadoff batter, setting the tone and topic for family conversations. And much of his material came straight from the newspaper. Long before Jay Leno made his living from the headlines, my father saw the comic potential of our local papers, *The Bridgeport Post* and *The Fairfield Town Crier*. Nobody read the newspaper like my father, except maybe Steve Allen, to whom my dad gave full credit. But at our house, it was my father's show, and I never wanted to miss it.

In the morning there was always an air of tension in the

kitchen. Would the hapless newspaper deliveryman toss the paper up our driveway before my father came down for breakfast? I was up early, on the lookout for the paper. I didn't mind running outside in my bathrobe in February to get the bagged treasure. Sometimes I would underestimate how cold it was outside and my bare feet would stick to the frozen flagstone walk.

If the paper wasn't there, my father could not eat his breakfast. He would pace around, constantly opening and closing the front door as if the newspaper deliveryman might have thrown the paper onto our front walk in the nanosecond since the last time my father had opened the door. (Later, when we moved to Southport, we had a more reliable papergirl and much of the morning tension about the newspaper disappeared.) When the paper finally did arrive, my father settled in for the event, his coffee within reach and his oldest daughter within earshot. I wonder if he knew how intently I was listening.

My father read *The New York Times* in the morning and *The Bridgeport Post* and *The Fairfield Town Crier* in the evening. In the morning he might remark on the latest crazy Khrushchev stunt or report a story about a guy in Brooklyn who had set up a parrot-breeding farm in his apartment. While the Cold War wasn't inherently funny, my father found a way to make it as interesting as the room full of parrots.

But the real fun began with his reading of *The Bridgeport Post* and *The Town Crier.* The lower the journalistic standards, the higher the comedic value. He would start laughing and say, "Oh this is good," or "Get a load of this," or "You gotta love this." While the police blotter or Ann Landers's letters were always sure bets for material, my father could even find hilarity in the Bridgeport Sanitation Workers' strike. He was particularly fond of reporting to my mother the latest hint from Heloise, especially those that involved old panty hose. The more preposterous the advice, the better. My mother would shake her head and beg, "Oh Jim, stop, that's ridiculous."

"No, no, it's true," he'd say. "It's in the paper." We'd all have a good laugh imagining my mother brewing coffee with used panty hose.

Sometimes I couldn't believe that it was the same paper I had just read. When I read *The Fairfield Town Crier,* I only saw the school lunch menus and pictures of our First Selectman. My father would read a one-inch column item about a man from Shelton who attempted to clip his hedge with a lawn mower and by the time he finished recapping the story to us at the dinner table, I could see the decimated hedge and the expression on the Shelton man's face from his near-death experience. We would veer off from the Shelton man's gardening techniques to recounting our own home-repair mishaps, which would lead to riotous reminiscence of how Jimmy and Dick, while trimming the top of our Christmas tree with a saw, managed to hack it in half. A one-inch column was all my father needed to inspire an evening's worth of conversation.

We tracked some stories over time, watching the paper for periodic installments of our local drama as if it were a Dickens novel. One of my favorites was the ongoing saga of a Westport woman who was being sued by her neighbors for having twenty-seven cats. My father would play all the parts of this epic, giving a dramatic reading of the Crazy Cat Lady's assertions that she was a cat lover, plain and simple, and the angry neighbors' complaints about the cats' midnight crying. One time we did a drive-by of the Crazy Cat Lady's house to see what a house with twenty-seven cats looked liked. From our dinner-table discussions, I had imagined a Dr. Seuss–like chalet with cats on the roof. We were disappointed to see not a single cat from the road.

My father's comic rendition of the local papers taught me that real life is funny. Daily drama is where the action's at. People all around us do crazy things, and then somebody writes about them in the paper. The next big laugh is right around the corner. My father taught me to look for laughs in the fine print.

I no longer get to hear my father read the paper every day, though he does save up his favorite stories for seasonal gatherings. Left to my own devices, I now look for laughs in the fine print of *The Bangkok Post*. I am tracking an ongoing story of a wayward Buddhist monk who stuffs his saffron robes into a fake Army officer's uniform before his nightly prowls for women and booze. I'm also following the claims of a Bangkok woman who uses a special back-slapping technique to enlarge a woman's bra size. That's right, one good slap on the back and she can take you from a B to a C cup, just ask one of her many satisfied customers. And then there's the story of the elephant band in northern Thailand who has just released its first CD. Ridiculous? No, no, it's true. It's right here, in the paper.

$\mathcal{A}$ttributes of a Good Audience

After learning how to tell a good story, the most important skill you can develop is how to be a good audience. Here are our thoughts on what we like in an audience, large or small.

1. Listen. This may be hard to do, but stop talking for five minutes.

2. Pay attention. Don't make the storyteller go back over details.

3. Don't be too literal. Let the storyteller elaborate, embellish, and lie. This isn't *60 Minutes*, for God's sake. It's a story.

4. Ask questions that move the story along, not drag the story in another direction. If the story is about a flat tire on the way to a "come as your favorite Muppet" party, it doesn't matter what color the car is.

5. Be generous. Laugh at the funny stuff. Go ahead and nod, knee-slap, and give verbal encouragement like, "Yeah, baby!" Even if you're the funniest person on the planet, give someone else a yuk every once in a while.

6. No eye rolling or whispering to your neighbor.

7. If your significant other is telling the story, don't keep correcting him/her. Man in a Muppet costume? We care. Exact tire pressure? We don't care.

8. Wait your turn. Let the storyteller finish before you launch into your own Elmo goes to Las Vegas story.

9. Don't ever scoop the punch line. That's just unsporting.

Men Stink and Other Lessons Learned from Our Brothers

by Julie, Liz, Sheila, Monica, and Lian

Brotherless girls are at a disadvantage. They never really get to see men from the inside out until it is too late—too late because they are already working with, living with, or in love with some man. It must be frightening to see the 3-D version of a man for the first time in your twenties. We had an early education in men and boys, and for that we are grateful. So now, for all our brotherless Satellite Sisters, we present the following list of things we learned from our brothers Jim, Dick, and Brendan.

1. Men stink. Literally. Our brothers were an eternal spring of bad odors. They really stank. Even if it was thirty below and sleeting outside, it wasn't too cold to roll down the car window after picking up a brother from football practice. We discovered it was possible to empty the contents of our brothers' hamper and make it downstairs to the washing machine all in one breath. Smelly sweat socks, cruddy jeans, foul football cleats, and a recently vacated bathroom—all stinky things that come with men. This is an invaluable truth that made living with roommates and husbands less shocking.

2. Life can be unfair. Take advantage of it. It was not really Jim, Dick, or Brendan's fault that their only household chores consisted of taking out the garbage and occasionally shoveling snow or raking a few leaves while the girls were assigned the never-ending task of table setting, plate passing, and clearing and washing dishes. Our brothers would lie around on the den couches watching a baseball game, completely oblivious to the fact that there were dishes to be done at all, while we would be feverishly trying to scrape off a baked-on bit of scalloped potato. Given the chance, we would have happily done the same, but we'd be watching *Love, American Style* while our brothers had kitchen duty.

3. Men and women are equal. You need only to watch your brother attempt to cook frozen fish sticks by putting them in a wood-handled frying pan and then putting the whole pan under the broiler to know that men are no more qualified to run the world than women are. Boys are great, but the more time you spend around them growing up, the more alarming the idea of an all-male Cabinet meeting becomes as an adult.

4. If you think you've already made dinner, think again. Brendan taught us that it is possible to eat half a pan of lasagna and maintain the façade of a full pan by scooping out the lasagna innards and leaving the top layer undisturbed. This operation was always perpetrated while standing in front of the open refrigerator. The knowledge that whole meals can mysteriously vanish from the fridge is very helpful for living with male housemates, husbands, and teenage sons.

5. It is never a good idea to shift from first to third. None of us sisters would be able to drive a stick shift if it wasn't for Dick's Toyota Celica with the loose clutch and his hearing loss in one ear. No driving instructor would have put up with so much gear grinding, but Dick was Mr. Patience. He taught us the release-parking-brake-and-ease-into-first-gear technique for starting on a hill. And he provided the kind of extra instruction that you don't often get at a licensed driving school. Like how to hold a beverage, light a cigarette, and shift at the same time. That's a good teacher.

6. Friendship = Teasing. Brendan once described his gang of college friends as "just guys who know each other well enough to pick on each other's insecurities." While this definition of friendship is dramatically different from the one most sisters would offer, it can be very helpful to understand it later in life. In business life, most employee orientations, strategy meetings, and job evaluations involve a lot of ritualized hazing adapted from early teasing training. This is an attempt to bond, even if it does not appear that way.

7. Understand the implications of an icing penalty. The hours, many under protest, we spent watching the New York Rangers, the Superstars, the Olympics, and the Yankees increased our Sports Intelligence Quotients (SIQs). This has paid off in many arenas. We have higher SIQ scores than the average girl and significantly higher scores than brotherless girls. We have all won Final Four office pools, and two of the sisters, Liz and Lian, turned this early sports education into a profession.

8. Take-out: It's not just food; it's a lifestyle. Someone without brothers would never believe you could live in an apartment by yourself for three years without *ever* turning on any major appliances, including the refrigerator or stove. We know this is possible, thanks to our brother Brendan. Also, miniature baseball helmets recycled from a Dairy Queen sundae can double as a chips 'n' dip plate.

9. Nice guys are nice. Living with brothers who are nice guys teaches sisters that the men in their lives need not be brooding bad boys who will ultimately break their hearts. Early exposure to nice guys builds a lifetime of seeking out nice guys to have around as friends, boyfriends, and husbands. Nice guys also make excellent fathers.

10. *Appropriate loungewear is important.* Brothers often have different definitions of "presentable" than sisters do. This is especially true when it comes to around-the-house, laying-on-the-couch, television-watching ensembles. As a teen, Jim favored one-piece jumpsuits with other's people's names on them that had been cast off by a friend who worked in a commercial laundry. Brendan once spent most of one year wearing cutoff green scrubs that he acquired after a bad biking accident. The hospital pants were full-length when he was released and sent home. He just thought they'd be more comfy cut off just below the knee. Very Jughead. We saw those "shorts" long after he made a complete recovery. Behind closed doors, nobody cares if you look like some kind of escapee. If it's comfortable, go with it.

11. *Specialize.* We often came home to find Jim spending hours boiling wooden hockey sticks in large pots of water on top of the kitchen stove in an effort to shape the sticks into a specified curvature, or Dick practicing three-point shots into the top of the lampshade with a duct-taped sock. What we learned was that excessive repetition of seemingly inexplicable and specialized tasks leads to expertise. This kind of obsessive repetition can also bring about the discovery of protease inhibitors, the Internet, and the human genome sequence.

12. *The signs at movie theaters that say "No Outside Food Allowed in Theater" don't really mean anything if you're wearing the right coat.* Our brothers taught us that certain laws beg to be bent or broken. Sure, you can bring a three-course Thai meal with beverages into the movies if your overcoat is big enough. Also, speeding is acceptable if you're late for a Springsteen concert, and rent-control regulations are irrelevant when your sister needs a place to stay.

13. Boys don't say what is on their minds. A silent scowl from your big brother after meeting your latest boyfriend means, "He's a jerk, stay away from him." Your brother will never tell you this. He will also never tell you that you're good at something, that you're fun to be around, or that he loves you. But they have facial expressions for those sentiments, too.

14. You can never block properly from an upright position. Jim, Dick, and Brendan made sure that all of us knew the correct way to throw a hipcheck, punch, or a pass. We took a lot of hits. The evening boxing matches held in the upstairs hallway and the not-quite-touch touch football games may have left us red-faced, bruised, and crying, but if we hadn't gotten used to playing with pain, we wouldn't have survived extended labors, miscellaneous surgeries, and far too many fractured ankles. We can dodge and weave whatever is coming at us, even a letter from our husband's corporation telling us to relocate in thirty days. Don't cry about it; just get low and brace for impact.

15. Men really don't like chick flicks, so don't push it. *Love Story*—our brothers never read the book and wouldn't be caught dead at the movie.

16. Live by your wit and humor. Our brothers had the overall age and size advantage. The sisters had to make up for this by out-thinking them or, at the very least, making them laugh hard enough that out of respect they would allow us to change the channel—when the game went to a commercial.

Funseeker vs. Funsucker

by Liz

Let's start with a definition of fun. For the purposes of this discussion, fun does not need to involve hilarity. We'll set the bar fairly
low. Funseeking is making the best of any situation. Whether it is a
corporate meeting, a family dinner, or a long delay at LaGuardia,
funseekers try to find the humor in the situation. Funsuckers? Well,
not only are they the "glass half empty" crowd, they are the ones
whose lives depend on bringing us down with them. If they would
just suffer in silence, the "glass half full" crowd could move on with
our lives. But no, funsuckers are the ones demanding a complete
reading of the minutes of the last board meeting (oh, please) or
ostentatiously pulling an item that does not belong in their salad
out for all at the table to see. Must they kill all our appetites? Funsuckers need to learn to keep it to themselves.

Some people believe that in order to be taken seriously, they
must be serious all the time. I have learned to avoid doing business
with these people whenever possible. You know these types. One is
the bully—the guy who must have the last word on any topic at
any meeting ever. He tends to like hierarchy and enforces it. He
defines his managerial role as shooting down or poking holes in
ideas presented by others, even his own team. Spare us. We all
know it is harder to nurture new ideas than it is to kill them, so
who made you the genius, Mr. Funsucker? Another type of funsucker in business is the woman who is so worried about her own
credibility that she can't make a joke or crack a smile when others
do. I can empathize with this woman. I really can. I've been there
and made that mistake. You have trouble getting taken seriously so

you think the key is to take yourself very seriously. Wrong. That just gives the people who don't want to see you succeed one more reason to root for your failure. I have rarely seen a man in business brought down for being humorless, but it is an accusation that torpedoes women's careers all the time. Ms. Funsucker wears a scowl instead of a cool new scarf and can never admit to caring about her hair or having a fascination with bad boy Russell Crowe.

Growing up, there was simply no upside to being a funsucker. A funsucker suffered the worst fate of all. A funsucker was *left home.*

As kids, the goal was to join in on the fun others were planning by being a low-stress addition to the group. No older brother or sister ever wants to take his or her little sister anywhere. The key to getting included was to strike the delicate balance between being easy to accommodate and allowing the older sibling to score points with the parents by graciously taking you along. If Julie, a licensed driver at sixteen, agreed to take you with her when she and her friends went to the movies, it allowed her to look like a good older sister. Your job was to be quiet and not humiliate her in front of Leslie and Beth. A funsucker might complain about not being able to see the screen or divulge that they were not going to the movies at all—they were meeting other friends at the Athena Diner to smoke cigarettes and drink Tab. A funseeker would recognize that this was much more educational than going to the movies.

In a big family, there were simply never enough slots for everyone to do everything. If a small group was headed to the nature museum, you did not want to jeopardize your slot by whining about the fact that Sheila was wearing your sweater. If this was your strategy to dislodge her from her place, it rarely worked and usually resulted in both of you missing the trip and other kids coming in off the bench to the two newly vacated slots.

In adult life, funsuckers do not appear to calculate any impact they have on the overall group fun quotient. They simply must be heard on any topic of interest to them. Socially, a funsucker will tell you about the latest research on the link between cell phones and brain cancer right after you've just told your hilarious tale of finding your now-dead cell phone in the dryer because you forgot to take it out of the pocket of your bathrobe when you did the laundry. Is that really necessary? This is just a few people having coffee together, not a scientific conference. A funsucker can never lighten up.

Some funsuckers believe funseekers are superficial. *Au contraire.* On an average Friday night stacked up at LaGuardia or Saturday afternoon in the emergency room with the three-year-old again, it can be really hard to be positive. It takes imagination and commitment. Any dopey funsucker can get mad when the toilets overflow on a plane that's still on the runway. It takes a skilled funseeker to withdraw into her Walkman-centric world and entertain herself for the next several hours, fantasizing about actually being Bonnie Raitt. When airplane reality intrudes, she writes it off, knowing in her bluesy heart that she's headed to a great gig with John Hiatt. When she actually deplanes in Chicago and finds her car completely snowed in, she must manufacture another positive fantasy. No, she's not really Bonnie Raitt. She's Susan Butcher and she is in the Iditarod!

My mother always said, "If you don't have something nice to say, don't say anything." I have learned as an adult that this applies as much to your own internal dialogue as it does to real conversation. If our faux Bonnie Raitt admitted to herself that it was the fourth time in two months that she spent a precious Friday night trapped on an airplane, she could be done for.

Lian calls funsuckers "negaholics," and I think the term is apt. It is a disease. Even worse, it is contagious.

I am willing to admit that being a funsucker can be hard, too. Any amateur can allow that Friday night on the runway to be a negative experience, but the skilled funsucker can ruin a wedding, a party to celebrate landing a big contract, or an episode of *Friends* for everyone involved. OK, of course struggling twenty-somethings in New York don't have apartments that really look like that. Could you just get over it? It's a damned TV show.

Maybe funsuckers get into ruts because they believe people care about what they think. Growing up in a big family, it was always clear that nobody did. No-o-o-body. Accept that and you are on the road to funseekerdom. Negaholics of the world, you have nothing to lose but your complaints.

Funsuckers vs. Funseekers

Funsuckers always bring the wrong clothes.

Funseekers are content to wear a garbage bag.

Funsuckers never have an opinion until it's too late.

Funseekers take charge or take direction.

Funsuckers think the event is about them.

Funseekers know the event is about the event.

Funsuckers think only "important films" should be
Oscar winners.

Funseekers consider *Titanic* an Oscar-worthy vessel.

Funsuckers are picky about their food.

Funseekers just like to pick.

Funsuckers count calories.

Funseekers count cannolis.

Funsuckers complain about the service.

Funseekers leave a big tip.

Funsuckers fight in public.

Funseekers save it for the drive home.

Funsuckers itemize the dinner check.

Funseekers throw an extra twenty in the pot.

Funsuckers arrive late.

Funseekers stay late.

Funsuckers think "adults only" is for other people's children.

Funseekers think "adults only" is a great excuse for a baby-sitter.

Funsuckers never allow eating in their car.

Funseekers offer to drive.

Funsuckers drag you through their preparatory stages.

Funseekers arrive ready.

Funsuckers edit your e-mail and send it back.

Funseekers congratulate you on your great idea.

Funsuckers give you the gruesome details of their upper-GI series.

Funseekers realize the comic value of the words "barium enema."

Funsuckers tell you about their cats.

Funseekers tell you about their dogs.

Me and Mr. Jones

by Monica

For fourteen years, I've worked as a nurse in various hospitals across the country. I've worked in the inner city and wealthy suburbs and all sorts of hospital environments in between. I've been a night nurse, a traveling nurse, and a head nurse. Over the years, I have worked on a medical ward in the ICU, the CCU, and the angiography lab. No matter where I worked and in what capacity, there were always two constants to being a hospital nurse: hard work and good humor.

An intern once remarked, after watching me rush around, care for patients, then plow through chart after chart, "Nursing must be a lot of paperwork."

"Mostly toilet paper," I replied.

The work was backbreaking and heartbreaking at the same time. Many nights, I left work in tears, thinking about my patients and their families and all the sadness inside that big building. Some days I'd climb onto the bus after the night shift and want to scream at the passengers, "Get up and give me that seat! I've been working all night while you've been sleeping!" But just as often, I left work smiling, recalling a hilarious moment shared with one of my patients or fellow nurses.

A hospital can be a fun place, but you have to make it that way. Like many work environments, we had a special language and coined code names for doctors and patients. We had Yankee-baseball-cap day and Hawaiian-shirt night. Birthdays were big deals, with drinks after work. In one hospital in New Orleans, I worked the night shift with a fun nursing crew that included all types, from grandmothers to transvestites. We even staged our own ICU version of Mardi Gras, riding the medication cart down the hall, tossing beads and doubloons. We'd do anything to stay awake during the shift, including holding our monthly Naughty Panty Night. The rules were pretty simple: Wear your raciest panties under your scrubs, model them before a discriminating jury at 2 A.M. in the ICU, and win a prize. Both men and women were allowed to enter, but there was only one grand-prize winner. The contest was so popular we had to open up entries to include the ER, the CCU, and the housekeeping staff. Only in New Orleans, only on the night shift. As in other workplaces, it was the laughter that brought us together and made it possible for everyone to get up and do it again the next day—nurses, orderlies, doctors, and patients.

I remember one patient, Joe, who unfortunately missed the notice in his local paper about the grand opening of the new light rail system downtown and was seriously injured by an oncoming train. I was his night nurse the first week after the accident. One night, I walked into his room at the beginning of my shift and asked how his day had been.

Joe said, "I feel like a wreck."

"Well, Joe," I said, "you *were* run over by a train." We busted up laughing. It made us both feel better.

Another time I helped an elderly man to the bathroom shortly after his surgery. He fainted and fell on top of me. In the process, the IV pole got firmly wedged between the commode and the bathroom door, trapping us in a tangled mess of IV tubing, EKG wires, and various surgical tubes. As I was calling for help, my patient, who'd come to shortly after we hit the ground, said, "This is the most ridiculous situation I've ever been in. How about you?" When the other nurses finally rescued us, my patient and I were both in tears, rolling with laughter on the bathroom floor.

Not everyone on staff wanted to play along. I remember one head nurse in Washington—let's just call her Suzy Rulebook— who brought down the fun factor on every shift. One beautiful Sunday afternoon, Suzy Rulebook called me in to work an extra shift in the CCU and look after a patient, Miss Ella Fitzgerald. Not much was going on with Miss Fitzgerald, but the hospital wanted a full staff there anyway. About 5:00, Frank Sinatra called to see if he could visit his dear friend Ella.

"No," said Suzy Rulebook. "You are not immediate family. Good-bye."

She hung up on Ol' Blue Eyes! The Chairman of the Board wanted to come to my CCU and funsucker Suzy said *no*. I think it's safe to say that Suzy would not have been an enthusiastic participant in Naughty Panty Night, either. (After her full recovery, Miss Fitzgerald came back to the hospital and sang "Thanks for the Memories" to the staff.)

My friends loved to hear my hospital stories because they worked in small, cramped offices with computers and copy machines. Their daily routine was never as crazy or action-packed as mine. "How was your day?" they'd ask me.

That was a tricky question to answer because the truth could be off-putting. How was my day? I didn't sit down for twelve hours, I never went to the bathroom, and I came close to tears a few times during my shift. My patients were really sick and in a lot of pain or out of it on drugs. The doctors snapped and so did the families. How was my day? My friends didn't really want to know and I didn't really want to tell them. Instead, I preferred to tell them one of the funny highlight stories of the week. I developed a repertoire of real-life anecdotes that were suitable for friends and family.

The most miraculous recovery I ever witnessed involved a very young patient in a drug and heart attack–induced coma. For four days, he was on a ventilator until he improved enough to breathe on his own. Still he remained in a deep coma, not responding to any stimuli, like voice or touch. We didn't think he was going to make it.

One evening, as I was helping out another nurse, I noticed the call light was on outside his room. *Hmm, that's curious,* I thought. I walked into his room. The patient was sitting up in a chair, having detached himself from all life-support systems, and climbed over the side rails of the bed—just sitting there, wide awake, watching Michael Jackson perform "Thriller" on the Grammy Awards.

"Hey," he said. "Can you go get me a Big Mac?"

There are lots of stories I can't tell outside the hospital. To people outside of the medical profession, they might seem in poor taste—gallows humor and worse. But to those of us inside this world, that sort of humor is a necessary survival skill. We didn't laugh at the patients because they were funny. We laughed at the situations because they were absurd.

The story of the escapee is one such situation that comes to mind. I was a graduate nurse working on a Saturday afternoon with another RN named Susan. We were swamped, running from room to room just trying to answer all the call bells and make sure the thirty-two patients under our care were bathed, fed, and received their medications. A typical day.

One of Susan's patients, Mr. Jones, wanted out of the hospital. He was fed up with the doctors, the nurses, the whole scene. He just wanted to be home watching TV in his favorite chair. The doctors determined that he was not well enough to be discharged. So Mr. Jones took matters into his own hands.

He made it down the back stairwell, dressed only in his hospital gown and an old cardigan sweater. He'd wrapped two pillowcases around his bare feet and secured them with surgical tape. Susan and I were so busy we hadn't noticed that he was on the lam until our floor secretary got a call from the chief security guard who

reported that Mr. Jones was across the street from the hospital, trying to hail a cab. Susan and I panicked. The thought crossed both
our minds that a lost patient was going to look very bad on our
year-end job evaluation.

We asked security to escort Mr. Jones inside and up to the third
floor, please. They said because he was off hospital property, technically, they could not do anything to help us. Mr. Jones was our
responsibility. It was cold, it was snowing, and he was wearing pillowcases on his feet. Susan, all ninety pounds of her, took charge of
the situation. She stood on that street corner for almost an hour,
trying to convince Mr. Jones to come back inside and get into bed.
She succeeded brilliantly. I smile every time I picture Susan and
Mr. Jones getting off the elevator and walking hand in hand down
the hall to his room.

I know how Mr. Jones felt. Sometimes I wanted out of that
hospital, too. The long hours on my feet, not having enough time
or help to finish my work, and the bedpans are but a few reasons.
Then I would remember a nurse in New Orleans, Mark, who
taught us all the songs in *South Pacific* to get us through the long
nights, or the patient in Portland, who mistook the defibrillator for
a phone and tried to make a long-distance call using the paddles,
and I would laugh a little, then get back to work.

*N*ever Start a Sentence With . . .

If you're really looking to strike up a conversation, here are a few opening lines to avoid. Conversely, if you're standing in the buffet line and someone starts a conversation with one of these, excuse yourself and head for the prime rib station.

My therapist told me that I'm . . .

On my daughter's ninth day of potty training, she . . .

As a life insurance salesman, I meet a lot of people like you, who . . .

Though the systems-integration project is progressing well, I believe . . .

After they drained my abscess, I . . .

My ex-wife always . . .

The Lord Jesus Christ tells us . . .

During our last visit to Tuscany, Frederica and I . . .

I want to share with you some of the collaborative statements from our subcommittee meeting . . .

My thesis topic was . . .

My daughter's violin teacher says . . .

Yesterday, Tabby did the cutest thing . . .

Dolan, Inc.

by Julie

Our radio show, Satellite Sisters, was not our first family business venture. Over the years, we have tried various schemes to make a little dough. You might assume that a ten-person family would have a huge talent pool to draw from for a group business enterprise. In fact, that wasn't the case. While we had an ample supply of potential business partners, our actual moneymaking skills were limited. Our talents lay in those areas that could only be categorized as "chores." My mother used to sigh as she handed out the money for miniature golf and say, "Why can't you kids just write one hit song?"

Fortunately, our financial goals were mostly small and short-term—such as raising enough cash to buy a post-tonsillectomy present for Jim or a fresh batch of love comics. Long-term financial goals were on the order of raising enough capital to go to Rye Playland at the end of the summer or, for Lian, selling enough Burpee seeds to purchase a bow and arrow that she'd use on Brendan.

What we lacked in talent, however, we made up for in ingenuity. With our Morningstar cousins, we once set up a tollbooth across Orchard Lane in Rye, New York. We barricaded the street with brooms, chairs, ladders, stepstools, and planks of wood and charged cars twenty-five cents to drive down the public street. We had a rotating crew of Dolan and Morningstar cousins working the booth. We had made about two dollars in two hours before a neighbor complained to our aunt, who was very surprised to learn about the new tollbooth on her street.

The key to a good business plan is minimal parental support. In fact, some of the best plans were executed without any parental knowledge whatsoever. It was reasonable to take supplies such as sugar, water, and flour from the kitchen without consent. Or you could help yourself to the one family hammer, or a bedspread to drape on the blueberry bushes for a talent show backdrop. But if your business plan involved a delivery service, you were out of luck unless you could carry it on your bike or your back. And don't even think about asking permission to use the living room coffee table, even if it was just the right height for your neighborhood casino roulette game.

Along the way, we experienced a number of setbacks—slightly burnt brownies that wouldn't sell, a poor location for our used magazine stand, or having no takers for the overly ripe apples that we picked up off the ground in our backyard. But the fallback business position was always to put on a show. I think it was the intense, short-term business cycle that appealed to us. We would practice and fight really hard for two days. The shows were fairly easy to mount because we had lots of coordinating outfits and Jim had an 8-track player. Most of our shows consisted of synchronized interpretive dancing. Sheila and Monica would do tumbling routines and occasionally Jim would perform magic tricks. One of the younger kids might read poetry left over from the previous year's recital to Dick's percussion accompaniment on the kitchen pots and pans. We would round up a few neighbors and friends and charge a hefty admission fee that my parents covered. It was a winning formula for raising a quick buck.

During our high-school years, Liz and I ran a summer day camp at the beach. Nine paying campers enrolled, and, of course, we had to take Lian. Normal barriers to business entry did not deter us. We didn't have a state license, any early-childhood developmental training, or a police record review. In fact, we didn't even have a driver's license between us, just a couple of junior lifesaving certificates. What we did have was some great tie-dyed T-shirts and a lot of arts-and-crafts projects that involved gluing sand onto things.

As we got older we diversified. We shifted away from group ventures to individual efforts. We sought the glamorous world of low-paying service jobs. We worked as painters, baby-sitters, caterers, waitresses, cooks, fence builders, pool cleaners, and house-sitters. Some of us were more naturally suited to the service sector than others. Those of us who successfully performed chores at home turned out to be successful performers of chores for other people. Not surprisingly, Sheila was perhaps the worst waitress of all time. She specialized in getting orders completely wrong, forgetting the beverages, undercharging, and giving incorrect change.

Brendan and Lian set up a house- and pet-sitting business. Their chief client was our next door neighbor Mrs. Lee, who had a cat and a dog. Not long after Mrs. Lee left town, quality control issues surfaced. Brendan started eating the ice cream in her freezer and Lian refused to feed the cat canned food because it made her gag. Mrs. Lee returned home to find her cat had been accidentally locked in the basement for five days. The cat turned out to be fine, but Brendan and Lian were out of business.

Others in the family, however, seemed to have natural business acumen. Dick was a maestro at price gouging. His "starving student" summer painting company charged more than many full-time professional painters. Monica's strong customer relations skills helped her land a couple key baby-sitting accounts, so she spent her high-school years on Easy Street. Jim succeeded in transition planning by passing on his pool-cleaning business to Brendan. It was Lian, though, who came up with the boldest business plan. She and her pal Sarah Ostheimer set up a lemonade stand. Their genius was to sell water as lemonade. Step right up and buy something to drink from these cute eight-year-old swindlers. What—not thirsty?

Then how about buying one of these leaves we've just picked up off the ground? Eventually they were busted by the kindly Mrs. Reeves.

Now, after years of going it on our own, we're back to working as a group again. While we certainly learned a thing or two from our grown-up jobs, a lot of the business basics came from our early training. The big difference is that these days we work together but live in different cities. People ask us if we were surprised that we were able to come up with a concept that we could turn into a business. No surprise at all, we say. We've been doing that for a long time. Anybody want to put on a show?

Always Sit with the Smart-Ass

by Liz

Always sit with the smart-ass. That's the best piece of business advice I can offer. At any meeting or company gathering, sit next to someone who will remind you not to take it all too seriously. After all, for most of us, work is not brain surgery or rocket science. If you are a brain surgeon or a rocket scientist, ignore everything I am about to say and please go back to your studies. For the rest of us in business, wouldn't we benefit from taking ourselves a little less seriously? I worked in the athletic shoe business and I always appreciated it when, after a heated debate about lacelocks, someone would say, "People, we're talking sneakers here." Right.

I have identified two strains of successful business humor: front of the room humor and back of the room humor. Front of the room humor is that which comes from the presenters, the so-called grown-ups. Back of the room humor comes from the smart-asses in the back. Back of the room humor takes us back to our days in seventh grade. For routine corporate meetings, the basic back-row behavior you mastered in the seventh grade can be helpful. Think same attitude minus the spitballs. If you can summon that spirit again, you will approach any grown-up corporate new-mission-and-values-statement-company-wide launch in the right frame of mind. I've been in the front of the room as a grown-up and the back of the room with the kids at these kinds of events, and I can assure you the back of the room is a lot more fun.

In the back of the room, I prefer to sit with the individuals who can draw cartoons lampooning whoever is speaking. It is a silent, discreet sort of subversion. It is also easier to get away with than outright misbehavior and disrespect. Best of all, it leaves a permanent record of the company's embarrassing moments. Learn who the artists are and seek them out.

My second choice for back of the room accomplice is the mistress or master of the mumbled aside. The person delivers their devastating critiques of the speaker in such a sly way that you are laughing before you realize you heard anything. This creates a secret bond in your row or at your end of the table. The risk here is that the mumbler never gets caught but those around the mumbler get shushed and pointed at for childish outbursts. Sitting next to the mumbler requires exquisite self-control.

Let's admit it. Business is funny. Or rather, it's not funny but it is incumbent upon us to make it funny. We spend an unbelievable amount of time doing things that are just not worth the effort. But if that's what they pay us for, we might as well have fun, right? What is the right response to realizing that you just spent the last four hours working on a flow chart about process improvement when everyone knows that if the process had any chance of being improved you'd start by not spending four hours on the flow chart?

Laughter is the only legitimate response. Admit it. It's funny. You thought you were going to change the world and now you spend every day selling sneakers.

Front of the room humor is harder to pull off because you have to be one of the grown-ups, not one of the seventh graders. If you play to the smart-ass factor in the back, you can lose the goody-goodies seated in the first few rows, who are actually paying attention and might actually do any of the things you are exhorting them to do from the podium. On the other hand, pandering to the goody-goodies means losing the respect of the cool kids and admitting that, yes, you are just a dorky member of management. This part feels like the seventh grade again, too, doesn't it? Cool kids. Smart kids. Nerds. Life doesn't change much.

After years of trying to be one of the grown-ups without losing the respect of the back row, I have but one piece of advice: Debase yourself. Do something really humiliating. Everyone loves to see the boss make a spectacle of herself, goody-goodies and smart-asses alike! It's a surefire crowd-pleaser. I learned this from two of my favorite bosses over the years.

Joan Parker ran the PR agency in New York where I worked. On one occasion, she hired a tango instructor to infiltrate a business dinner we were hosting for a client. Pablo (I think that was his name) was introduced as a new account executive. When dinner ended, the restaurant suddenly filled with tango music and the "account executive" leapt to his feet, stripped off his jacket, and led Joan in a very energetic and erotic tango. Why? I have no idea why. I am sure there was an excuse but I no longer recall it. Joan was not the most skilled tango partner in the world, but she looked great with that rose clenched in her teeth. Everyone who was there will always remember it. Isn't that enough? How many business dinners can you say *that* about?

The other boss who taught me the value of having fun at your own expense was Phil Knight, CEO of Nike, for whom I worked for almost a decade. In the winter of 1992, we needed to record his remarks on video for a major meeting he would not be able to attend in person. It happened that our planning meeting for that video took place the week after the opening ceremonies for the Albertville Olympics. For those of you who may not be the opening-ceremony aficionados that my sisters and I are, let me just say that the Albertville O.C. might have been the best, strangest, funniest, most whimsical ever. It was considered a triumph in the Dolan household, where these things are closely watched and hotly debated. The stars of the show were the snow-globe people—creatures with clear, snowy orbs around their torsos, like Woody Allen in *Sleeper* but see-through and with downy flakes inside. In a fit of Olympic enthusiasm, the team convinced Phil Knight that he should wear such an orb while he made his speech. After all, Nike is a sports company. Why not give a subtle nod to an enduring image from the biggest sporting event of the year? We got a Plexiglas bubble, cut it open, put Phil Knight and some Ivory Snow inside it, then sealed it shut and yelled, "Roll 'em." It is a sign of his truly warped and wonderful spirit that Phil did not fire us all on the spot. Our snow globe had none of the artfulness of the French version, but it did have a big-time American CEO stuck inside, trying to deliver remarks on the state of the industry. Best of all? The video was for an audience of sporting-goods retailers in Germany. I will leave it to you to imagine what they might have thought of this American captain of industry covered in Ivory Snow. Sublime.

There is, however, one kind of workplace humor I would like to denounce. Staged silliness, the kind often perpetrated by human resources departments or outside team-building consultants, is just not funny. If I walk into a room and see that the meeting organizers have Super Soakers stacked in the corner, I turn and leave. That's it. Making employees feign childlike exuberance in a corporate conference room is just not funny. The key to workplace humor is finding humor in the actual situation, not in creating a false scenario that suggests we are all friends, just here for a good time. There is no such thing as human-resources humor.

So, whether humiliating others or humiliating ourselves, always remember that the average agenda of the average business meeting is not sacred. Subvert it. Undermine it. Laugh at it. Ditch the PowerPoint. Don the snow globe. Find your inner seventh grader.

All Rise:

OUR NOMINEES FOR THE SUPREME COURT

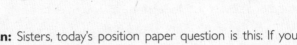

Lian: Sisters, today's position paper question is this: If you really wanted to shake up the Supreme Court, who would you nominate as a justice? Julie?

Julie: That's easy. *Any* high school senior. Reason number one: They know it all. There's nothing you can tell them. They know it *all*. Reason number two: They have *only* strong opinions about *everything*. They are not interested in anyone else's interpretation of anything. And reason number three: They know far more about Napster, the Internet, and software than the eight other justices combined.

Lian: Very nice choice, Julie. And let's face it, it would look really impressive on a college application if you were, in fact, a Supreme Court justice. Liz?

Liz: Well, I would start by asking myself what I would want to change about the way the Supreme Court does business. And I guess I would just want them to be more businesslike, actually. In business, if someone comes to you for a decision in October, you don't get to say, "Well, let's see. OK, we'll get back to you in May." It doesn't work that way. And you certainly don't get to say, "You know what? We've decided not to decide about this."

So I think we need somebody to crack the whip a little bit, get a little more productivity out of the brethren. So I think I'd go with the woman who has been called the most powerful businesswoman in America—Carly Fiorina, the CEO of Hewlett-Packard. I think she would make a big contribution on the bench.

Lian: I'm sure she would. Those justices would be in cross-functional teams in no time. No more of these five-to-four decisions. Monica, what about you? Who would get your nomination?

Monica: I would nominate Olympian Janet Evans. She has a lot of gold medals. She's personable and patriotic, and she did such an excellent job running with that torch in Atlanta. It's hard, tiring work to make all those decisions, and I think Janet, as a distance swimmer, would be up for it. I believe Justice Janet would add a lot of vigor and stamina to the bench. She gets my vote.

Lian: Very persuasive argument, but I think the Supreme Court needs some levity. I mean, for God's sake, it isn't life and death.

Liz: Actually, it is. But you're right, they do seem a little uptight.

Lian: That's what I'm talking about, Liz. So, my choice is Tony Award–winner Nathan Lane, because he's fun.

Julie: He's fun, fun, fun. He's Mr. Fun.

Lian: A little song, a little dance, a little seltzer down your pants. Every session, Nathan gets one big number and you could sell tickets to all those ladies on the theater buses. A little showbiz, that's what we need on the Supreme Court.

Julie: Not just justice, but increased production values. Intriguing notion. Last but not least, Sheila. Who gets your nod?

Sheila: Well, Julie, my nominee has a lot of common sense, likes to tell other people what to do, and loves a uniform. My nominee is Her Honor, Liz Dolan.

Lian: Now that's thinking. A sister as a Supreme Court justice. She could take care of a few parking tickets. . . .

Julie: Get us into the employee cafeteria. . . .

Monica: I bet she could score us some VIP tickets to the White House Tour!

Lian: Excellent choice, Sheila. I think you have the support of all the Satellite Sisters. Liz? What do you think?

Liz: I like working in a robe. Currently I work in a bathrobe, but I could transition to black. OK, I'm in.

Lian: There you have it. Five sisters with the same parents *and* the same opinion on who we would nominate to the Supreme Court.

The Teen Commandments

by Julie

I was a pretty good mother when my sons were young. I was particularly good at instituting naps, preparing balanced meals, and reading at bedtime, but my parental confidence started to slip away when my oldest son entered junior high. Suddenly more was required of me than arranging stimulating play dates; I had to come up with on-the-spot rulings about attending co-ed parties, going to PG-13 movies without an adult, and buying rock CDs with explicit lyrics.

For me, raising teenagers has been a humbling experience. So when a friend asked me for advice on dealing with her three teenagers, I decided to compile a very short list of what I have learned. Here are my Teen Commandments, counsel for any adult who has the good fortune to live with an adolescent.

1. Nothing good happens after midnight. There is no social, educational, athletic, or spiritual event—at least none that you want your kids participating in—that begins that late at night.

2. No sleepovers. Innocent slumber parties in the preteen years become, for teenagers, the equivalent of parent-sanctioned AWOL status for twelve to fourteen hours.

3. Just call. No matter how late the hour or how much trouble he or she is in, your teenager should always call you when they get there or when they need a ride. No excuses.

4. Only one electronic device—phone, CD player, blow dryer, computer, etc.—may be operated at a time. I am not sure of the medical or scientific rationale, but I know multiple electronics usage can't be good for teenagers, and it's murder on parents. My son had the habit of simultaneously playing his electric guitar and answering e-mail.

5. No piercing, no tattoos. One of our listeners amended this commandment by adding that corrective surgeries to undo body piercings and tattoos should not be financed with family funds. Let me just say that I am in favor of hair dying. It will wash or wear out and will make a great picture to blow up for his or her fortieth birthday party.

6. The presence of an older sibling does not make it better. When your fourteen-year-old says, "Don't worry, Mom, John's older brother will pick us up," just remember that John's older brother is probably sixteen (see Commandment number 7).

7. No sixteen-year-old can actually drive a car. Oh, they have a license, they're behind the wheel, and they're on the road, but they are not "driving" as we know it. Driving doesn't happen until seventeen or eighteen. That first year is a total free-for-all.

8. Eat dinner with your kids. My son's high-school principal gave me this piece of advice at the freshman orientation. I thought he was crazy, but making time for this group activity really pays off.

9. Find your son or daughter an adult friend. Face it, you're the parent, not the friend. So find them an aunt, an uncle, a coach, a teacher, a minister, a neighbor, or some other adult to whom they can talk.

10. Don't forget to laugh. Someday you are going to appreciate how funny it was that your son hosted a graduation party at your house and invited everyone in the world but you.

11. Be ready. Conversation, real conversation, between you and your teen usually comes at times when you least expect it.

The Halloween Week Massacre

by Liz

Halloween was a major holiday at our house. Imagine a normal day in a house with eight kids between the ages of two and fourteen. Now imagine that same household on Halloween afternoon. Costumes were taken very seriously, from the orange pumpkin outfit with the green stem hat for the baby (that would be Lian) to the menacing gangster getups for the two oldest boys. In between, an array of princesses, Raggedy Anns, superheroes, and hobos. No backstage operation at the Metropolitan Opera was this complicated in its sheer range.

Halloween was also exciting because we spent it with our cousins in Rye, New York. Our neighborhood in Connecticut was very sparsely populated and without streetlights or sidewalks, so my parents would pack us in the car and take us to our cousins' much more densely packed neighborhood. They, too, had a big family (nine kids between the ages of two and sixteen). When we hit the streets together, it was quite an assault.

The beautiful thing about trick-or-treating in a neighborhood not your own is that you can behave very badly. You can grab huge handfuls of candy. You can push little kids out of the way. You can cut through the hedges instead of using the sidewalk. All of this is possible because the parents in the neighborhood do not recognize you. Not only are you not local, you are masked. It was a license to misbehave. We felt like a marauding army, even in our princess costumes.

The aftermath back in the Morningstar living room was the dangerous part. We'd come back to the house and count, sort, and trade candy. "I'll give you two marshmallow pumpkins for one Milky Way." It got a little competitive. Little kids were duped into all kinds of foolish trades because they overvalued candy corn. During the Year of the Gangster, my brothers Dick and Jim and my cousin Joe carried guitar cases as part of their costumes. They knew from the movies that real gangsters carried their tommy guns in violin cases, but this was the late 60s. We had guitars, not violins, around the house.

The older boys' haul was impressive, with Dick bringing in the biggest of the night. They taunted us, lording it over the rest of the group that they had pulled off the heist of the century. "This loot will last us until Christmas," they cackled. Or so we thought.

My mother had a rule that every night after Halloween, one child would get their candy bag and give everyone else one piece for dessert. We took turns, and it was always a blow, sometimes a lethal one, to our individual supplies to give out seven additional servings. I suspect it was part of my mother's grand plan to wipe out the candy supply as quickly as possible.

On the night it was Dick's turn, he went to his room to get the locked and hidden guitar case. Shortly, much yelling was heard from upstairs. It was gone. *Gone.* The whole guitar case was missing.

Interrogations followed, with each child at the dinner table closely questioned by Dick about his or her activities that after-

noon. Could we account for our whereabouts? Did we have wit-
nesses? Could he examine our hands? (I can't explain this last one.
Was he looking for chocolate stains?)

Next, a room-to-room search was conducted. I knew I hadn't
stolen Dick's candy, but I couldn't be sure that Sheila, with whom
I shared a room, had not. What if the candy was in our closet? I was
worried. I could be implicated as some kind of accessory or
accomplice.

I looked around the dinner table, trying to suss out who the
perpetrator might be. Jim, the oldest? Hard to believe. Jim and
Dick always banded together. Julie? Unlikely. Dick made her life
hell every day; she would not want to provoke him further. Me?
No. Sheila? Not impossible, but I think she had Brownies that
afternoon as her alibi. Monica? Did that sniffling betray guilt, fear,
or just allergies? Brendan? The baby boy? It would be foolhardy
and shocking for one brother to plot against another. Usually, they
united against the girls. Lian? Too young to be under suspicion.

A cry went up. The guitar case had been found. Unbelievably,
the thief had slit it open from end to end to get at its locked contents. The guilty party? Little Brendan! He had gone from Batman
on Halloween to candy crook a mere week later. It was a plot twist
worthy of the great Perry Mason himself. One brother turns
against another, upsetting the entire Boys Against Girls family balance of power. Secretly, the girls were thrilled to see the crack in
the brothers' solidarity. Publicly, we were too terrified of Dick's
retribution to support Brendan. Personally, I was impressed that the
biggest caper in our family history had been pulled off by a calm,
cool, and collected five-year-old.

Divorce, Dating, and Dogs

by Sheila

Dating after a divorce is really not very funny. All of a sudden you wear strange clothes and act like a teenager. Friends who have never had a successful time of it or are in the process of breaking up with somebody are wildly endorsing your choices. Yes, they shout, an accountant with three kids is great! So is the personal trainer who knows your body-fat percentage. You are so damaged that it doesn't occur to you that such friends may not be the picture of emotional health. "Get back out there," they say. Out where, exactly? In my former life, I'd find men in out-of-the-way places like the semiotics section of the bookstore or bird watching in Central Park. When you are divorced, you get this strange surge of courage mixed with the fear that you'll never be in a relationship again. So you take your friends' advice and date anyone, anywhere, at least once. The danger is that one date can lead to marriage, at least in my experience.

Bars and gyms were definitely out when I first started dating because I could not afford either. So were macrobiotic potluck suppers and adult choirs. I'm obsessive about food cleanliness and I can't sing. I preferred to wear a scarlet "D" on my chest as long as I was able, but the truth is that I did have a few select dates after the divorce. They were awkward, over-the-top, and doomed from the start. For me, it doesn't really matter where or when I find a man I like because I always find a way to blow up a relationship all by myself. Sometimes it takes fourteen years and other times it just takes quick three months, like it did with the dog walker.

I was introduced to the man who walked dogs by a friend one

day at a Starbucks on the Upper East Side. We all sat down together
at a small, round table, where I proceeded to down two vanilla cap-
puccinos in rapid succession. I get that way—and they think that
the glow on my face means we are meant to be together. I tend to
have a severe reaction to the caffeine and sugar, so that breathless
quality that men find so sexy may actually be hyperventilation. The
dog walker walked me home and asked if he could call me sometime. "Sure," I said. How about giving me a ring when I get
upstairs?

That's pretty much my interpretation of *The Rules*. There are
no rules once I get going; it's just search and destroy. Besides, he
was ten years younger than I, and I was newly divorced. Is there a
special set of rules for that situation? Apparently he didn't see any
reason to wait, either, because my phone rang a few minutes after I
had come inside and washed my face and hands, which were still
sweating from the caffeine hot flash. I planned my outfit on the
phone as we planned a dinner date for the following evening. I
assembled a hideous blend of decades in one fell swoop, which
included spandex, corduroy, and pashmina. I was stepping out, even
though I felt like throwing up as I walked down Second Avenue to
meet him for dinner.

We went to his favorite restaurant, which featured steak, orange
lights, and sawdust. The steak tasted like sawdust, and two televi-
sions at the bar blasted basketball games throughout dinner. He
asked the waitress for three different kinds of steak sauce, which
should have been a red flag for me. Rule Number 1: What to do
when your man exhibits excessive condiment use on the first date.
Then I remembered: He's twenty-nine; that's what men in their
twenties do, I guess.

I invited him back to my place, where I made coffee and put
on, of all things, a film version of *Hamlet*. That should have been a
red flag for him, but he agreed to watch it with me in my empty

apartment. I didn't have proper furniture back then, so he sat on the floor while I leaned back uncomfortably in a black leather reading chair that came with the divorce. We endured half the movie before he got up and announced, "I have to get up early tomorrow. I have a lot of dogs." Forget the red flag on that one, and just bring out the banner that reads, "You can't compete with a cairn terrier."

The dogs were a part of his life long before I arrived at Starbucks on that fateful day. He walked dogs professionally, lots of dogs, and he loved every one of them. He especially loved the ones that were big, sloppy, noisy, and annoying. I know, because they entered our lives the very next night, when I was invited to dinner. By the way, we spent every night together in some capacity from the first date until we broke up three months later.

The first time I went to his place for dinner there was a one-hundred-forty-pound Rhodesian Ridgeback waiting to greet me as I stomped up the stairs in inappropriately young chunky shoes. My date made eyes at the dog all night and laughed when it charged at me and leaped up on the bed. I hated the dog walker at that moment and cursed the dog under my breath. We then ordered take-out from the steakhouse on the corner, where we had eaten the night before.

This time I sat on the floor, while he and the dog sat side by side on the couch. We hardly had room on the table for the ten mini-cups of condiments, various sides, and the plethora of plastic utensils. *This is my life,* I thought. I am here with a man, doing what my friends suggested. I am dating a young man who enjoys dogs and steak. I still wasn't sure if he enjoyed me, because every time we got romantic, the dog would jump up between us, which would make him laugh. I was miserable, but I forged ahead in my new life as a single woman.

Things got worse. Next came the terriers, Labradors, and shepherds. Big dogs, little dogs, everywhere there were dogs and more dogs. There were even cats (I am allergic) being boarded in his apartment on the weekends. I overlooked the litter trays, wagging tails, and miles of leashes just to be with this guy. On the few occasions he visited me at my apartment, it was equally uncomfortable because of my limitations and pet peeves, if you will. First, the lack of furniture and lack of condiments cut into the good time we could have been having. One time I served my mother's famous Irish stew (a real hit with my former love interest), and he asked for ketchup. When I lied and said I didn't have any, he requested Worcestershire. This was payback time for the dogs, so I deliberately stopped buying sauces of any kind. You get the picture. It was not about love; it was about power. Pitting a dog against a Dolan tradition was not a constructive way to build a new relationship. As I said, it was doomed.

Finally, it was my daughter, Ruth, who was instrumental in helping me break off the relationship. At age fourteen, she was the voice of reason I needed to end this charade. The last time I invited him for dinner, I made Japanese food just to really throw him off. There was absolutely nothing on the dinner table that warranted Western condiment use and yet halfway through the evening, I noticed him looking around for something to put on the rice. I asked my daughter to meet me in the kitchen, and here is where my weakness really lies. I was still worried about what she thought, because I was still willing to make a go of this. I whispered, "What do you think?" She shook her head and looked down. She was speechless. The next day the dog walker and I had a painful phone conversation, which involved barking on his end and crying on mine. It was over. I had put myself out there and so had he and we both deserved a little credit for trying. We parted rather clumsily. He went back to his dogs, and I sat alone, in my pet-free apartment with old movies no one watches anymore except divorced women who are between relationships.

Today, I live with a great guy in a building that does not allow animals. Still, anytime my boyfriend and I pass a cute dog on the street I get nervous, wondering if he'll leave me for a miniature schnauzer or, worse, a pug. At least I know he'll never request ketchup for my mother's recipes because as fate would have it, he's Japanese!

Like Eric with a B

by Lian

Every six months or so, I look across the dinner table at my husband as he is going on and on about fifteen- vs. thirty-year mortgages or how George Steinbrenner cheats, and I blurt out, "Oh my God, I married Berick Treidler!"

It's hard to believe that after nine years, the identity of my groom could continue to shock me. Perhaps this is a common phenomenon, referred to by marriage counseling professionals as the Oh-My-God-I-Married-What's-His-Name syndrome. And, to be fair, my husband has been struck by similar moments of clarity, shouting out at odd intervals, "Oh my God, I married Lian Dolan!" It's not that we didn't expect to get married one day; we just didn't expect to get married to each other.

Berick was a year ahead of me at college. The school was small enough so that we had intersecting circles of friends, even though we did not have intersecting interests. He ran cross country, studied math and economics, and wore sweater vests. I played lacrosse, studied archaeology, and wore flip-flops. Our history together started my freshman year when he doused my roomate Ann with beer. Ann snuck into a party at Berick's house, refusing to pay the fifty-cent cover charge. Then Ann had the audacity to change the tape on his stereo during the party. Despite the fact that Ann was an anthropology major, she did not appreciate the sacred bond between man and stereo. If nineteen-year-old men ruled the world, this offense would have resulted in the amputation of Ann's hands, but the pesky Constitution prohibits that sort of retribution, so Berick simply lobbed a plastic cup of beer at Ann's head. Berick maintains that the beer didn't actually hit her, it just soaked her as it crashed into the wall above her. When Ann returned to our room, wet and angry, I supported her cause. Dramatically, I vowed never again to speak to Berick Treidler. And I didn't for ten years. The next vow I took with Berick in mind was to have and to hold 'til death do us part. *Hmm*. Life's funny.

In the decade between The Beer Vow and The Wedding Vow, I lurched along the romance trail. I had my heart broken and I broke a few hearts. All right, I didn't break any hearts, but I think I bruised one or two. I learned enough about the opposite sex to create a checklist of attributes that I admired (hard-working, willing to dance at parties, likes college basketball) and those that I didn't (self-absorbed, possessing a limited vocabulary, eats with mouth open). I was in my late twenties when I started looking around for real, with very low expectations. I lived in Portland, Oregon, and worked in the sports business. I was surrounded by men all day, but I couldn't buy a date. Was it the unfortunate haircut of winter 1991? I'm not sure. All I know is that I turned to my tarot-card reader Alexa for the answer.

Shockingly, she had one. "I never say this to anyone, but you will be married within a year," Alexa predicted, "to someone you had a problem with in the past. Just give him another try." (Just in case you think this is revisionist hokum, I have the reading on tape.)

Someone from the past. Just give him another try. The words echoed in my head. An old college boyfriend had recently started calling again, so I thought for sure Alexa meant him. I went off to ol' beer-soaked Ann's wedding with that on my mind—that and how was I going to stuff myself into the ill-fitting bridesmaid's dress. Reenter the culprit Berick after ten years, a wedding guest, too, because he was a good friend of the groom.

It seems Berick had learned a few things in the intervening decade as well. He was living in Los Angeles, working in real estate, and serial dating. He'd developed several complicated theories about women over time as a result of his frequent lunches and dinners with the opposite sex. He believed most women did not date to find a husband, despite what other men thought, and that there is no need to be friends with old girlfriends. Once it's over, it's over. He also practiced the Ladder Theory of relationships, a strategy that involved climbing back into dating after a bad breakup, one rung at a time. He started with easy-to-get, one-time-only dates on the bottom rung, advancing higher with more challenging, stimulating partners as he regained his confidence. Apparently, I came along when he had reached the top rung.

I think of the wedding weekend as love at second sight. Yes, he still had a few sweater vests in his closet and I retained some flip-flop tendencies, but we were in sync on the big issues—I mean the really big issues, like John Hiatt and dogs vs. cats. There were lots of differences in lesser-impact categories like Anita Hill, career goals, and personal neatness; and big gaps in other areas, like home ownership (he saved and bought a house at twenty-five; everything I owned fit in the back of my VW) and religion (I had one; he had distance running). But, all in all, we hit it off the second time around.

To say that our relationship progressed quickly is an understatement. Is there a land-speed record for romance? We remet in

March, announced our engagement by July, and married New Years' weekend. Remember, he lived in L.A. and I lived in Portland. All told, we had spent thirteen days together before we decided to spend the rest of our lives together. On the Fourth of July, Berick told me he had bought me something that was hard to ship. I thought it was chair—a comfy blue armchair with a big sunflower on it that we had seen in a furniture store. He told me it was something quite a bit smaller, and it sparkled. I'm decisive, but Berick's decision-making abilities impressed even me. How could I say no? That's when I realized I could never go back to Alexa the tarot-card reader. What if she told me, "No! Not this guy with the ring. Some *other* guy you had a problem with."

Family reaction varied. When I called home, my mother cooed and applauded at the news. "Lian's getting married," she shouted to my father. "To who?" he bellowed back. With my Berick sitting next to me, I had to spell my future husband's name over the phone, "Yes, Dad, that's B-E-R-I-C-K. Like Eric with a B."

Monica countered, "But you hardly know him." *So?* I thought. I have the rest of my life to get to know him.

And Liz's response was the best of all. She said, "Here I was, thinking that it was going to take me years to find a man, fall in love, then decide to get married and have a wedding. Now I know I can wrap the whole thing up in eleven months! You have given me such hope." Then she asked, "You aren't doing this just because Alexa said so, are you?"

No, I was doing this because he's hard-working, likes to dance at parties, and follows college basketball. Why the rush? At the time, it seemed like a good idea just to get going with the whole shebang. We realize now that we were crazy. "What were we thinking?" we howl. Marriage is so serious, so permanent. We spent thirteen days together and then announced, sign us up for the whole package—kids, house, disability insurance. We were idiots.

But that's what keeps it lively—the constant sense of disbelief and amusement that here we are, together. Even our disagreements have a tinge of laughter because our union is so unlikely. Best of all, we get a kick out of the confusion on the faces of our classmates at reunions when they try to comprehend that Lian Dolan and Berick Treidler are married. To each other. What a riot.

The Family Laugh

by Sheila

Sometimes I think my family laughs too much. Granted, when all of us are together in one place, there are a lot of individuals (eight to ten) laughing at the same time. Still, I would bet that we laugh more than the average family. We are laughers and the more we laugh, the harder it is to stop laughing. We started young, in church, where we would often burst out laughing at absolutely nothing. There was nothing comical going on in church, just a faintly heard sermon, a few dramatics with the wine and wafer, and the endless parade during communion. It was during communion when things got out of hand. When folks started getting up to walk toward the altar, it was almost a signal for us to start laughing. The choir would begin singing and we assumed, incorrectly, that their shrill voices would drown out the snorting and stifled laughter coming from our pew.

Jim and Dick would make goofy faces just as the organ would play the first three notes of "Come Thank Thee All Our Lord," and that would set off a chain reaction that began with Julie and worked its way down the line to whomever was the baby at that time. We knew from experience that there were consequences to our laughing fits, but hard as we tried, we couldn't extinguish the laughter once it started. Our shoulders would be shaking, our hands would be signaling "stop," and our heads would be bowed—we were praying to a higher power to stop the affliction of uncontrolled laughter.

There was only one person who could put us out of our misery, and that was our mother. With one sharp look down the pew, she would send the message necessary to break the chain of laughter. One by one, we would straighten up, get a grip, and then miraculously stop laughing. At that point, I would try to focus my eyes on something far, far away at the front of the church and pretend that I couldn't feel Monica still smiling (which she was).

After church we would drive home down the Post Road in Fairfield, always stopping at Devore's for our weekly supply of glazed and jelly donuts. During the cramped car ride we would relive our laughing jag. There was some kind of demented pleasure we had in laughing even more about our laughing. So in addition to laughing all the time, we also indulged in talking about how much we'd laughed or who had laughed most or loudest, and we would start laughing all over again. Lots of laughing.

Because I have spent so many years listening to my family laugh, I have come up with a list of the various laughs in our family. Everyone has their own individual laugh, as you will see, but there are also crossover laughs that have been genetically handed down. I will start with my father and work my way down to the baby, Lian, who loves to laugh more than anyone. I would be laughing all the time, too, if I had gotten out of that family trip to Washington, D.C., where the temperature hit 100, we had no air conditioning, and I was throwing up not only in the car but also at the Mint.

1. Dad: A laugh that starts about a half an hour before the real thing. Dad thinks he is the funniest of us all, and very often he is. He chuckles while telling his long stories, and then suddenly stops, mid-anecdote, as if to warn you that a big laugh is coming. You grow impatient as he starts to laugh harder, pursing his lips into an elongated "O." He will accompany this with a light bang on the table, several "ho, ho, hos," and conclude by sitting back, crossing his legs, and laughing uproariously at himself.

2. Mom: A refined but open laugh that is the counterpart to Dad's. Mom does some head shaking, and will often murmur, "Oh, Jim, stop," or just, "Oh dear," as she tries to control her own laughter. Mom often acknowledges the person who is making her laugh with a pat on the back as if to say, "Thank you for the joke," and sometimes claps her hands together when she totally lets loose.

3. Jim: A head shaker. Makes a definite attempt to control his laughter but can't. Jim immediately breaks into a wide smile when he laughs. He also has been known to do some patting on the back, and then disappears into the other room to try to gain composure. Loves to recap the laughing jags and will sadistically throw one word out to the crowd to tempt you into taking the joke bait. We always take it and run with it.

4. Dick: Laughs at his own material and at others. Has an unusually deep and loud "hah, hah, hah." Has been known to say things like "Jeez" and "Oh, God" while laughing. These apparent protestations do not take away from the fact that Dick is funny, loves to laugh, and has a son who is a major cutup.

5. Julie: Enjoys laughing but controls it for the sake of her family. Rubs you on the back and does a downward head shake while she lets a sweet "ha, ha, ha" ring out. Can lose control occasionally with the "oh, ho, ho" variation, though she'll quickly try to regain a semblance of order by making coffee for everyone.

6. Liz: A unique silent laugh that is distinguished by closed eyes and a head thrown back. Liz looks like she is in pain when she laughs, which we love. Making Liz laugh is our goal, because we can wipe out her businesslike veneer with one stupid joke. Yes, if we can succeed in making Liz totally spaz out, we have done our job.

7. Me: Like a chameleon, I have many laughs. I will laugh the way you want me to laugh. I can do the full belly laugh or the silent scream. I have observed, though, how unpleasant one can look while laughing, and so I try to adjust my laughs accordingly.

8. Monica: A one-of-a-kind laugh that indicates that Monica herself is her own biggest fan. Laughs with the Dolan "ho, ho, ho," and then stretches the final "oh" into an "ooooooh, my God," then repeats the process, just in case you didn't laugh with her. Finds people and dogs funny. We find her dog funny, too.

9. Brendan: He was the cutest laugher in the family when he was little. Does he still like to be tickled?

10. Lian: Guffaw, guffaw, guffaw. Loves to tell jokes, reenact stories, and laugh. Lian slaps her knee, wiggles her hips, and loses weight while she laughs. She snorts, sneezes, and does other physically unattractive things while she cracks up at herself. We let her do whatever she wants because she didn't get to go on the trip to Washington.

a sense of

adventure

A Sense of Adventure

by Monica

Every day after school our mother bundled us up in play clothes, hats, and mittens, sent us out the back door, and told us to play outside until dinnertime. It was up to us to entertain ourselves. We were free to explore our back-yard, climb trees, ride bikes, or play in the stream. We did not live in a conventional neighborhood or at the end of a cul-de-sac. Around us were empty fields and narrow country lanes. Those hours of unsupervised play instilled a sense of adventure in all of us Dolan children.

From our surroundings we created a playground of adventure. In winter we knew just how to position flashlights at the top of our back hill, lighting up the night so we'd be able to sled after dark during a big snowfall that we knew would close down the school the next day. We spent hours skating on a nearby pond, tramping down the street in our skates (no skate guards for us). In summer we would strip down to our underwear and "swim" in the stream that ran alongside our house.

The fields behind our house were a big draw. An abandoned and allegedly haunted house sat in a field down the street. Once, our brothers dared us to go inside and upstairs. We younger sisters were allowed to cover our heads with our blue cardigan sweaters in the "scary parts." Thank goodness for blue cardigan sweaters. Even today, there are times when I'd appreciate a blue cardigan to cover my head.

What I loved the most was the freedom to ride my bike alone to my closest schoolmate's house, two miles away. It was a long journey for a ten-year-old, but I was determined to get to my destination. My friend Jennifer Bullard had two things that seemed very exotic to me: a leaky rowboat in the pond behind her house and her own bedroom. One afternoon, I tried the shortcut, riding down Merwin's Lane, but two giant German shepherds came out of nowhere and chased me down the street, so I changed my route, which made the trip twice as long but a little less scary. I'm not even sure my mother knew where I was every day.

One cold fall afternoon, I rode home as it was getting dark. I remember thinking to myself, "I'm all alone out here on this road." And I loved that feeling.

To this day, I still cherish being able to say to myself, "I'm all alone out here."

Having a sense of adventure means you're willing to take some risks in order to get to where you want to go and you're not afraid to be alone. When I was little it meant getting to Jennifer Bullard's house and back. Now, as an adult, it could mean the excitement of traveling to a foreign country alone.

My father was a big believer in adventure. When I was five years old, he established a new family tradition. One Sunday after mass, with all eight children in their church clothes piled in the back of the family station wagon, my father announced, "We're going on an adventure." That's exactly what he called it—an adventure.

My father surprised us with a road trip to New York City and a ride on the Staten Island Ferry to see the Manhattan skyline. In the weeks and years that followed, we made other post-mass trips to the Central Park Zoo, the Statue of Liberty, and Pepe's Pizza in New Haven. With a couple of notable exceptions, the logistics of a full-blown family vacation were too overwhelming for my parents, but that was ok—single-afternoon adventures were good enough for me. It was the element of surprise that made these journeys so memorable. And, honestly, what kid wouldn't be wowed by the Manhattan skyline?

My own sense of adventure really surfaced several years after I had finished college. I was working as a nurse, and one night I had a life-changing conversation with a fellow RN, Janet Gray. Janet must have sensed that I was in a rut and, frankly, I was. I had lived in the same city for nine years and had been working at the same hospital for five of those. All of my college friends were starting to move away—taking new jobs, going to graduate school, or getting married—and I was feeling left behind. I realized there was nothing keeping me in Washington, D.C., except my own lack of gumption.

Janet suggested that I look into becoming a traveling nurse. I didn't even know such a thing existed. She hooked me up with a nursing employment agency that would place me in a temporary job and provide housing anywhere in the country.

Those were the key words—"anywhere in the country." I was ready to see more of the world than just the East Coast. My dream was to live at the beach in the summer and near the mountains in the winter. Part of the plan was to allow for surprises along the way. Where do I sign up?

The more I talked with her, the more I knew I could do it.

Sometimes you just need a little push from a Satellite Sister to get you out the door. Sometimes your sense of adventure needs a kick-start. I gave away everything I owned—the beat-up couch I inherited from an old roommate, the unmatched set of plates from my mother, and my circa 1970s stereo. It was totally liberating. I bought a Rand McNally road map and pointed my VW west. My only possessions were a stethoscope, a bike, and a beach chair. It turned into a four-year road trip. Along the way I lived in Southern California, Northern California, Louisiana, and Oregon—my "Huck Finn days" as I fondly refer to them.

Along the way, I met up with other like-minded adventurous nurses. We worked in the hospital at night and by day learned to surf and cross-country ski together. We were constantly planning our next road trip. There was always some uncertainty about the next destination, but it was exciting all the same. Everything always seemed to work out in the end. I learned that where you live doesn't have to define who you are.

Eventually, I parked my car, bought a couch, and settled into life in Portland, Oregon. I was ready for a permanent address. But I still have adventure in my heart. Given the offer of a good road trip, I'm the first in the car.

My brothers and sisters are living examples of adventurous souls. Collectively, we have lived in thirty-nine different places around the globe. They taught me that it's a good thing to shake your life up every once in a while. Go ahead, move to a foreign country, quit your old job, embark on a new career, learn a new language, and have the courage to leave when things don't work out the way you thought they would.

Having a sense of adventure doesn't mean you have to climb Mt. Kilimanjaro every year. That's something that most of us will never experience, because it requires a combination of stamina and a willingness to die. No thanks. But being adventurous does involve a willingness to take the risks that come with trying something new—to take the scenic route down a country road instead of the shortcut. To pack up your life in a VW and hit the road every once in a while. To understand that settling down doesn't mean sitting still.

A sense of adventure can involve weighing pros and cons, factoring in economics and life-expectancy rates, and calculating risks, or it can be expressed as simply as the everyday lesson we learned growing up: Go outside and play.

Under Your Own Steam

by Liz

One day in 1993, I found myself wandering alone on the back streets of Beijing. All of a sudden the thought crossed my mind: "If I disappeared right now, no one would know I was gone." What was shocking about this thought was not that I was thinking it, but how rarely it ever entered my mind. Yes, I was on vacation alone for a few days in Beijing, having been in Hong Kong on business the week before, but I had spent much of my career working in new places and trying to squeeze in my own adventures between meetings. Sometimes I managed to convince friends or coworkers to join me. Other times that wasn't possible. Given the choice between not visiting Beijing and going there alone, it was easy. I was as close as I was ever going to get to China, and I had saved a few dollars. It never dawned on me not to go.

I was in the habit of calling my parents every Friday just to check in. In fact, I think I had called them from China the day before. So, by my calculations, with my parents not expecting to hear from me and my office not expecting to see me, I would be gone for a week before anyone really noticed my disappearance. And, once they did, it would be unlikely that they would start to look for me on the back streets of Beijing.

But what was I supposed to do? Leave breadcrumbs?

Our parents have always encouraged us to explore our world, be it solo, in pairs, or in larger groups, whether riding our bikes to the beach together or choosing to move to a new city across the country or half a world away. My mother was willing to consider any plan we proposed as long as we could do it "under our own steam." That was her phrase and that was always the goal: to concoct a plan you could pull off largely through your own resources—some combination of public transportation, baby-sitting proceeds, and a bit of sibling support. That is not to say that my parents did not loan the family station wagon or a few dollars if the idea merited it. It's just that the perfect plan would always be "under your own steam." If you could pull it off on your own, it was much harder for them to say no.

When Lian went off to college in California, it was under her own steam. When Monica hit the road as a traveling nurse, living in southern California, northern California, and Louisiana over several years, it was under her own steam. When Sheila went back to finish her college degree when her daughter, Ruthie, was three, it was totally under her own steam.

I have carried this concept throughout my life. When I moved from New York City to Portland, Oregon, in 1988, I arranged for all the movers, travel, and temporary housing on my own. It wasn't until after someone in charge of relocations in the human resources department of my new company called to check in on me that I realized a relocation specialist even existed. Who knew? I assumed I had to do it under my own steam.

Each time we figured something out ourselves, we were a little less intimidated by the unknown parts of the world. Of course, not all these plans worked out perfectly. For example, the time that I ended up spending Christmas Eve in a jail cell in Bergen, Norway, comes to mind. (It's not as bad as it sounds, but it was certainly not what I had planned for the night. My plan ran out of steam.) But each time you try something and it works, you are a little more adventurous the next time. Each time you try something and it fails, you are a little smarter the next time.

So there I was, by myself in Beijing. I had spent a wonderful morning touring the Forbidden City, listening to Peter Ustinov on the Acoustiguide explaining its history to me. I only knew what I had seen in *The Last Emperor*. I wandered around Tiananmen Square, trying to conjure up the images I had seen on the news just a few years before. Where had the Goddess of Democracy been erected? Where had the lone individual faced off against the tank? And finally I found myself on that back street thinking about how removed I was from my own world. It was great and scary at the same moment, and I had gotten there completely under my own steam.

The best adventures have a delicate balance of planning and risk. It's my opinion that there needs to be more adventure in one's life than just the occasional, off-the-beaten-path vacation. Most of my biggest adventures have been job-related. I never had much of a career plan, but I was always up for something new.

Before I moved to Oregon to work at Nike, I was working and living in Manhattan. When the recruiter first called, I declined. "Beaverton, Oregon? Is there any airport anywhere nearby? Oh, Portland! Right. Well, thanks but no thanks. If I think of anyone who wants to move to Beaverville, I'll have them call you." That was the first conversation about the job, but over that weekend the idea started to grow on me.

I had just turned thirty and I had a few goals for the next chapter of my life. I wanted to: (1) live in a smaller city; (2) buy my own house; (3) work in a fun environment, and (4) be somewhere where I could go skiing on the weekends—all this, of course, under my own steam. Surprisingly, Oregon was starting to sound perfect. It is absolutely OK to make a major career change based on the recreational opportunities nearby.

So I went on the interview but only after several days of coaching from siblings (Lian, Brendan, and Dick), who knew more about professional sports than I did. By the end of the interview day, I was hooked. By the end of the following day, I had a job offer, and by the end of the month, I was packing to leave Manhattan. Green Acres, here I come.

A more thoughtful person might have hesitated before switching industries, switching coasts, and going to a place she had only visited twice and where she had no friends.

Under the circumstances, I did what any sane Satellite Sister would do. I called my sister Monica and suggested she come with me. She was working at a hospital in New Orleans at the time, having moved all over the country under her own steam. She had the perfect reaction: "I was thinking of moving to Seattle, but Portland sounds just as good." Sold. She had never been to either place. I now had the right balance of planning and risk. Plus, I had an accomplice.

It did not take long for us to get on our feet. Monica drove her VW Rabbit west and I got us a room at a motel along Highway 217 in Beaverton. I started my new job at Nike and Monica got one in the ICU at Good Samaritan Hospital—Good Sam in Portland parlance. We spent the evenings exploring Portland and the weekends exploring the rest of Oregon: the Columbia River Gorge, the coast, the Cascades. Our years of training in operating under our own steam had really paid off. We loved it. Before long, we had a new house and new skis. I even bought a car (my first) and Monica bought a dog (her first).

Not every leap of faith is as rewarding as our decision to move to Oregon, but what's the worst that could have happened? If it hadn't worked out, we knew that some combination of public transportation, baby-sitting proceeds, and sibling support could lead us to our next adventure under our own steam. Trust me, it's a short hop from Beaverton to Beijing. You'd be surprised.

You'll Be Fine, Dear

by Julie

We were not all-singing, all-laughing Dolans. We spent plenty of time fighting and inflicting cruelties on each other. There are only so many hours that you can spend outside playing dodgeball with your brothers and sisters before someone gets a ball in the face. The combinations of who was fighting with whom were endless: boys vs. girls, Jimmy vs. Dick, Lian vs. Brendan, and on and on. We would fight with anything—long, beanlike things that hung from a tree we dubbed the Captain Kidney Bean tree, rotten apples, even dried cow manure from the field behind our house. We threw books, legos, and rocks. We punched, kicked, poked, and shoved. We teased, mocked, picked at, shouted at, and ridiculed each other.

We all did it, even me. I remember pinning Brendan, eight years my junior, on the floor with my knees and spitting in his face for no good reason other than that I could. Monica threw a clog at Sheila (or maybe it was Sheila who threw it at Monica) that left a sizable dent in the bathroom door. Even Jimmy—the oldest and therefore usually above the fray—snapped one night and systematically captured each of the girls, tied them up with his ties, and threw them in his closet.

As a means of channeling some of the aggression, my father bought boxing gloves and set up a makeshift ring in the upstairs hall. Jimmy and Dick would parade into the ring in their bathrobes, relinquish them to Liz and Monica, who were acting as their handlers, and duke it out. Sometimes Monica and Sheila would put the gloves on and wildly throw punches at each other in their flannel nightgowns. Unassuming Monica with her sweet smile was the best fighter among the girls.

I was always getting hurt. After one touch football game when I was thrown face first into the dirt by the force of either Dick or Jimmy's tag, I got up, crying, and ran to my mother in the kitchen. I had a fat, red, bulbous splitting lip that, to my mind, was unequivocal proof of my brothers' cruelty, but my mother's response was, "You'll be fine, dear." I couldn't believe what I was hearing. I had just gone through one of the most horrifically cruel moments of my life, and my mother's response was "You'll be fine"? No mention of Jimmy and Dick, just "You'll be fine, dear"? I am not sure she even looked very closely at my lip. She just handed me some ice wrapped in an old dishcloth.

This line became one of my parents' mantras. I was angry when my mother said I would be fine. It wasn't fair. I hadn't done anything wrong. It was my brothers who had pushed me down. I was the injured party, but still she expected me to get up, stop crying, wash my face, and go back outside and play. No matter how hurt I thought I was, I was to stop whining because I was going to be fine.

Later, when my wounds were more emotional than physical, my parents used the same phrase. In seventh grade I was the first in our

family to go to the giant junior high school in the center of Fairfield. There were eight hundred students at Tomlinson Junior
High, and I was petrified. Some of the eighth-grade boys had hair
on their faces. Girls wore makeup, chewed gum, and smoked in the
bathroom. Scary. After the first day, I didn't want to go back. I just
wanted to stay at Timothy Dwight Elementary School with all of
my brothers and sisters. I told my mother that Tomlinson was really
the wrong place for me. I just wanted her to drive by and see all
the scary students. I was sure that she would see what I was going
through and immediately pull me out of this juvenile detention
center and find somewhere else for me to go to school. But instead
she just said, "You'll be fine, dear."

Later, in college, I was panicked the night before I was to leave
for a whole year to study in France. It was so far away, and I really
didn't know how to speak French. I was thinking that I should just
stay home and go back to my nice, safe college. Why did I ever
think I could study in France? It was a terrible mistake. This time it
was my father who said, "You'll be fine." Obviously, he wasn't listening to what I was saying that night. I told him that I had been
faking it—I really couldn't speak French, so how was I ever going
to be able to go to school? He wasn't impressed. He just repeated,
"You'll be fine." And I was thinking, *Oh, sure. Easy for you to say—
you don't have to go to* France.

My mother said these words to me again after my second son
was born, on the day she was leaving to return home. On that hot,
sweaty morning I didn't believe that I was going to be fine. I was
standing at the door of our three-bedroom yellow brick ranch
house on Riviera Avenue in New Orleans, watching my mother
get into the car to go to the airport. I was holding two-week-old
Will in my arms. Nick, who was eighteen months, was around my
knees. I was tired and shaky. I was wearing a dress that my mother
had ironed for me and thinking that was the last time I was going

to be wearing clean clothes for the rest of my life. I didn't think I could cope with kids and laundry. I was living in this strange city with no family and few friends and two small children and a husband who was away on business a lot. I did not think I was going to be fine.

Somehow, I was fine in seventh grade, on my junior year abroad, and on Riviera Avenue. How did my parents know? Did they really think I was going to be OK or weren't they listening? Whatever the case, because they didn't give in to my whining, it made me stop crying, wash my face, and go back out and play. I think you need people in your life who will listen to you and reassure you when things look bleak. You also need people who don't really listen to you because it forces you to pull yourself together. When I see no possible way for things to turn out fine, I say these very words to myself. You can't stop playing a game or trying new experiences just because it doesn't look too good or someone was unfair or mean to you or what you're up against is hard. Remember, you'll be fine.

Get Up and Get Going

by Sheila

I was sick a lot as a child. There were times when I was "sick" and other times when I was sick. I was "sick" for tests and quizzes, flute practice, church, and watching my little brothers and sisters for an hour. You could say I had performance anxiety with a touch of self-centered sloth. I was also legitimately sick with common childhood illnesses, including colds, chicken pox, and the flu. Our mother, being smart and sensitive and having raised four children before me, knew the difference between the two kinds of sick. She would take one look at me in the morning and say the magic words that revealed she knew what my real condition was without even having to take my temperature. "Just get up and get going, dear." It worked every time.

Get up and get going. Mom said it with a smile and made it sound like it was a good thing to do, a painless choice. "Get up" meant get out of bed and "get going" meant brush your teeth and wash your face. Put some clothes on. Once Mom helped you out of bed, you really didn't have any other choice but to get dressed. "Just get up and get going, dear," she'd say, "and then we'll see." This addendum was the perfect antidote for a whiny child with low-level anxiety like me. She didn't have time to indulge my apprehension because the whole family had places to go and things to do.

The most compelling part of Mom's action plan included what might happen once you got going. There was always the assurance of something better happening downstairs with my brothers and sisters, who were already getting revved up for the day. A car trip to Stew Leonard's, a walk down to the pharmacy, or a spontaneous game of Monopoly were obvious improvements over solitary inactivity. It just took me a little longer to make that leap of faith. Sometimes, I would get up, get dressed, and slump back into bed with all my clothes on.

At that point, Mom would reappear in my room and ask, "So, how are we doing?"

"Oh fine, Mom," I'd say. "I'm up and dressed. I just can't get going." There was no time for that, so Mom would cinch the deal with her last few words of warning, which were, "I'll meet you downstairs." And then she was off, out of the room before you had the chance to make your case again. There was nowhere to hide, so

I surrendered to what I knew was right. Walking slowly downstairs, I'd overhear my brother Dick giving a dramatic reading from the Wheaties box and my sisters laughing. I'd poke my head around the corner, unsteadily assessing the situation, which was just another morning unfolding around the kitchen table. One of my sisters or brothers would finally notice me, look up, unimpressed, and then someone would shout out, "Sheila's ready!" I took my seat with the others and, without knowing what hit me, I would be swept up into the promise of a new day.

Get up and get going. It worked back then and it continues to work now. I instinctively used it as a mother with my own daughter, who also suffered from occasional school/life "sickness." Ruth, being Ruth, always asked, "Get going where, Mommy?" I turned my mother's wise words on myself to make it out of bed in the morning and get to work. In fact, I used the phrase every day for ten years when I taught public school in New York City. If I could just get up and get going, there would always be something exciting waiting for me in the classroom. Teaching was a daily thrill ride from start to finish, which left me exhausted but never bored. My choice of career probably had a lot to do with the sense of adventure that permeated the Dolan way of life. "Rise and shine" was too *Pollyanna* for our family. Mom taught us that a day was filled with responsibilities as well as small, unexpected pleasures. Just get up and get going, and then you'll see.

Presently, my three-pronged plan includes getting up, getting coffee, and getting going. I hope Mom won't mind the added step.

Ruts

Everyone gets into ruts, except our sister Sheila, who claims to reinvent herself every day. She has *habits*, she argues, but not ruts. What's the difference? A habit is a semiconscious choice; a rut is a lazy choice. We'll go along with that, because we believe that a rut is easy to get out of—all you need is little gumption. Let's hear it for ruts!

JULIE

1. Tuna fish sandwiches every day for lunch for twenty years. Literally every day.
2. Owns many pairs of earrings. Wears the same pair every day.
3. Has had essentially the same haircut since high school.

LIZ

1. Black pants and black shoes for the last decade.
2. Balsamic vinegar as the condiment of choice.
3. Rediscovered Fresca in midlife. Rehooked.
4. Fashion look: long over short or big over small.

SHEILA

As noted above, no ruts, only habits, which include the following.

1. A little laundry every day.
2. All coffee before noon.
3. No shoes in the apartment.

4. Personal space management that guards against loved ones who gesticulate wildly.

MONICA

1. Won't go out on a work night or the night before a trip.

2. Home vegetable consumption limited to spinach and broccoli.

3. Never manages to wash all the dishes in the sink.

LIAN

1. Cottage cheese, three meals a day for months at a time.

2. Sweatpants that go on in the morning and sometimes stay on until bedtime.

3. Too much coffee. Nice with cottage cheese.

4. Romance novels. I'm not proud, just easily amused during times of great stress.

5. Ponytails. They eliminate the need to comb, wash, cut, or highlight.

On the Road Again

by Lian

We were not a big car-trip family. Understandably so. Piling eight kids into a station wagon and driving anywhere is not a vacation. Our family trips were usually mandatory and involved several hours of hitting and at least one stop for carsickness. Our family motto was "Don't touch me." For vacation, my parents put us all onto camp buses and stayed home by themselves. A very sensible approach, if you ask me.

As I grew older, I began to associate the car less with throwing up and more with transition. As the youngest, I became the ultimate passenger. My parents gave the station wagon keys to my brothers and sisters, and they took turns driving each other to college in Rhode Island, summer jobs in Boston, and new apartments in Washington. I went along for many of these rides and learned a lot about life's rites of passage. I discovered that road trips meant Tab, Bruce Springsteen, and inside jokes. And being a good passenger meant staying awake and knowing when to shut up. By the time my turn came to drive away to college in California, I was a seasoned traveler.

I didn't own a car until I was twenty-four, but my love of being a passenger kept me on the road. These trips were not joyrides, but comings and goings of import; life changes that were best begun slowly, over a few thousand miles and lots of conversation. With my friend Andy, I saw Graceland, bought a coonskin cap, and listened to the other Elvis—Costello, that is—sing "Imperial Bedroom" thirty-four times on the way back from Christmas break. I accompanied Monica on her migration west and spent five hours in a

Carl's Jr. in Las Vegas, waiting for the sun to go down while praying that her overpacked Rabbit would survive the climb out of Death Valley. After college, I moved to Wyoming with my friend Alison, giving myself over to the wonders of biscuits and gravy and John Hiatt. And I wept for fourteen straight hours as I drove from a Single Girl's life with my sisters in Portland to a Married Woman's life in Pasadena with my new husband.

My own family is much smaller and more car-trip-ready. My two boys love to belt in and drive for hours, and my husband is skilled behind the wheel. Our vacation plans more often than not involve a car rather than a plane. I like it that way. I hope my children will learn that a good road trip is not just about getting from here to there and back. A good road trip is about getting from here to there and never looking back.

*I*t's Never a Perfect Time To . . .

If you're waiting around for the perfect time to make that big life transition, to get a jump on your future or achieve your goals, don't bother. There's never a perfect time for that stuff. Now is as good a time as any other. Remember, it's never a perfect time to:

- Get married.
- Get divorced.
- Go back to school.
- Have a baby.
- Quit your job.
- Get fired.
- Ask for a raise.
- Take a vacation.
- Talk to your kids about sex and drugs.
- Get a physical.
- Get adult braces.
- Redo your résumé.
- Clean out your closets.
- Move.
- Get in shape.
- Write a will.
- Go on a blind date.
- Set three new goals for the year.

The Middle Seat Peace Plan

by Julie

I couldn't believe our family was actually going to take a car trip that required driving through multiple states. Our only previous experiences with family car trips were short one- to two-hour trips to visit our relatives. On the trip to Washington, D.C., we were going to bring luggage. We were going to strap things to the roof of our car. We were going to stay in a hotel and eat at restaurants. I was ecstatic. I was finally taking a family vacation like the family vacations my friends took. I always felt different because we didn't go on camping trips to national parks or drive to exotic places like the Blue Ridge Mountains or Lake Winnepesaukee. We did lots of fun things as a family but never all together in a car.

The day we left, Jim and Dick collected the suitcases from each bedroom and lined them up in the driveway. My father stood out front, supervising the project and considering how best to stack and secure the suitcases on the roof of the car. I don't know how my father knew how to stack luggage on the roof of a car, since we'd never done anything like this before. Yet there he stood with his arms folded across his chest, commenting on Jim and Dick's work. Working as a team, my brothers confidently made decisions about which suitcases should go on top of the car, which ones were best in the back seat, and which types of knots would work best with Samsonite luggage. It was as if they had taken some special class in luggage roping. Maybe they learned it at summer camp.

Finally everything and everybody had a place in the car. I managed to get a window seat in the second row of seats along with Sheila and Monica. Liz, Dick, and Brendan were in the way back. I was happy to settle in and watch the world as we set out down our driveway. I don't think we made it to the on-ramp of the Connecticut Turnpike before a minor skirmish had broken out between Sheila and Monica about how close Monica could put her leg to where Sheila's hand was resting on the seat. Every time Monica would shift her leg over to reclaim an inch or two of the seat, Sheila would elbow Monica in the ribs. It began silently, with Monica jerking her leg over to Sheila slightly harder each time and Sheila responding with a corresponding shove or an elbow. Sheila was using her hand to define her personal space, creating her own Maginot Line that Monica was not to cross. I could see that neither of them were going to let this go. It took a lot to incite Monica, but once engaged, she was relentless. She was going to put her leg on that two-inch strip of car seat or else.

My parents in the front seat were oblivious to the escalating violence. What was currently a small isolated exchange was about to erupt into something much worse. I didn't really care if Sheila and Monica hit each other. The two of them lived in their own world where they constantly fought but were inseparable. I just didn't want the noise of their fight to draw my mother's—or worse, my father's—attention. If my mother caught a glimpse of the second-seat border war, she might shoot a glare at Monica and Sheila. If my father heard the commotion, the stakes were much higher. He was less tolerant of our daily bickering. If he heard the unrest, he might conclude that we were all selfish and spoiled and not worthy of a car trip to Washington, D.C.

As far as I was concerned, the family vacation was at risk. If Sheila and Monica didn't stop, my parents might turn the car around, head home, untie the luggage, and make us sweep the patio for four days straight. I was not going to let that happen, even if it meant giving up my window seat. Without acknowledging my sisters, I swung my leg across Monica, jammed my hand up against

Sheila, and in one swift move inserted myself between them. Sheila and Monica were stunned. I said nothing and looked straight ahead. As their older sister, I knew neither of them would dare to say or do anything. I sat on the hump with my knees up and the sun beating down on my thigh from the sunroof of our Buick station wagon for six hours, knowing that I had single-handedly saved the family trip to Washington.

Once we safely made it to Washington, our trip was everything

that I had hoped for. For me, Washington was a glamorous city of beautiful monuments, fancy hotels, and sophisticated people doing important things, and I felt like one of those people. You see, it was the first time I was allowed to wear clothes that didn't match or even coordinate with Liz, Sheila, or Monica at an official family outing. While my sisters were trudging up the Washington Monument in white shorts and blue shirts, I was in a pink floral Qiana shift. Standing in line at the White House, I was sure that someone passing by would not associate me with the group of girls in matching turquoise-and-white striped dresses. I felt older, special, different.

On our trip we visited the Supreme Court. I told my father that I wanted to be the first woman Supreme Court justice when I grew up. My father looked down at me, smiled, and said that would be nice because he would like to come and have lunch with me in the Supreme Court's beautiful courtyard. At fourteen, standing there in my own clothes and hearing my father's encouraging words, I felt like someday I could do something important. After all, I had just negotiated the middle seat peace plan.

June 1969

by Liz

In a big family you often do things in shifts. One parent and four kids go off on an adventure together while the other parent and the leftover kids stay home, waiting their turn. The first overnight trip we ever took all together with both parents was our family trip to Washington, D.C. Dad, Mom, and a station wagon full of kids drove the six hours to our nation's capital for a four-day visit in June 1969, after school let out. I had just finished the sixth grade. Seven out of eight of us went. Lian, age four, was home alone.

Despite all of its educational highlights, my favorite part of the trip was staying in a hotel with elevators. All the girls (Julie, Sheila, Monica, me) were in one room, all the boys (Jim, Dick, Brendan) were in another, and our parents were in the middle. In theory, this allowed them to monitor our behavior. In fact, our brothers were busted by hotel security for lighting a roman candle and holding it out the window of their room, aiming it at the Russian Embassy. Meanwhile, we girls secretly held a contest to see who was brave enough to walk around the hotel in pajamas. Two by two we would venture out, first running up and down the hallway, then actually riding the elevator down to the lobby. We would rush back to the room to deliver breathless reports on our daring exploits, then the next team would set out and try to top it.

I was feeling pretty cool in my bare feet and bathrobe in the lobby of the Hilton until I bumped into Chief Justice Earl Warren. Busted—by a Supreme Court justice, no less. I knew it was him because we had studied Warren Court decisions like *Brown v. Board of Education* in social studies that year. Plus, we had just visited the Supreme Court the day before. It was not in session, but I studied the photographs, thinking Supreme Court justice seemed like a job I might enjoy. It was fitting that I was wearing a robe when Mr. Chief Justice and I met, even if mine was a to-the-knee flowered number, not the ankle-length black one I aspired to.

Once we got dressed and out of the hotel, we did all the great Washington stuff—visiting the Capitol, the White House, the FBI, the Washington and Jefferson monuments, the Mint, and the Smithsonian. It was very hot and we were frequently lost, but I loved it and was impressed with the law-making and law enforcement stuff of government. It had never dawned on me that someone actually had to *make* the money. We also studied the first ladies' gowns. We couldn't believe how tiny they were. Our favorite, of course, was Jackie Kennedy's.

At the Capitol, we sat in the Senate Gallery. There was nothing happening, but it was nice to get in from the heat. As I looked down into the chamber, I thought that senator might also be a good job. There were no gowns involved, like justices or first ladies, but there were other benefits. Actually, given a choice between first lady or senator, the latter seemed far more interesting. At the time, there was only one woman in the Senate—Margaret Chase Smith of Maine. She was always mentioned in school, too, because she was The One. I calculated the odds. The Senate had one hundred slots vs. the Supreme Court's nine. The Senate had one woman. The Supreme Court had none. Not in its entire history. One out of one hundred. Zero out of nine. I still had years before I could get through junior high, high school, college, and law school. Would those numbers change in the interim?

The most emotional stop on the tour was Arlington Cemetery. At the Tomb of the Unknown Soldier, we watched the Changing of the Guard. We were aware of the great sacrifices that had been made by many, including my mother's brother Dick who had been killed in World War II. We were also aware of the controversy raging over America's involvement in Vietnam. My own brothers Dick and Jim were fifteen and seventeen. It was 1969. I was twelve. At that moment, I was not sure what to think about war.

Our final stop that day was at John and Robert F. Kennedy's graves. Beside John Kennedy's grave, an eternal flame burned. Robert Kennedy's was new. We knelt down and said our prayers, just as we had seen their families do on television. The kids stayed quiet, just as we had learned to do watching their funerals on television. Our parents cried, just as we had seen them do in 1963 and again in 1968. They told us about the great promise that had been lost, then we got in our station wagon and went home.

The next time my brother Jim was in Washington, he was arrested on the steps of the Pentagon demonstrating against the war. The next time I was in Washington, I was an intern in the office of Senator Lowell Weicker, a member of the Watergate committee. Monica spent four years at college in Washington and four years following college working in the hospital where they brought Ronald Reagan the day he was shot.

In 1969, when we were all in Washington together, we had no idea such things were ahead of us. I was twelve. In my short lifetime, I had seen the government work well and work poorly, protect its citizens and harm them, and open its halls to some as it prevented others from being heard. I did not know how to make sense of all of this, but I knew I wanted to.

The D.C. Blues

by Sheila

Gather 'round folks and lend me your ears,
I'll tell you 'bout a family that hadn't been in years,
On any vacation that might involve a car,
Or boat or a plane that took them very far.

No vacation, no vacation, no vacation, you say?
Why can't eight kids find some time to get away?
The Dolans had a rule, and it was plain to see,
That ten bodies on a trip was truly heresy.

Well, it was Dad's idea to break all the rules,
He plotted and planned until the kids were out of school.
He sprung it on Mom on a hot June day,
We're going to the Hilton via Chesapeake Bay!

We're going to the capital, yes, the heart of D.C.
The history, the Hilton, the land of the V.P.
It was the summer, a bummer, the summer of '69,
We were told to dress lightly and, baby, not to whine.

So it was Mom and Dad and Jim in the front,
In the middle were Monica and me, with Julie on the hump,
The way back was saved for Brendy and Dickie,
With Liz as a buffer on the way down to D.C.

Did I forget to mention Lian? Little Lian wasn't there.
She was home with a sitter in the big easy chair.
How come she got the chair to herself and could just sit
and watch TV?
"Little Lian is too little to appreciate D.C."

D.C., D.C., it's not very far,
Just six hours straight in an air-conditioned car.
If the air isn't there, roll the windows down wide,
We're going on vacation and to see the countryside.

The temperature climbed as we neared the Jersey shore,
We played "License Plate" for three hours, maybe four.
The next few hours we were repositioning
Our bodies on the seat for we had lost conditioning.

Air-conditioning that is, oh the words we couldn't say,
On the six-hour trip to D.C. that fateful day.
We could say "window down" and "New Jersey looks nice."
But we couldn't mention air or conditioning or ice.

D.C., D.C., it's not very far,
Just six hours straight in an air-conditioned car.
If the air isn't there roll the windows down wide,
We're going on vacation and to see the countryside.

We steamed into town with a car full of kids,
The Hilton awaited and would be our digs.
We prayed we'd have a/c sometime soon on this vacation,
Mercifully the hotel had some fine refrigeration.

Liz was in heaven, Julie wore us out,
Her outfits were endless as she strutted about.
I melted at the Mint and pressed my head against the marble.
Was there any way to watch all this on film? I felt sort of horrible.

D.C., D.C., it's not very far,
Just six hours straight in an air-conditioned car.
If the air isn't there roll the windows down wide,
We're going on vacation and to see the countryside.

I don't remember much from our family's D.C. spree,
I was eleven, it was hot, and I watched some TV.
In the Hilton hotel, which I loved very much,
The thermostat read fifty, which Julie told us not to touch.

D.C., D.C., it wasn't very far,
Our Dad was a trouper in our nine-person car.
We saw everything that a family could see,
In the hottest summer on record in our nation's history.

I Didn't See the Arrows

by Monica

Too bad our family vacation to Washington, D.C., did not take place ten years later. By 1979, the Washington metro had opened and we could have relied on public transportation to take us to the major sites. We could have ridden in air-conditioned comfort to the Mall, the Supreme Court Building, and the Mint. But we went to Washington in 1969, so we spent our vacation trapped in the hot family station wagon, getting lost.

The trip from Connecticut to Washington was pretty much a straight shot down I-95. My father had no trouble navigating this part of the trip. But when we entered the District, the one-way streets and traffic circles posed a challenge. We didn't have many of those in suburban Connecticut. In the space of four days, it seemed like my father managed to go down every one-way street in Washington the wrong way. That's just the kind of thing that embarrasses a ten-year-old girl. For me, it was the most vivid memory of our vacation. I'm sure it didn't help that seven children were screaming, "Turn around!" at my dad from the back seats.

His reply was always the same: "Shoot, I'm sorry. I didn't see the arrows."

We spent a lot of time in Washington traveling in reverse. Thank goodness we had out-of-state plates.

Every morning of our vacation went something like this: Seven children and two adults would pile into the hot station wagon with a list of monuments and sites to see for the day. Our father would drop us off at the corner of 15th and Constitution and say, "I'll park the car and be right back." One hour, three bridges, and two states later, he would return. And each time, he was amazed at how easy it was to cross from Virginia to Maryland and back into D.C., all in search of a single parking space. Dad did not believe in maps.

One memorable morning, we set off to see the embassies on Massachusetts Avenue. After spending what seemed like several hours circling Dupont Circle, we headed back to the hotel without seeing a single embassy. Just a lot of Dupont Circle.

The next day, the nine of us were headed for the Lincoln Memorial when my father eyed a deluxe parking place, probably intended for descendants of Lincoln, right in front of the monument. My father was determined to nab it. Unfortunately, he was in the wrong lane. The next thing you know, we were on the Memorial Bridge with my father saying, "Hold on, kids! We're going to Virginia!"

Our only outing without incident was to Mt. Vernon. They have a parking lot.

Once we reached our destination and the parking brake was set, my father made up for the driving mishaps by being an incredibly enthusiastic tour guide. My father loves American history, so Washington, D.C., was the perfect place to share that passion with his children. He knew all kinds of great stories about the presidents' lives and the history of the city's monuments. Maybe he made some of the stories up, or embellished them a little (another one of his specialties), but he made Washington come alive.

Years later, I was lucky enough to live in that beautiful city for nine years, for college and then work. I think the epic family vacation in 1969 had something to do with this. I didn't own a car, so I used the new metro and avoided accidental travel to Virginia. But I did share my father's stories with friends.

I spent many spring evenings, sitting on the steps of the Lincoln Memorial, watching the tourist buses come and go. I shared countless picnics with friends by the reflecting pool. And every night for years, I walked home from work up Massachusetts Avenue along Embassy Row, slowly taking in the embassies we had missed in 1969. I saw the arrows; I just saw them on foot and on my own.

The Vacation of a Lifetime

by Lian

I did not go on the fabled Dolan family trip to Washington, D.C., in the summer of 1969. I was four years old and would have, as my mother correctly predicted, been too little to appreciate our nation's capital and too hot to do anything but whine. But, at the time, being four, I flung myself on the kitchen floor and threw a tantrum while my seven brothers and sisters loaded up the car and headed off to The Vacation of a Lifetime. This particular tantrum is one of my earliest memories.

While my family was enjoying The Vacation of a Lifetime, I stayed home with a baby-sitter in a house that was strangely quiet. I don't remember much about that week, except this: the baby-sitter *let me eat in the TV room*! This was unheard of in our house, where food was consumed in one of three places: at the kitchen table, at the dining room table, or, in the case of some contagious disease, on a tray in our rooms. But *eating in the TV room? Never!*

This was amazing. I was doing something that my brothers and sisters didn't get to do. Who cared about the Mint when I could eat SpaghettiOs on a tray in the TV room while watching *Underdog*? I was the one having The Vacation of a Lifetime.

When my family returned, I listened to the stories, laughed at the right spots, and played along as the tales of D.C. turned from memory to myth. I studied the Washington Trip pages in the family photo album so many times, I felt like I was the one in the light blue shorts set, not Monica. Sometimes I would even recount the stories as my own, only to be reminded by a sibling that I was "too little to go to Washington."

By my early teens, I discovered that I had the ultimate bargaining chip in my back pocket—the "I didn't get to go to Washington" defense. Whenever I was about to get aced out of some event or be given a litany of good reasons why something would not be possible, I could look up at my mother and say, "But I never got to go to Washington."

It worked like magic. That early family injustice was parlayed into many trips to the theater in New York, weekends in Boston, even a trip to the Olympics. I found I could use the Trip Not Taken as leverage for a new pair of jeans or a better bike. I played the Washington card long into adolesence to get first dibs on the bedrooms during family vacations.

Not too long ago, when I felt that, in good conscience, I had played the Washington chip for the last time, I revealed to my mother that staying home had not really been that bad. In fact, the baby-sitter had allowed me to eat SpaghettiOs on a tray in the TV room while watching *Underdog*, so actually I had had a fine time all by myself. My mother was astounded, horrified really. I'm not sure what bothered her more, the thought of me eating in the TV room or the fact that I had conned her for so many years. She gasped, "Maybe we should have taken you on the Washington Trip after all."

My First Car

JULIE

1977 MUSTANG HARDTOP. The ugliest Mustang ever produced. Had to have an American car in order to work at U.S. Steel. COLOR: chamois. NICKNAME: The Honey Car. NUMBER OF SIBLINGS WHO SUBSEQUENTLY OWNED THE CAR: 6. EVENTUAL DEMISE: overburdened by tickets and abandoned in Boston parking lot by sibling who shall remain nameless.

LIZ

1972 CHEVY IMPALA, purchased in 1985. Bought at church auction for $500 to use as a "station car." COLOR: brown and Bondo. Featured in the independent film *Bailjumper* in which it was hit by an asteroid. EVENTUAL DEMISE: donated to demolition derby by filmmakers to raise cash.

SHEILA

Has never owned a car.

MONICA

1982 VW RABBIT. COLOR: tan. Made the financial decision to get the good tape deck instead of air-conditioning. Regrettable. Survived three cross-country trips and flooding. Forced to bail out back seat with a saucepan after a New Orleans rainstorm. EVENTUAL DEMISE: traded in for VW Golf with air-conditioning and self-bailer.

LIAN

1974 VW BUG bought in 1988. COLOR: green. Purchased for $350 in quarters, saved in coffee cans during a winter season of waitressing in Jackson Hole. No reverse made parallel parking tricky. Lug nuts on tires not too reliable. Wheels had a tendency to fall off at stop signs. EVENTUAL DEMISE: sold to fellow waitress for $350 in quarters.

Good Planning Makes Good Fun

by Julie

I didn't realize that other people didn't celebrate Thanksgiving the way we did until I was older and had Thanksgiving dinner at a friend's house. It was a very delicious meal, but nothing like what went on in our house. We didn't have Thanksgiving dinner; we had a Thanksgiving pageant complete with acts, costumes, and specific roles for all of the participants.

Thanksgiving was always at our house. My mother's three sisters, uncles, and approximately twenty-five cousins would come. The count for dinner, including boyfriends or college roommates, was usually thirty-five.

My mother was a master planner who did most of her work on the back of the envelope with a crayon. We always seemed to be short on writing materials and utensils at our house. But what she didn't have down on paper, she carried around in her head. I am sure she worked on Thanksgiving mentally all year long, but things would really start to heat up after Halloween. The entire month of November was devoted to Thanksgiving. Each day my mother worked on some task associated with the big day. As she used to say, "Good planning makes good fun." Even tasks that weren't technically associated with Thanksgiving, such as cleaning windows or repainting the back gate, got reclassified as Thanksgiving imperatives in which we were all expected to take part.

We had the same menu every year: pâté, potted shrimp dip, carrots, celery, and olives as hors d'oeuvres; and for the main course, two turkeys, a capon for my father (who had a theory that the hormones injected into turkeys were making him ill), mashed potatoes, stuffing, gravy, butternut squash, turnips, creamed onions, cranberry bread, cranberry relish, and peas. Pies, ice-cream turkeys, fudge, nuts, and tangerines were served for dessert. The only debate was about the peas. My mother never seemed satisfied with the peas.

My mother or one of my aunts would provide matching aprons, usually in some Pilgrim motif, for all the sisters to wear, with coordinated potholders or dishtowels. Everyone else arrived in good clothes. Our Boston cousins would even stop at a rest station so they could change out of their travel clothes and arrive at our home in their good clothes. No one ever asked them to do this, but somehow it became part of the plan. When some of my older cousins were in high school and college, my mother sent out word in advance of the event that "no funny clothes" were to be worn at Thanksgiving. The cultural revolution of the 70s was not going to intrude on the Dolan Thanksgiving.

Although there was no official schedule, there was a time for everything. There was a point during the hors d'oeuvres period and prior to mashing the potatoes and carving the turkeys that we

would pause to take the "sisters picture." My mother and her three sisters would take their aprons off and stand on the front porch to take their annual Thanksgiving picture. The "sisters picture" was part of the pageant.

Everyone had a role to play. My father and my uncle Harry carved the turkeys. When electric carving knives were all the rage, it would sound like a logging operation in the kitchen, with dueling electric knives and the electric beater mashing the potatoes all at the same time. My uncle Dick brought novelty items like rubber noses, yo-yos, boomerangs, and plastic finger puppets. He kept the items in a paper bag and would move around the party, surreptitiously distributing the gags individually to the kids. Even if you were twenty-five years old and married, you got a novelty item. Cousins Sue and Patty were in charge of making place cards. I always mashed the potatoes. My brother Jim took the official event photos while cousin Tommy took candids. And so on, down the line. Everyone had an assignment, from passing the pâté to finding the projector for the after-dinner slide show.

There were four tables organized by age group—adults, teenagers, preteens, and the little kids. With this seating arrangement it was clear that some of the people at the little kids table were never going to make the adult table in this lifetime. A revised seating plan was developed in later years so that the little kids, who were now in their late teens and early twenties, would be rotated to the adult table.

After dinner, we would all crowd into the den and watch old family slides and howl with laughter at our funny hair or bad clothes. We showed the same slides every year, but it didn't matter. One year my cousin's boyfriend had the bad judgment to fall asleep during the family slide show. When my cousin and her boyfriend broke up, many in the family pointed to this moment as the turning point.

For all the people and food, it was never chaotic. We sat down, said grace, and ate a hot meal. Then all the aunts, uncles, and cousins took their plates, pots, oven mitts, and serving spoons and went home. Nobody spent the night. That was part of the plan.

While everyone else in America goes shopping on the Friday after Thanksgiving, we would sit around, too tired to even consider it. We would eat turkey sandwiches, review the events of the day before, and begin the planning for the following year—perhaps reassigning the making of the cranberry relish to another family member or discussing what to do about the peas. My mother would make a mental note to remember to take the ice-cream turkeys out of the freezer earlier.

Long before I went to business school and knew what a PERT chart was, I was aware of advanced planning. You couldn't wait until the Monday before Thanksgiving to polish the silver. You had to order the turkeys from Rippe's Farm two weeks in advance. The leaves had to be raked on the Saturday and then again on the Wednesday before Thanksgiving. From Monday on, you weren't really allowed to eat anything in the refrigerator. And, of course, the tables for Thanksgiving dinner had to be set the night before.

When I think about my career in academic administration, every big project that I have managed, from developing a recruiting schedule for admissions to planning an annual meeting for my professional association, was essentially the Dolan Thanksgiving without the turkeys.

When I was hired as a director of admissions, one of my first assignments was to plan the admissions recruiting schedule. This is where my Thanksgiving training really paid off. I set the dates, developed a work back schedule, figured out the tasks, assigned jobs, designated roles for the day of the event, picked out menus, printed nametags, had a tablecloth with the school name made, and set the table with school brochures well in advance of the event. When prospective students arrived at our event, I fed them cheese cubes, crackers, coffee, and tea, and had a slide show.

Thanksgiving taught me not to be intimidated by scale. I actually find staging big events or taking on big tasks to be fun, and because of it, I am always raising my hand to volunteer. This lack of intimidation has led to a slight problem of overcommitting myself. Even when I was living in San Francisco and working in Los Angeles and trying to monitor the movements of two teenage boys, I raised my hand to serve as cochair of the school auction committee. That year three hundred fifty people attended the school event rather than thirty-five, but if you're used to a large group, what's a few more people?

Working with volunteers or staff is not that different than working with your family. Like all groups, a core inner group seems to do most of the work. Why was it that Sheila always had to make an urgent phone call right as we were scraping, stacking, washing, and drying the holiday dishes? She was twelve—who could she be calling? It always seemed to me that some of my brothers and sisters were MIA just when I was polishing the silver, or they needed to go to the library just when the front porch needed washing. If you simply accept this and try to get a lot out of your core group and at least a little something out of the rest, the work will get done.

Back then I couldn't understand why my mother was ironing the Thanksgiving napkins in October, but now I see—she had a plan.

Thanksgiving Recipes

Turkey Tetrazzini

8 ounces spaghetti, broken into 2-inch pieces

4 tablespoons butter

4 tablespoons flour

1 teaspoon salt

¼ teaspoon nutmeg

2 cups chicken broth
1 cup light cream
¼ to ½ cup sherry or Marsala wine
⅓ cup grated Parmesan cheese
2 cups cooked turkey (or chicken), cubed
½ pound mushrooms sliced
1 egg yolk
1 can (7¼ ounces) black olives
   packed in water, drained

Drop spaghetti into 6 cups of rapidly boiling water. Bring water to a boil again and cook until tender, about 12 to 15 minutes. Drain. Meanwhile, melt butter over low heat, blend in flour, salt, and nutmeg, and stir constantly until mixture is smooth and bubbly. Remove from heat; stir in chicken broth and cream, bring to a boil, and cook, stirring, for 1 minute. Stir in wine and cheese. Add sauce to cooked spaghetti. To the chicken, add mushrooms and egg yolks. Add turkey mixture to spaghetti and sauce, blending thoroughly. Pour into buttered 2½–quart casserole. Top with black olives and bake, uncovered, at 350°F for 25 to 30 minutes. Let stand for 10 minutes before serving. Yield: 4 to 6 servings.

NOTE #1: The original recipe is from *The Cookbook,* Worcester Art Museum, Worcester, MA, 1976. The cookbook was a Mother's Day gift from our brother Jim to our mother. Our mother *always* doubled this recipe. She also always added more cheese and mushrooms than the recipe called for. Sometimes she would top the Turkey Tetrazzini with ¼ to ½ cup of breadcrumbs.

NOTE #2: Turkey or Chicken Tetrazzini was our dog Tor's favorite dish. I think that's why our mother always doubled the recipe so that there would be plenty of leftovers for Tor. Tor was a black

Lab that our brother Jim brought home one summer from Camp Monadnock, where he had been a counselor in training. Tor was devoted to our mother and her tetrazzini.

Thanksgiving Pâté

1 pound sausage
1 pound chicken livers
1 clove garlic, mashed
1 large onion, finely chopped
1½ tablespoons tarragon
1½ tablespoons parsley
½ cup tawny port
¼ pound mushrooms, chopped
2 tablespoons butter
½ cup heavy cream

Slowly brown sausage in a frying pan. Drain on paper towel. In the sausage fat, sauté chicken livers with garlic and onion. Add tarragon, parsley, and port. Put sausage meat and chicken liver mixture in blender or food processor and mix until smooth. Sauté mushrooms in the butter. Add cream. Mix everything together and pour into a 2-pound loaf pan. Place pan in a larger pan. Add water to the larger pan until it comes 2 inches up around the loaf pan. Bake at 325°F for 1 hour covered, then ½ hour uncovered. Refrigerate a day or two so that pâté will solidify and reach its full flavor. Serve at room temperature with thin slices of French bread lightly toasted with olive oil and herbs and cornichons.

NOTE #1: The original pâté recipe came from *The Cookbook,* Worcester Art Museum, Worcester, MA, 1976. Our mother always added more tarragon and parsley than the original recipe called for.

NOTE #2: Next to tetrazzini, pâté was Tor's second favorite dish. One Thanksgiving, my mother put the pâté in the garage to cool overnight, because our refrigerator was full with other Thanksgiving preparations. Unfortunately, Tor was also put in the garage. We didn't have pâté that Thanksgiving.

Another year, the pâté was served on the coffee table in the family room. The coffee table was the same height as Tor. He managed to eat about half of the pâté before someone noticed. Tor was placed in the garage for the rest of the Thanksgiving meal.

Christmas 1977

by Liz

The first Christmas you spend away from your family is a big deal. Mine was spent in jail. I was twenty. Let me explain.

On Christmas Eve 1977, my friend Ellen and I found ourselves in the train station in Bergen, Norway. We had met in Paris, where we were both students studying at the university for the year. During the holidays, all the foreign students head home or somewhere cheap and exotic. Actually, most students head somewhere sunny, cheap, and exotic, but we thought we'd be more adventuresome. Plus, how cold and dark could it really be?

To save money, we purchased unlimited student interrail passes and planned an itinerary through Scandinavia that included the maximum number of nights on a train and the minimum number of nights in a hotel. We were girls on the move, slowed only by the extra layers of clothes we had to wear or carry in our huge aluminum-frame backpacks. There were a few moments when I realized that my classmates who headed for Rome probably did not have to bring mittens, but everyone goes to Rome. Scandinavia would be so much more . . . *Christmas-y.*

On December 24, we took a beautiful train ride from Oslo to Bergen. During the few moments of actual daylight, it was everything we wanted it to be—fjords, actual live reindeer frolicking, everything. When we arrived in Bergen, we began a late-afternoon hunt for a hostel or cheap hotel. This is when we discovered the real reason that students don't come to Bergen for Christmas—nothing is open. Or maybe it is the other way around. Nothing is open because nobody comes. Anyway, that afternoon we had a crash course in Norwegian holiday customs. It seems that Christmas Eve is the big holiday in Norway, not Christmas Day. On the 24th, everything is closed down and everyone has gone home. Restaurants, shops, inns—all closed. There are no blaring "One Day Left 'Til Christmas" announcements broadcast from mall loudspeakers. There are no malls. There are no days left. Christmas is about Christmas Eve and on Christmas Eve, everyone is at home.

When you travel in foreign countries you realize that one of the hardest things to do is use the phone. It seems so simple, but when you can't read the instructions, don't have the right coins, can't figure out the dialing codes, and can't understand the person who picks up on the other end if by some miracle you should get all the other steps right, it can lead to much frustration. As we called around to hotels, we got nowhere. The locals seemed truly puzzled that we would not be at our own homes. One Bergener asked Ellen, "Don't you have family in Bergen?" Her reply was "Bergen County, New Jersey, yes. Bergen, Norway, no." It cracked me up at the time—maybe hypothermia was already setting in. The Bergener did not fully appreciate Ellen's answer.

The only hotels that were actually open were the ones well outside our price range—the ones where to check in we would have had to have a credit card, which neither of us possessed. We sat on the bench in the train station and considered our options.

Option #1: Get back on the train and go back to Oslo. This had the advantage of being free. The disadvantage was that we would never see Bergen in daylight. It would also leave us looking for lodging in Oslo around midnight. We had just come from there and knew our way around a little, but walking the streets at night with our backpacks looking for a warm, dry place to stay the night was a little too close to the original Christmas story for my taste.

Option #2 was to present ourselves to the authorities and beg for mercy. We chose Option #2. A short walk through dark, deserted downtown Bergen brought us to a clean, lovely, warm police station. Inside that station, we found four officers who had drawn the short straws and had gotten stuck working Christmas Eve. We may have been sheepish in asking for their assistance, but they could not have been happier to see us. The evening's entertainment had just arrived with two big backpacks on. *Skol!*

We had a great night. They shared their Christmas feast with us (free!), poured us glasses of their traditional glug (free!), and taught us Norwegian carols and phrases. They got such a kick out of it when Ellen and I repeated the phrases that it became clear that what they were teaching us was not exactly polite conversation, but we played along. After all, we were warm and safe and everything was free!

Things were going fantastically well until there came another rap at the door and two American boys in a similar predicament showed up. Apparently, they had taken the later train from Oslo. They were nice and we were happy they, too, had found refuge, but their presence had consequences for us. The Bergen P.D. graciously lodged both pairs of Americans in empty cells that night, but because the officers did not want to leave us alone downstairs in the jail with these unknown boys, we all had to be locked in. Luckily, the girls got the deluxe cell with down comforters and a small window. This must have been where they put the real criminals. The boys got the stripped-down cell where they throw the drunks. It had two cots and very limited linens. There was nothing particularly scary about being locked in our cell except this: It only had a urinal. The real bathroom was down the hall on the other side of the locked door. We made one last visit around midnight. We knew the police would be back at 8 A.M. to let us out, but just knowing that we couldn't reach a real toilet prevented me from thinking about anything else all night.

On Christmas morning, the day shift sprang us from our cells, fed us, and set us free into the still-dark, still-deserted streets of Bergen. We trudged around for a while, appreciated the day as the sun rose, then headed back to the train station. To our surprise, it was packed with families: grandparents, parents, and kids, all bundled up with skis in hand, headed to the wide-open spaces that fill most of Norway. On the train, the mood was festive and the picnics freely shared. Strangers told us about how they had spent Christmas Eve and we did the same. We got laughs, strange looks, and herring.

The train would occasionally stop in the middle of nowhere and families would climb down, strap on their skis, and whoosh away toward the hills and herds of reindeer. Christmas in Norway? See it from the train! It was the best day of our trip, and it was free.

Later that night I placed a collect call home to Connecticut from a pay phone in the hallway of the latest cheap hotel in which Ellen and I had landed. It would politely be called a "seaman's hotel" and we laughed that this was where we should have been locked in! Jail was safer.

As I spoke to my family for the first time in four months, I could picture where they all were, what they had done on Christmas Eve, and when they would leave to go to my cousins' after Mass. I could imagine every detail of their Christmas at home, which was a great feeling. I also knew that they could not imagine any of the details of mine. That was a great feeling, too.

My Olympic Moment

by Lian

For my fifteenth birthday, my mother promised me a trip to Lake Placid to see my heroes, Tai Babilonia and Randy Gardner, end the Russian domination of pair figure skating and capture Olympic gold. It was the perfect present for someone like me. I thought of myself as just a few missed school figures away from Dorothy Hamill's gold medal. If I couldn't have her medal, then I could have her hair. My Olympic chances may have been over, but my Olympic dream lived, and its name was Tai and Randy.

Just a few small problems with the plan. There was no plan. My birthday had somehow slipped under the "Good Planning Makes Good Fun" radar. With the opening ceremonies just days away, I had no tickets, no hotel, and no one to take me—nothing but a dream. Then, the Games opened, a huge snowstorm closed the New York State Thruway, and the town of Lake Placid reported that the transportation system was a disaster. Only ticket holders would be allowed into the town, and all tickets were sold out for the pair-skating finals. Things looked bleak until Liz stepped up and offered to drive. Sheila and Monica, eager for any road trip that might get them out of doing the dishes, offered to ride shotgun. We had momentum, even if we had no plan. No tickets, no hotel, and no thruway, but we were going to the Olympics.

It's easy to talk yourself out of spontaneity. There are always a million reasons not to go somewhere or do something. Time, traffic, tickets—all valid excuses. Work, money, or just plain old "too much trouble"—those rate, too, when a half-baked plan looks barely baked. And, believe me, there have been times when I wished I had listened to those inner wet blankets warning me, "Don't to go to Vegas without hotel reservations during the computer industry convention!" or, "Kids don't appreciate Kabuki!" But I didn't listen and the spontaneity backfired.

Sheila claims that most sporting events are more dramatic on TV. A warm fire, a bowl of artichoke dip, and a nineteen-inch TV—does that qualify as an Olympic dream? I don't think so. And, while no one enjoys Olympic coverage more than I do (I lap up every "Up Close and Personal"), nothing is more thrilling than being there, and nothing is more fun than getting there.

While my mother is a great advocate of planning, she is also a great practitioner of improvisation. Things don't always go right when traveling with ten people, even if you're only going to the grocery store. In fact, some of the best-laid plans go awry. We learned from my mother to think creatively about alternate arrangements. What to do when the battery won't start, or you miss the train, or all the chocolate bunnies for the Easter-egg hunt melt in an unseasonable heat wave? Second to planning, improvisation makes good fun.

So we improvised my birthday trip. Instead of tickets to the figure-skating finals, we secured some cheap tickets to the women's downhill, which would at least buy us entry into Lake Placid. We could buy tickets to the finals from scalpers once we got there. We drove over hill and dale instead of on the thruway to make it to upstate New York. We spent the night in Saratoga Springs, a town nowhere near any Olympic venue whatsoever. And, while hordes of event-goers waited like lemmings at specially designated bus stops for buses that never came, we stood at a lone bus stop and lucked out with what seemed to be the only working bus in town. We were at the Olympics!

Of course, as any figure-skating fan knows, Tai and Randy never even got to compete for the gold medal that year. We heard the news when we got to town. Randy had pulled a groin muscle before the short program, so the pair had pulled out of the Games. At that moment I thought my Olympic dreams had come to an end, too. But then I did what any Olympian would do: I persevered. I played with pain. I did what I had to do. While Randy spent the night with an icepack on his privates and my sisters spent the evening in a Lake Placid bar with Sheila impersonating downhill winner Annemarie Moser-Proell, I bought a standing-room–only ticket from a scalper for forty dollars and watched the Russian pair win their third straight gold medal. It was one of the great thrills of my life.

Now I am the mother, the planner, the improviser. Whenever I am about to utter the words "bad traffic" or "we'll never get in," I stop and think about Lake Placid. No tickets, no hotel, no thruway. Just a girl and her Olympic dream. Get in the car, kids.

*F*or No Amount of Money Would We ...

There's risk-taking and then there's stupidity. It's important to draw your own personal line between the two.

For no amount of money would I:

JULIE

1. Live in New York City.
2. Change my hair color.
3. Get behind the wheel of a semi.
4. Engage in any subsurface activity, like mining or spelunking.
5. Jump out of a plane.

LIZ

1. Hang from a rope or a ledge.
2. Inject myself or someone else with anything.
3. Pierce my tongue.
4. Work at an airport security checkpoint.
5. Expose my navel.

SHEILA

1. Live in a foreign country.
2. Be involved in a high-speed chase.
3. Go ice fishing.
4. Walk on stilts or ride a unicycle.
5. Artificially implant anything in my body.

MONICA

1. Work the night shift again.
2. Go on a blind date.
3. Scuba dive, high dive, or cliff dive.
4. Wear a bustier in public.
5. Engage in any activity where I could not easily blow my nose.

LIAN

1. Perform surgery.
2. Eat a sea slug.
3. Teach preschool.
4. Sail anywhere single-handedly.
5. Paint the Golden Gate Bridge.

Car Sick

by Sheila

As the only sister who got car, bus, and boat sick, I was adventure-challenged as a youngster. It was hard to fake a gung-ho spirit when it meant getting into or on one of these means of transportation. My standard emergency kit included a plastic bag, gum, Dramamine, and ginger ale. Despite the humiliation of being the only child to say, "Can we pull over please?" I survived all the excursions we had as kids, and there were even a few that I enjoyed.

I loved the trips that promised dining on the other end, like the time we drove to Little Italy for dinner and sat at a table where a man "had been shot." A little more upscale—and not as dangerous—was the old Brasserie restaurant in midtown, where my father would stun the maître d' by saying, "Table for ten, please." We also drove all the way to Coney Island just to sample birch beer, which my brothers insisted was real beer, pretending to be tipsy after a few sips. Also enjoyable were the shorter trips, like going to New Haven to visit my father's childhood home, after which we would eat at the world famous Pepe's Pizza Parlor. These adventures represented my father's love of a great, out-of-the-way meal and his remarkable confidence in our social skills.

Our main means of daily transportation was our mother's Buick station wagon. The everyday short trips to swim team practice or church were no problem. When I got to sit in the front seat and could stare "straight at the road," like my mother said, I wouldn't get sick. The longer trips, though, to visit our Morningstar cousins in Rye, were riskier. We visited the Morningstars throughout the year, for Thanksgiving, Christmas, summer vacations, and birthdays.

The hardest trip for me, though, was the annual Halloween jaunt. Halloween was an all-out, one night up and back adventure hell. I could handle the overnight trips because I knew I could just crash in my cousin Beth's room with some ginger ale and potato chips; I had to build in recovery time for these car trips. But the one on Halloween was long and loud. Jim and Dick would be arguing about their strategy for that year, which concerned how to hit every house in a twenty-mile radius in lower Westchester. The girls would get excited as Dick and Jim would shout directions on how to hold our pillowcases so that we could get the most candy and what to do if the house had a "one per person" policy. I'd stumble out of the car, dizzy from the anticipation and sick from the fumes coming from the "way back" where I sat with Monica. I'd be all dressed up in my Egyptian princess costume, my face completely white under the blue-sequined mask. I insisted on looking glamorous, though, even in the dark, and so in my below-the-knee costume and black patent-leather shoes, I struggled to keep up with the wild hours-long scavenger hunts. I didn't even care that much about the candy; I knew I could always steal some of Monica's if I changed my mind.

The bus trips we took to Otis Ridge Ski Camp in Massachusetts during winter vacations were even worse. I probably could have been arrested for the illegal amounts of Dramamine I ingested, and I would still throw up in the back of the bus. The older boys and girls would go to Otis for an intensive long week-end after we learned the basics on Powder Ridge in Connecticut. At Otis we would sleep in separate barracks, ski all day, and only see each other at night during dinner, which was always Dinty Moore stew. At the end of these long days on the slopes, I'd drift off to sleep, wondering how I was going to score some more Dramamine for the ride home.

I'm lucky we weren't a sailing family, because boats are my least favorite means of transport. Our uncle, however, had a boat and would invite us out for fishing trips once a year. It would always be the hottest day of the summer; we would be slathered with sunscreen, strapped into orange life jackets, and squeezed into the semicircular bench in the back of the boat. The boys got to sit up front with Uncle Tom, to try out the steering wheel and pretend they were driving the boat. There's nothing like the wind in your face, the pounding force of the waves, and the overwhelming fumes of gas and dead sea life to make you wish you were back at home under the covers. Moving made it even worse, so I stayed stuck on the seat cushion, my eyes closed, trying to figure out how my hero Harriet the Spy would handle this situation.

(At the risk of sounding like a whiner, it should be noted that I never refused to go on any major adventures with my family, except for OpSail in New York. Again, boats. I don't know how I got out of OpSail. To this day, I'm not sure if my family even realizes I wasn't there.)

By the time I got to college, I had experienced a wide variety of people, places, and things in spite of my delicate stomach and thanks to our parents. I even decided to embark on an adventure of my own that involved taking a plane. I took some "time off" from college in 1982, and cooked up a scheme to go to Ireland with my friend Ellen McCurley. I had saved up some money I'd earned working in a bookstore in Westport for six months. Luckily, Ellen had some relatives and friends in Ireland whom we planned to stay with along the way. My parents helped me buy the plane ticket, and I'm sure said some extra prayers at night, as we counted down to my departure.

I knew this was going to be a tough trip for me, considering my handicap, but away I went with my first backpack, a pair of leather pants, and a punk-rock haircut. What I didn't anticipate was how hard it was to look good in wet Irish weather, when your clothes got wet *inside* your backpack. Plus, you hadn't slept all night because the youth hostel had no heat and you lost your favorite hair products back in Tipperary. We did manage to see the Pope in Limerick, where I committed a sin by wearing the leather pants. Ellen and I kissed the Blarney Stone and climbed the amazing Cliffs of Moher. After that it was all downhill. I spiraled into a traveler's nightmare, which was really just a bad case of homesickness. If I were with my family, they would have this thing all planned out and organized. We would be having fun. Alone, I had very little motivation (and money) to keep going. I tried to keep in mind what our father taught us, and so I spent lots of time eating crumpets in obscure tea shops, where I could mingle with the natives and rest for a while, but all I really wanted to do was come home. In the end, Ellen and I stuck it out for three months. When I finally returned home, my hair had grown, the pants didn't fit, and all I wanted to do was wash my clothes in peace.

Unfortunately, I have passed down my travel disability to my daughter, Ruth. She took an ambitious trip to Europe last summer with her four best friends. I remember feeling a pang of recognition during a phone call I got from Tuscany. "How is it?" I asked her. "What have you seen?"

"Well, we're eating a lot of cheese, Mom," she said.

"Cheese?"

"Yes. I'm doing my laundry, finally, and eating cheese."

I understood completely and asked her what kind.

The Zen of Business Travel

by Liz

Early in my career, the phrase "business trip" had an exotic ring to it. The very thought that someone else was paying for me to fly somewhere, stay in a hotel, and dine out was part of the thrill. I lived in a New York City apartment that was tinier than most of the Marriott or Ramada rooms in which I found myself, and my main meal at home was a tuna fish sandwich.

More important, business travel usually involved going somewhere I had never gone before and doing something I had never done before. A business trip was an adventure.

After a decade or so, this all began to change. My blood ran cold when sentences began, "Liz, can you attend a meeting in . . ." The phrase "business trip" now summoned images of lying on the floor at O'Hare waiting for "late inbound equipment," wandering around Denver in a rental car at midnight trying to find my hotel, or realizing that I may be in Orlando, but none of my clothes or business materials were.

So, over twenty years I have developed my own Zen of Travel guidelines that are designed to preserve my mental health. I share them with my Satellite Sisters so that we may all find the Way of the Road Warrior to be more peaceful.

Never think about what time it is where you came from. This is the surest route to mental exhaustion. Do not constantly remind yourself, as you are making your way to an 8 A.M. breakfast meeting, that it is really 5 A.M. for you. This is not healthy thinking.

Never think about what time your flight is scheduled to arrive. Flight schedules are irrelevant. When I arrive at an airport, I put myself into a Zen state wherein the journey has its own life that I can neither predict nor change. If I constantly remind myself of what time I was *supposed* to get somewhere, I will go mad. My Zen of Travel maxim goes like this: When I get there, I am there, and not a moment before. This concept may be difficult at first, but it will save you from possible incarceration when you are tempted to slug the reservations agent who tells you your delayed flight has been rescheduled . . . for tomorrow.

Never wear clothes on the plane that you could not reasonably wear to your business meeting. This is true even on night flights when pajamalike garments are *so* tempting. Bags go awry. We all know this, but I can tell you from experience that the more important the contents of your luggage, the more likely it is to get lost. I am not sure how the airlines pull this off, but miraculously they do. A corollary to this is never, ever pack the presentation you are to deliver at your destination. A final warning related to lost luggage: Never pack your house keys or car keys. Nothing is worse than getting home but not being able to actually go home. I once came home from a three-week trip and had to sleep on my neighbor's couch. No one should have to see me *that* cranky.

Never compare the hours of sleep you are not getting with what you normally get. Forget about sleep altogether. Between flights at dawn, late-night convention socializing in the hotel bar, jet lag that wakes you in the middle of the night, early morning meetings you would never schedule if you were home, and the banging noise coming from the room next door, you can abandon all hope of real slumber. Nap when you can. Sleeping through the airline meal is particularly useful because it accomplishes two goals: catching some shut-eye and sparing yourself the dreadful chickenlike substance masquerading as dinner.

Never think you have hit rock bottom. If you travel for business, you have a long life of late planes, missed meetings, broken-down A-V equipment, botched presentations, and bad nights' sleep ahead of you. Telling yourself that it could never be worse than it is right at this moment in the snowy airport parking lot in the middle of the night just invites further disappointment. Manage your own expectations—the lower, the better.

Never cut it too close. It is a proven scientific fact that most heart attacks that occur on business trips are not the result of the apocryphal Too Much Fun. They happen to individuals who believe their plane will land on time, their luggage and rental car will be readily available, the traffic won't be too bad, and they will be able to find their meeting site according to the driving instructions the organizers have provided. Simply too many variables. Don't count on any of it. I beg you.

Gravy Boat

by Julie

When we decided to move to Thailand for my husband's job, it was up to me to pack up the house. I had to sort all of our household items into six categories: (1) permanent storage, or as it is known in the expat/overseas assignment world, "perm storage." Our company relocation sponsor kept referring to my perm storage. At first, I didn't know what he was saying. I thought he was saying "berm" which really had me confused. I kept imagining a tunnel storage system. The second category (2) is air shipment. I was allowed to air freight a certain cubic measurement of our belongings to our apartment in Bangkok. This shipment would arrive within two to three weeks of our departure. The third category (3) is the bulk of our household contents, which are packed in a container and come to Thailand by boat. The container shipment can take up to three months to arrive. The fourth category (4) is the items I was going to bring over in my suitcases. The fifth category (5) is the household items I intended to sell or donate, and the sixth category (6) is a domestic shipment that could be sent to a relative or friend within the United States. The thought behind the sixth category is that you might want access to certain items when you were back in the United States on home leave.

I had to work through each room in my house with form 470-1 Household Contents Inventory Worksheet and write down the name of each and every household item ("one glass bottle of beach sand with cork top") and then assign it to one of the six categories above and also estimate what the replacement value of one glass bottle of beach sand from our honeymoon in Bermuda twenty-one years ago would be—a simple process. Of course, this process didn't include the three items that would not be appearing on the Household Contents Inventory Worksheet. One eighteen-year-old firstborn son, whom I dropped at freshman orientation before getting on the plane to Bangkok, and two dogs. I am sure my husband would have listed Mardi as a "flat-haired golden retriever," which is how he always identified him when people asked what breed he was. The truth is he is a mutt from the Japonica Street SPCA in New Orleans who had made five moves with us so far, but was not going to make the cut this time and come to Thailand. Our other dog, Teller, is a not-too-bright black Lab. Teller goes wherever

Mardi goes. Both dogs were moving to my in-laws' in Colorado and therefore would not be appearing on the inventory worksheet. To say good-bye to my son and my two dogs was not too bad, but it was the gravy boat that got me.

I didn't get stuck on the description or the estimated replacement value, but on what to do with the gravy boat. This was a gravy boat my mother had given me and that I used only on Thanksgiving. Would I be celebrating Thanksgiving in Thailand? And if I were celebrating Thanksgiving, would I eat turkey in Bangkok? Would I need a gravy boat? Maybe I would be eating something else. If I were eating something else, would it require gravy? I could just put the gravy boat in perm storage and not worry about it, because maybe I wouldn't celebrate Thanksgiving at all. But I would feel pretty bad if, when I got to Thailand and found out that people do get together for Thanksgiving, I wouldn't have the gravy boat. What's the point of having a gravy boat if you can't use it on Thanksgiving? I could put the gravy boat in my container shipment, but then I'd run the risk that it might not arrive in time for Thanksgiving. The gravy boat wouldn't be of much use to me if it arrived after Thanksgiving. I also considered sending it in my air shipment because then I would know for sure that I had the gravy boat in time for Thanksgiving, but sending the gravy boat in the air shipment seemed like an overreaction because I only got a very limited amount of space. Should I waste any of my valuable cubic feet on a gravy boat for a holiday that I didn't even know I was going to celebrate? I considered sending it to my mother-in-law, who was receiving our domestic shipment; that way, when I got to Thailand and found out if people bothered to celebrate Thanksgiving, I could call her and she could ship the gravy boat to me. But how would she send it to me? Was I going to have to pay customs fees on my gravy boat? Are you allowed to import gravy boats?

The only two choices that I was able to eliminate were that I wasn't going to sell or give away the gravy boat, and I wasn't planning on bringing the gravy boat in my suitcase. Well, actually, it would have had to go in my carry-on bag because it was breakable. I thought maybe I could bring the gravy boat in my carry-on, but I still had the problem of not knowing if I was going to be celebrating Thanksgiving.

I thought about contacting my relocation sponsor because it was her job to assist me, the trailing spouse, with any questions about relocating to my husband's assignment. Would she know what I should do with the gravy boat? What did she know about Thanksgiving in Thailand? Maybe she'd think I was incompetent because I couldn't complete my Household Contents Inventory Worksheet form. Would she write something in my husband's employment file like "confused trailing spouse inquired about gravy boat"? It was too risky.

I wondered if I should call our favorite local Thai restaurant with the really spicy chicken wings. Would they know if Americans living in Bangkok celebrate Thanksgiving? Or would they think I was some crazed customer? I was not going to mention the problem to my husband when he called from Bangkok. If I started talking about the gravy boat, which I was sure he didn't even know we owned, it would be a clear signal to him that I had lost it. No, I had to figure out this gravy boat mess by myself.

I was paralyzed. I couldn't move on to the wood-and-brass salt and pepper shakers that we got as wedding gifts and have never used until I made up my mind. The gravy boat had to go somewhere. I had to make a decision and I had to write it down next to the gravy boat description and estimated value on my form 470-1 Household Contents Inventory Worksheet and I had to make five copies of all my inventory sheets and send one set to my moving coordinator, one set to my relocation sponsor, one set to my mother-in-law, and keep two sets for myself. So I wasn't going anywhere until I came to a decision about the gravy boat. The movers would have to pack the house around me because I would still be standing here with this gravy boat in my hand. I would miss the plane because I couldn't make up my mind about the pitcher. My husband and my younger son, who went ahead to Bangkok, would be waiting in the sweltering heat at the Don Muang International Airport, and I wouldn't be there because of this damn boat. My son would not be able to enroll in high school, he'd become a dropout, and he'd drift into a life of crime in Bangkok because I had the school forms he needed to register and I couldn't make the trip because I didn't know if they celebrated Thanksgiving in Thailand. My husband most likely would lose his job because his trailing spouse couldn't fill out the Household Inventory Worksheet form correctly. It all came down to the gravy boat.

I didn't ask for this. This is not what I agreed to. I agreed to move to Asia because it was a great opportunity for both my husband and my son. I did not agree to lose my mind over a sauce server.

In my married life, I have moved eleven times. I never thought of myself as the moving type. I did not have *Wanderlust*. I really thought that I would live in Connecticut forever. As the oldest daughter and the most traditional, I would have been very happy to live down the street from my parents and eat Sunday dinner at their house. In fact, when we were first married, I spent a lot of time trying to create a situation whereby my husband and I would move back to Connecticut. It didn't work out that way.

I know my family is closer, wiser, and more flexible as a result of all our moving. We've learned to depend on each other and to adapt to a wide range of living experiences. I never would have eaten an oyster po'boy or hiked in the Angeles National Forest or seen a monk collecting morning offerings if we had not moved.

We all have our gravy-boat moments. It is natural to have trep-idation about making changes in our lives and what the impact of those changes will be. It is easy to get stuck because you don't know what the future will be like. Sometimes things are not as dra-matic as a move halfway around the world, but the feelings are the same.

The gravy boat is here with me in Bangkok. In a desperate last-ditch move, I assigned the boat to the container ship. It arrived in plenty of time for Thanksgiving. It sits in a glass-and-teak wood cabinet over the bar in our living room. It doesn't really belong in the living room, but I put it there when I was unpacking and just left it. So far it has been filled twice with delicious hot gravy at two wonderful Thanksgiving celebrations with friends. I see it every day. I'm glad I brought it.

a sense of

direction

A Sense of Direction

by Sheila

Me? "A Sense of Direction"? The idea that of all the Dolan sisters I was the one chosen to introduce the chapter on finding direction in life initially struck me as absurd. I felt the least qualified. After all, I have led a very loosely organized existence for more than thirty years, guided only by a desire to be happy and a willingness to try new things. If I'm not happy with the path I've taken, I'll go a new way. People who move their lives forward in a straight line have always baffled me. How do they know where to go? I have made many detours in my life, always with my brothers and sisters supporting me and urging me along toward each new goal. In our large family, we were encouraged to strike out on our own and wander about with the safety net of knowing there was always a couch to crash on until we found our way again.

There have been times in my life when I felt that the road ahead was clear and I had a clue about where I was going. When I discovered swimming at age eight was one such time. Racing in the pool was an instant passion for me. All I needed to do was go up one lane and back. Strangely, this clear path that allowed for no deviation felt like freedom to me. There was only one direction—straight ahead—and the short distance made it the perfect trip. (I have to say that I was also pretty cute in my team suit and cap.)

By age nine or ten, decisions about school, friends, and life in general started piling up. Life was looking more like a wild water polo game. My simple routine in the pool didn't work for me anymore. During those years and throughout my adolescence, I would periodically sit down with our dad for a little chat. (I have always been a seeker of advice, if not always a taker.) Our father would say things like, "You've got the weight of the world on your shoulders, dear."

"Well, yes, I'm with you on that one, Dad," I'd say. "But should I go to the dance or not?"

Later, when I couldn't decide whether or not to go to college, I sat down with my dad once again for a talk. "Don't lead your life, follow it," he told me. Now that was a concept. I was in a state of teenage angst over school, boyfriends, and miserable SAT scores. I had begun thinking that a nunnery might hold me for a few years until I got my bearings. That fall, I did go to college with my class, the class of '76, but I graduated with the class of '90, summa cum laude, while holding the hand of my beautiful eight-year-old daughter, Ruth. As you might imagine, there were lots of couches and Satellite Sister conversations in between.

My earliest memory of feeling like I was in the wrong place was when I joined the Girl Scouts. Scouting had but one main purpose and that was to earn as many badges as you could in the shortest period of time. As we stood in the auditorium each week, pretending to be one big happy troop, I knew that the sewing badge loomed large in every girl's head. The Dolans were not sewers because our mother was not a sewer. The only sewing notions we owned were crammed into an old cookie tin in the kitchen. It also held the sole pair of scissors in the family and hundreds of missing buttons from our clothes. I had to give up on the idea of earning the sewing badge, but there was one that seemed within my reach: the cooking badge. Our mom was a great cook! I decided that we would have the troop over to our house—my turf. My mother could organize everything. This I could handle. And so, with my troop sitting around the kitchen table, we cooked hamburgers, french fries, and salad. Or, I should say, my mother prepared hamburgers, frozen french fries, and iceberg lettuce. This was a classic meal of the late 60s, complete with extra ketchup and a big glass of chocolate milk. The meal was a hit, the troop was happy, and I was on my way toward my first badge. After the girls left, reflecting back on our special meal, I knew life didn't get any better than this. My contentment was cut short, though, at our next meeting—a badge ceremony in the school gym, to which parents were invited. I stood there humbly, looking fondly over at our mother, picturing those Ore-Ida shoestrings. I earned the badge, but I knew full well that the cooking badge was pretty much the end of the line for me. The girls on either side of me had gorgeous green sashes laden with awards, including the much-coveted sewing badge. I spiraled into a kind of panic state that I would later identify as the period right before I decide to change direction.

My compass indicator was no longer pointing in any one direction, but spinning uncontrollably around the dial. I had to quit Girl Scouts. I could not go on living that lie. With our mother's blessing, I was allowed to stop, but only if I took up the flute—not an entirely successful alternate plan. I entered the panic state again during the tryout competition to play a solo at the school assembly. Suffice to say my music career was cut short by a growing overbite and too many missed rehearsals.

Over the years, I tried to follow the paths that my older sisters had paved before me. They were politically inclined, so I ran for class vice president in tenth grade. I won the election but started getting those sick feelings only days after taking office. To make matters worse, a casual comment made by a classmate in the restroom awakened me to the cruel reality of party politics. The only reason I got the job was because I was "a Dolan," the girl in the stall next to mine bitterly remarked to her friend. Now, I had to admit that 1974 was a banner year for us girls. Julie was president of the school and Liz was president of her class. Whether or not you get the job because you are a Dolan doesn't mean, necessarily, that you want to keep the job. It doesn't mean that you're going to be happy.

I preferred to see it this way—your chances of finding direction are better if you stick with the winners, so to speak. The more kids in your family, the more chances you have to find a solid role model. My older sisters were obvious winners. They had a purpose and a sense of direction in life. They both had the leadership-skill thing down, and that was something I wanted. Only my platform was a movement to defy school policy by wearing black socks instead of blue. I felt I could reach more people and spread the love of black even further in an elected office. I realized that, while it was important to have good role models, I had to listen to my heart as well—and my fashion sense. If you are a black-sock agitator, you'll never be happy in a blue-sock world. I was vice president, but I needed a change—a change of wardrobe. Tenth grade ended up being my last year at that particular school. Maybe it was that pesky girl who dissed our family, but I honestly think it had more to do with bell-bottoms and discovering boys.

My last two years of high school consisted of finding distractions rather than finding my own way. To begin with, I could wear anything I wanted at my new school. No more uniforms. That brought a tremendous opportunity to obsess on something new every day. If my entire reality meant finding a cool outfit every morning, then I would have a sense of direction on a daily basis. Sometimes you just need to look down at what you have on to find a new purpose. What was I going to wear? Black socks gave way to black tights, Indian wrap skirts, and red clogs. To top if off, I'd steal a shirt from one of my sisters and then pull the outfit together with my old school uniform jacket, sans patch. I remember facing a life-and-death struggle every morning to assemble the perfect outfit. Raiding my sisters' closets, either at night or at 7:30 A.M., was a way for me to stay focused on my new vocation—clotheshorse. This led to some classic fights, including the time I threw a clog at Monica's head, only to hear it thwap the door, which she slammed seconds before it could have hit her in the eye. After that episode, it was strongly suggested by Mom that I "lay out my clothes the night before."

Boys were my other distraction. My first victim was the older brother of a friend. I had heard that he actually lived on his own in Boston where he was a "rock star." Boston was to Fairfield what New York was to—well, you make the analogy because that in fact was my worst section on the SATs. This guy seemed very mature (I was too scared to ask how old he really was) and very laid back—so laid back that he fell asleep on most of our dates. Mostly, I would sit in his garage on a lawn chair, watching his band rehearse and fretting about how late the time was getting. We had a strict dinner curfew. He would take a nap; I would fix sodas and chips for the band and then run home just in time for dinner. No one in my family told me to ditch the sleepy bass player because I'm not sure they actually knew I was seeing him. The directions in this case were simple—from our kitchen to his garage and back again. I remained a groupie of his band until it was time to go to college.

I floundered for two more years, in and out of college, until I came upon a huge fork in the road and my future husband, sitting in a coffee shop in Greenwich Village. By that time, I had moved to New York City to take up acting, and even though I was working nine to five and had never been on an audition and didn't plan on auditioning anywhere, I still thought of myself as an actress. Sometimes your sense of direction is pure fantasy. At age twenty-four, I decided to get married. I say decided because it seemed like the first time in my life that I was applying myself. I thought, *I can do this,* and the belief that I could actually succeed at something set my compass in a new direction. If you can envision yourself playing that role, so to speak, then you may have found your way. Lucky for me, I had a great role model—our mother.

When our daughter, Ruth, was born, my purpose in life became tangible. I had but one job and that was to assist her in discovering life itself, moment by moment, day after day. I wanted to do everything right, so I read books, took classes, joined mothers' groups, taught her to swim, and cleaned all day long. Cleaning was a great way for me to fill in the blanks in my plan. In a fourth-floor walk-up in New York City, cleaning can be a twenty-four-hour-a-day proposition. I cleaned for a good four years until that old familiar itch started up again in my soul. A change was upon me, and this time, it was going to be a major, life-altering U-turn. With my family's encouragement, I enrolled at Hunter College as a twenty-eight-year-old undergraduate. I was going to go after that BA after all.

As soon as I entered college, I discovered that the idea of *more* could, in itself, provide direction. I pursued a teaching career, sat on neighborhood organizations, got straight As, and cleaned. More friends, more responsibilities, more, more, more. Warning signs started popping up everywhere, but I didn't want to slow down to read them. In pursuit of more degrees, better jobs, and more recognition, I gave up housework, cooking, reading with my child, being nice—anything and everything I once cared about. I discarded all of the good stuff I had learned from my mother and my siblings about putting family first.

There are times in life when you simply lose your way. Other times, you abandon the map altogether and plow through the wilderness, armed with the only tool you are familiar with: your will. For six years of my life (though it felt much longer) I was out there all on my own. The momentum of the ride at that point was all that was carrying me. I could have rested on someone's couch if I really wanted to, but no one in my family had any idea that I needed it. I wasn't talking to anyone about anything real; I just wanted to keep going. Then, after a six-year nosedive, that built-in compass of mine finally kicked in. There had to be something better than this. I made a move that wasn't in my plan, but turned out to be part of a greater plan. After fourteen years of marriage, I separated from my husband and crash-landed on a futon uptown in an apartment of my own on 97th Street. I found the apartment through a free paper I picked up at a candy store. It was the first and only ad I responded to because it was the only place I could afford. The listing read, "large one-bedroom with fireplace," and the rent was cheap. At that point, I just wanted space to breathe and move around in, someplace I could call my own. I hardly noticed the neighborhood when I went to look at the place and meet the landlord. The lobby looked a little dark, but you really wouldn't want to see the dingy unwashed floors anyway. It didn't matter that the fireplace was sealed or that some of the windows were shattered. Everything in my life was either shutting down or blowing apart, so when I sat in my new place on that first day, I felt right at home. My daughter, Ruth, and I stayed very close throughout this time, despite the seismic changes taking place. You see, I had broken away from the warm security of Greenwich Village to a cold, unsafe neighborhood uptown. My apartment was empty, except for a chair, the futon, and a television. I never slept in the "bed-room" because I was too scared someone might climb through the windows in the living room.

There was nothing up there for a teenager to do, so Ruth and I spent a lot of time talking about how dreary the apartment was. I couldn't let her go outside on her own, either, because it was too dangerous. I lived across the street from housing projects, a notori-ous park, and the even scarier Metropolitan Hospital, which loomed like a monolith outside my window. I would run to the corner to get a quart of milk and run back. Ruth resented not hav-ing her independence, and I felt guilty for taking that away from her. I promised us that I would fix the place up and that things would get better. It was hard for me to believe in anything at that time, but I kept talking, trying to convince us that by making the place beautiful, we could be happy.

I remember one night in particular when we sat and cried, fully clothed, in the bathtub for hours and then got up and went out for ice cream. Even if you don't know exactly where you're going, you can always take a break for something sweet. The two of us found comfort in small things, and so we took a lot of breaks during that time.

Day by day, we stopped thinking about our dismal surroundings and began to look inward. We started seeing ourselves as mother and daughter, not just two-thirds of the family unit we once were. I started speaking up, asking for what I needed, and Ruth found her voice as well. We started having real conversations that mattered. After two short years, I moved back downtown where I belonged. I never did fix up that place on 97th Street because it wasn't worth fixing. My relationships were, though, so that is where I put all my energy. The payoff far exceeds any decorating tip I could have fol-lowed.

This story ends happily for now right here, even though there really isn't an ending. Coming through that time didn't point the way toward some ultimate destination, but instead it offered me another chance to get back on the road, a new road. A psychic change allowed me to stop running and to begin looking at life in a whole new way. My family showed up for me in the countless ways that a big family does in a time of crisis. They helped pay my bills, took my daughter for the summer while I moved into a new apartment, gave me legal advice, sent me to a spa, and started calling regularly. Like the victim of an accident, I just needed to sit and rest. The long road of recuperation stretched before me, and I am still walking that road today, gratefully.

I have no original wisdom to impart about finding direction in one's life except for this: At the most confusing and scary time in my adult life, I finally understood what my father had shared with me some thirty years before on the living room couch, "Don't lead your life. Just follow it." I got it now, Dad. Thanks. The only map I look at now is the tattered directions I keep on my refrigerator that show me how to get from New York to Ruth's college, which I visit quite often. No longer do I need or want to take up the reins of my life. I am very happy being a passenger for now. Every morning when I wake up, I look out the window and see another day of uncharted waters. It's a good thing I know how to stay in the middle of the boat.

Curricula Vitae

Julie Dolan Smith

OBJECTIVE   Be everything to everybody and retain sanity while doing so.

EXPERIENCE   1999—present   Bangkok, Thailand
Trailing Spouse
• Pack up house, say good-bye to friends and family, ship dogs to in-laws, drop oldest child at college, and move with husband and teenager to foreign country.

• Overcommit to volunteer work, struggle through Thai language classes, and take up yoga.

• Maintain double life as Satellite Sister. Talk to siblings at odd hours.

1986–99   Various Locations: New Orleans, Los Angeles, Washington, D.C., and San Francisco
Admissions Director/Career Counselor
• Started back at work at Tulane as career counselor. Made perfect sense as I had no career of my own. Began twelve-year period of juggling work, children, and child-care.

• Moved, moved, moved. Unfortunately, for my husband's work, not mine. Moves often resulted in having to commute to different states for work. Held various positions at Graduate Management Admissions Council, Tulane, and UCLA. Briefly at Stanford.

• Achieved dubious distinction of the highest status on my airline frequent-flyer program. This is code for not spending enough time at home. Talked to sister Liz about doing something different with our lives. Radio show, perhaps?

1982–86   State College, PA/New Orleans
Stay-at-home mother
• Very little recollection of this period. Constant stream of birthday parties, mommies' coffees, school bake sales, and juice pouring.

1977   United States Steel Company   Pennsylvania
Management Trainee
• Third woman ever hired as trainee. Gender barrier–breaking experience as first female lifeguard in high school clinched job.

• First assignment in steel mill. Remember *Flashdance*? Well, not quite.

EDUCATION   1977   Smith College   Northampton, MA
A.B., Government

1981 Pennsylvania State University State College, PA
MBA

INTERESTS   •Maintaining surveillance on college-age sons

• Beginner bunco

LIZ DOLAN

OBJECTIVE   I'll get back to you.

EXPERIENCE   2000–present   New York, NY, and Portland, OR
Satellite Sisters on Public Radio International (PRI)
• Cohost, with equally opinionated sisters, of public radio show created with WNYC Radio in New York City. Main responsibility is to talk with sisters and guests about what's important in real life. Additional responsibilities include trying to find underwriters for the show and figuring out who is bringing the coffee to the sessions.

• In addition to Satellite Sisters, manage a marketing consulting practice for clients who don't mind the fact that I occasionally complain about them on the air.

1997–99   New York, NY, and Portland, OR
Marketing Consultant
• Contributed to the marketing effort for Women's World Cup Soccer Tournament, a dream project.

• First experience of life outside of the corporate world. Found that I spent much more time on my couch watching *Oprah* and C-SPAN 2 than I ever would have guessed. Loved it.

• Started to actually look like my couch due to new relaxed lifestyle. Even "relaxed fit" jeans stopped fitting.

1988–97   Portland, OR
Vice President, Global Marketing, NIKE, Inc.
• OK, I may be loafing in the current millennium, but I
worked really hard in the last. Ran Nike marketing and
communications. Learned a great deal about sports and
feet. Was inspired/intimidated enough to take up running and complete two marathons.

• Depended on network of brothers, sisters, and Satellite
Sisters to create illusion that I had a life in addition to
having a job.

1980–88
Just Out of College, Living It Up in New York, NY
• Held several fun jobs in advertising and public relations,
but they were completely beside the point. Explored
New York. Subsisted on free hors d'oeuvres. Learned that
no professional woman actually wears jumpers.

EDUCATION   1979   Brown University   Providence, RI
B.A., Comparative Literature
• Changed major every semester. Sampled European
History, Classics, Semiotics, French. Managed to gradu-
ate without a single course in math or science—a source
of much regret to me now.

1965
Line Leader, Second Grade, Timothy Dwight School
• My academic peak came in Miss Sorchiotti's second-
grade class. My favorite teacher, ever. She read *The Secret
Garden* aloud.

Huh? Oh, you mean what do I do when I am not working? Let me think. Does napping count? I could always
use a little extra shut-eye.

I am also a member of the Board of Trustees of the
Kips Bay Boys & Girls Club, Bronx, NY. I have been
affiliated with this organization both nationally and local-
ly for more than a decade and can't pass up an opportunity to get a plug in for their work.

And I try to stay informed about what's going on in
the world by keeping up with *The Daily Show* on
Comedy Central.

SHEILA DOLAN

OBJECTIVE   Spend more time alone.

EXPERIENCE   2000–present   New York City
Arts and Entertainment Satellite Sister
• Hook up with my Satellite Sisters. Move back to
Greenwich Village, my favorite place on earth. Winnow
down credit card debt. Go back to my maiden name.
Find a new love and less stress.

1994–99   Bridges School   New York City
Director/Founder
• Started and ran my own New York City public school
for grades three though five. Great experience.

• Ended fourteen-year marriage. Not that great an experience. Moved to a bad apartment. Accumulated, but did
not pay, much credit card debt. Suffered though several
rebound romances.

1990–94   Various schools   South Bronx/Chelsea
Classroom teacher
• Taught every grade and combination of grades from
kindergarten through sixth. Believe that everyone can
learn, just not on the same day.

EDUCATION   1969–99   This gets complicated   Many schools
• Graduated from Tomlinson Junior High with one true
friend and a bad haircut.

• Attended several very fine high schools. Graduated
from Roger Ludlowe High School in white Mexican

wedding dress that would be passed down to several sisters and various cousins.

• Attended many very fine colleges with long periods of off-time in between. First attempt, 1977. Second attempt, 1979. Third attempt, 1989, with new attitude and juggling classes and childcare. Graduated from Hunter College, summa cum laude, in 1990.

• Back at school, incurring debt and masters degree in 1996. More debt and second masters in administration in 1999 from Baruch College.

• More college in 2000, but this time for daughter, Ruth.

INTERESTS Daughter, Ruthie, born in 1982 on a full eclipse of the moon.

FAVORITE
BEATLE Paul

MONICA DOLAN

OBJECTIVE   Less stress, more vacations.

EXPERIENCE   1994–present Pacemaker Company Portland, OR
Full-time Clinical Specialist, Part-time Satellite Sister
• Initiate, manage, and monitor clinical device trials for pacemakers. Not as boring as that sounds. Lots of travel and patient interaction.

• Get to be a nurse without the white shoes and with expense account.

• Started job with no computer or typing skills.

• Cohost of radio show between medical emergencies.

1981–94   Various Hospitals   All Over the Country
Nurse
• Worked in trenches for nine years. Evenings, nights, weekends, holidays. Last job in hospital: cushy cardiac cath lab. We got to eat lunch.

• Never sat down on the job for fourteen years.

• Worked as traveling nurse for four years. Southern California, Northern California, New Orleans, Portland. Moved every nine months, inadvertently dodging bills and IRS notices, creating spotty credit history. Everything I owned fit inside a VW Rabbit. Looked for permanent gig after crazed man with gun to my head robbed me at ATM.

EDUCATION   1981   Georgetown University   Washington, D.C.
B.S., Nursing
• Attended during the Patrick Ewing era.

• Still best friends with freshman-year roommate.

INTERESTS   Trying to keep up with upkeep on my own house while accumulating record frequent-flyer miles. Contemplating gardening, but rarely actually gardening. Bark maintenance on dog.

PETS   Yellow Lab, Quin.

LIAN DOLAN

Maintain sharp verbal skills while simultaneously cooking dinner, assisting with homework, and scheduling dental appointments.

1995–present   Pasadena, California
Faux Stay-at-Home Mom
• Full-time mother/part-time radio host and writer. Gave up great job, decent wardrobe, and any and all outside interests to stay at home with two sons. Remind my husband of this weekly.

• Continue freelance writing career at naptimes. My children rarely nap and freelance writing suffers. Complete two spec screenplays and several thank-you notes in five years.

• Develop Satellite Sisters radio show as a way to get out of the house a couple afternoons a week and talk to adults. Sometimes I even get to sit down for lunch.

1988–1995   Portland, OR/Los Angeles
Writer/Producer
• Had great job traveling all over the world producing film and live events for various sporting-goods manufacturers. Saw many famous athletes in sports briefs. Gave this all up to move to Los Angeles and get married. (Remind my husband of this weekly.)

1987–88   New York City/Jackson Hole, WY
Floundering College Grad
• Accumulated an amazing number of job titles in two-

year period, including urban archaeologist, advertising assistant, cocktail waitress, ski host, and folk art salesperson. Always paid my own rent (except for short stint on Liz's couch).

• For two years in a row, skied more than one hundred days a year. Haven't skied once in the last six years. (Remind my husband of this weekly.)

| EDUCATION | 1987 | Pomona College | Claremont, CA |

B.A., Classics
• One of only two Classics majors in my year. The other candidate won all four Classics prizes. I took home college equivalent of Miss Congeniality.

INTERESTS   Gardening, grocery shopping, and my family. (Remind my husband of this weekly.)

Guinea Pig

by Lian

As the youngest of eight children, I thought of my older siblings not as role models so much as guinea pigs. Imagine the luxury of having seven trial runs at life before you got your turn. Seven guinea pigs in earth shoes or Mexican-print wrap skirts slogging through adolescence, college, grad school, work, marriage, and parenthood, all just a few steps ahead of you. Somebody almost like you, but not quite, making mistakes, finding success, falling in love. There was almost nothing in which my brothers and sisters engaged that I didn't absorb. I took it all in—the good, the bad, and the E Street Band—then made my own choices. From the ashes of their confusion, I forged my own sense of direction.

At most of the major turning points in my life, a feeling of déjà vu would wash over me, and for good reason—I had been there, done that seven times before. Well, I hadn't exactly been there or done that, but somebody a lot like me had, and I had been in the car, or heard the stories, or helped them make the move. Applying to college, finding a job, deciding to get married, having children. Done, done, done, done by my sisters and brothers. Sometimes it was a good experience; sometimes it was a bad experience. But it had all been done before me, and that was key. There were times when I felt like I got to live parts of my life over because I had experienced so much vicariously. Imagine that. Actually taking what you've learned and getting a do-over. Well, I felt that way. And as a result, I made untraditional choices.

My siblings might think that I took these radical turns just to be different, but actually it was because I didn't want to be the same.

There's a difference. I admired my siblings, but I didn't need to re-create their lives. I wanted to be like them, but not quite. And having had the luxury of watching and participating in their lives, I felt like my brothers and sisters had given me the freedom to make even bolder choices. In truth, they softened up my parents a bit, so I could take the risk that hadn't quite been taken.

It really wouldn't be until I was eighteen that I made any life-altering choices that called upon a sense of direction. Until then, I just watched and waited and developed the twin defining traits of my adolescent self—personal style and musical taste. Again, a nod to my siblings for their forerunning in these arenas. Because, let's face it, before you know where you are headed or what you're going to do, you have to know what to wear and what to put in the tape deck.

In the fashion arena, Sheila was a risk taker who inspired me to embrace capes and jumpsuits at a time when the preppy look was actually in style. (Sheila also kindly offered to rent me some of her clothes once when she was trying to raise some cash for a trip to Europe. For seven bucks, I could wear her cape for three weeks. I passed, knowing I could wear it for free once she left.) Liz understood my need to be on the cutting edge of my suburban-high-school existence and supplied me with cool T-shirts from London and my very first Norma Kamali sweatshirt—a black-and-white striped cowl neck that worked as a dress (with hot-pink tights) or tunic, when it eventually shrank under my mother's maniacal hot-cycle drying system. From Monica, I inherited a lifelong love of clogs.

And Julie? Well, she was always a little conservative for me, favoring Fair Isle sweaters over the *Flashdance* look. But she did come home from her junior year abroad wearing the first Laura Ashley sundress I had ever seen and ankle-wrap espadrilles. To me, she looked fabulously French. It may have been Julie's greatest fashion moment. From these far-flung fashion influences and the habit of borrowing from each other's closets, I developed my own fashion identity.

My brothers became my musical mentors, not because their taste was more refined than my sisters', but because their stereo was louder and I lived in the room next door. Thanks to my older brothers, I embraced broader musical sensibilities than most of my peers from small families who thought that musical greatness started with Billy Joel's *The Stranger*. I knew better. First of all, we had the ultimate listening venue—my brothers' bedroom with a sun porch off the back of the house—our own musical oasis, complete with a red, white, and blue shag carpet. And, secondly, the thirteen-year age difference between me and my brother Jimmy meant that we had a record collection that ranged from Sly & The Family Stone to Steely Dan to Elvis Costello by the time I was thirteen.

My brother Brendan brought home *London Calling* by The Clash in 1979 and changed my world. From then on, I had the go-ahead to reject all the Top 40 had to offer. On my own I discovered alternative college radio and the joys of early REM, U2, the Ramones, and Talking Heads.

Of course, from my sisters I gained an appreciation for the perfect girl-drinking-tea-and-burning-incense music—Joni Mitchell and Rickie Lee Jones. Donna Summer and Earth, Wind, & Fire were dance-party favorites, and the Isley Brothers made washing the dishes go faster. Liz took me to see my first concert, Rufus and Chaka Khan, in the infield of the Belmont Park racetrack. Looking back, that's the sort of thing I can't believe my parents let us do, but they did.

Of all the musical muses in our house, though, it was really the Boss who ruled. Bruce Springsteen brought the boys and girls together musically despite our differences in every other area of life. At times, the Boss was our family glue, the only thing we had in common besides our parents. I can remember the reverent silence in the car when WNEW, the major rock station in New York, would devote the whole weekend to Bruce, A to Z. I always knew that one of my brothers was in transition when I heard "Thunder Road" being played over and over and over again. And the Christmas *The River* came out, five copies changed hands at gift-giving time.

The music of my own coming-of-age period was the 80s, but I had a solid 60s and 70s foundation behind me. I was ready to test myself. I was eighteen. I had clogs. I had Bruce. I was born to run.

So I ran to California for college, whereas my sisters and brothers had not ventured west of I-95. After seven college tours, a bunch of freshman orientations, multiple parents' weekends and alumni events, and many graduations, I felt like I had seen every school in New England. By the time I was set to apply, I knew which schools would be too preppy, which would be too groovy, and which I didn't dare apply to because my brothers or sisters had been previously rejected. I eliminated the whole state of Massachusetts from my list simply because I had already spent too much time on the Mass Pike. When I looked at my list, that old/new feeling of déjà vu set in. Hadn't I already been to college at some of these places?

Liz, of course, took me on the college tour. Liz was a veteran of many college tours and a veteran of college itself, so she was well in command of the trip. Liz's alma mater was high on my list because I liked Liz and she seemed to have perfectly fine friends. People thought Liz and I were alike, so, fine, I'll apply there. (I wore a jumpsuit to the interview, by the way, which may account for why I did not get in.)

I had a pretty good idea of what college would be like on the East Coast, but the West Coast? No idea. Never been there! So I applied to Pomona and got in. It didn't really seem that crazy to me to go to school three thousand miles away to a place my parents had never heard of until I received my admissions letter. My friends, the ones without older siblings, who ventured off cautiously to Boston or New York to fine schools a train ride away from home, thought my goal was to get as far away a possible. It wasn't. I just thought a small liberal arts school in California sounded like a good place to spend four years. Enough the same, but enough different.

When Liz dropped me off my first day of college, I was wearing a Laura Ashley sundress and listening to Prince on my first-generation, big-as-a-suitcase Walkman. Right away, I knew that I had made the right choice. I was completely without fear because of my guinea pigs. I would have a college experience like my brothers and sisters, but not exactly. Déjà new, not déjà vu.

I made career decisions following that same model. I thought of my brothers and sisters as a graph that illustrated the range of career possibilities, but none of them had exactly the job I wanted. My siblings had gone out and done different things. It didn't really matter what exactly, but I had seven examples of what you could do after college, most of which did not involve grad school but an actual job. My classmates, those without siblings, seemed to think that doctor, lawyer, or investment banker were the only three careers available in 1987. This was the Reagan 80s, after all. I watched in horror as 75 percent of my frantic classmates committed themselves to one of these three careers at age twenty-two. I knew better, because I had my guinea pig, Liz.

Liz lived in New York and worked in public relations. She had the kind of job that wouldn't show up on some career center bulletin board, but it was fun and creative. I wanted to do something like that, so I moved to New York. After a brief stint in Urban Archaeology (no kidding), I ended up in an entry-level advertising job. I was sleeping on Liz's couch because that was all I could afford—nothing. I paid her no rent. On the subway to work one day, that creeping sensation came over me. Haven't I worked in advertising before and had this young New York lifestyle? Not really, but Liz and Brendan did. *Hmm.*

The next day, I gave notice and, because I was that kind of employee, I found my own replacement. One month later, I moved to Jackson Hole, Wyoming, to ski, waitress, and have the adventure my sisters and brothers had not quite taken. I was wearing a black beret and vintage wool ski pants and listening to the first 10,000 Maniacs album when I pulled into town. I would have been perfectly happy to carry my own skis, but I didn't actually own any skis at the time. I did have a few hundred bucks and a roommate with a Subaru, so that was a good start. I knew I was in the right place. I didn't know what my life would be like after Wyoming, but I knew exactly what my life would be like if I stayed in New York. That's the value of a guinea pig.

Julie and my sister-in-law Mary became my work/family/balance guinea pigs. The term "mommy track" didn't exist when Julie and Mary pulled off to the side career-wise and had children in the early 80s. Julie was a newly minted MBA and Mary was a corporate lawyer when they had their first children. Both put their careers on hold while they had baby number two and raised their kids to school age. And then, both Julie and Mary went back to work when the time was right and found their careers had taken unexpected but fulfilling turns. Julie went into business school administration and Mary opened her own legal practice, specializing in children's advocacy. I watched and learned. I could quit, have children, and then go back to work. I might not go back to the same job, but I'd find something else to do. And, most important, my children would be great because I could be there for them, but they would also be great when I went back to work. My nephews and nieces taught me that.

My guinea pigs had shown me this was possible. Again, I felt sorry for my sisterless friends who didn't have the frame of reference I had. They struggled with the decision of when to have children and then what to do. I saw the fear in their eyes when they thought about losing their career momentum or letting their multiple degrees languish. I wasn't afraid at all because I had the guinea pigs. For me it was no struggle. I was a producer of sports films. It was a career that was completely incompatible with children—long, intense hours, usually on the weekends, with stretches of downtime in between. I would work, have children, stay home for a while, and then I would figure out what I was going to do.

I thought screenwriting might be fun and child-friendly. (It isn't either of those things, but I didn't know that then.) I had the full support of my husband. We tightened our financial belts and took a risk on my career. I quit my job, listened to a lot of Nirvana, and wore the same red sweatpants every day for two years. I wrote a couple of mediocre screenplays that never sold and had two children along the way. And you know what? When it was time, another career option did come along—radio. Just like I figured it would.

To me, your sense of direction is only a good as your guinea pigs and your powers of observation. Most people don't grow up with seven others two steps ahead. I was lucky. My guinea pigs lived in the same house. But if you look around, you can find people a lot like you, just a couple years your senior. Your mother's coworkers, your best friend's big sister, your young, cool uncle. They are out there, making all the same choices that you will eventually have to make. Watch what they do, learn from their successes and failures, and then chart your own path, maybe a little broader, a little bolder. But before you do, get the clogs. And always bring the Boss with you.

The Way-Station Sibling and Safe-House System

by Liz

I counted once. Since we've left home, my brothers and sisters have lived in thirty-nine cities, not counting the town where we grew up. There are many reasons for this—schools, jobs, mates, general restlessness, and great curiosity.

There are at least two really good benefits to having siblings spread out all over the world. First, they provide excellent vacation options. When my older brother Dick lived in Tesuque, New Mexico, Monica and I used his home as a base of operations for several fine holidays exploring the Sangre de Cristo Mountains. When my brother Jim and his family were living in Casablanca, Morocco, it was a wonderful opportunity to visit North Africa. My nieces, ages eleven and seven at the time, had each learned enough Arabic and French to show the grown-ups around. I also remember the ultimate cross-cultural experience during my visit there, sitting on cushions in their living room watching Tonya Harding and Nancy Kerrigan on satellite television competing at the Lillehammer Olympics. Even in a foreign language, the look on Tonya's face when her lace broke and the look on Nancy's when young upstart Oksana Baiul took the gold were completely priceless. These were two embarrassing moments for the United States, but kind of funny in Morocco in Norwegian.

Julie's ten-year stint with her family in New Orleans was also a holiday bonanza for the rest of us that included many great meals, Mardi Gras costumes, Jazz Fest, oyster po'boys, and outdoor showers. I regret not having visited Brendan while he lived in Montreal or Dick while he lived in Juneau, Alaska, but time simply ran out. While some would make the case that it is great to have your family close by, I would argue that it is even better when they live in places you want to visit.

The second and more important benefit to having brothers and sisters all over the world is that they provide way stations—sibling safe houses, so to speak. Let me explain.

Any sibling can be a way-station sibling. It simply requires opening your couch, basement, or attic to a sibling who is between gigs. Any brother or sister who has recently graduated or dropped out of high school, graduated or dropped out of college, quit their job and has time off before the next one begins, or quit their job and has no idea where to get the next one, needs a sibling safe house. Financial reversals and relationship unravelings can also create the need for a safe house for some length of time. The way-station sibling is an all-important alternative to Moving Home. We owe this much to each other. Home is great, but not when you are twenty-five or thirty-five and feel like wearing your pajamas all day while you ponder your future.

On September 11, 1994, my younger brother, Brendan, arrived in New York and asked if he could camp out on my couch for a few weeks. He had recently finished college and was embarking on a Manhattan job search. As Thanksgiving, Christmas, and Easter came and went, Brendan's pile of belongings behind the living room couch (his bed) grew. He got a job, got a few suits, quit his job, got another job, and got robbed—all-important rites of passage for the new grad in the big city. One thing he did not get was his own apartment. We enjoyed a lot of MTV, *Miami Vice,* and Chinese food together for a year and a half. It was the *first* season of *Miami Vice,* before everyone else caught on and Bloomingdale's featured the fashions in their windows. On the whole, we peacefully coexisted, especially once I ruled that he had to keep his stinky running shoes out in the hall. When he did finally get his own apartment, it was directly next door. Not next door as in the next building down the street. Next door, as in, I was 2A and he was 2B. The hours of MTV continued, which was great, and his stinky running shoes moved from my front door to his—not totally out of range, but an improvement. Brendan's stay in a sibling safe house was longer than most, but I was happy to provide the way station.

A few months later, Lian arrived, taking up the same spot on the same couch, but she had already made use of several other sibling safe houses. Julie was Lian's first way-station sibling. High school got kind of tedious for Lian, so she finished early and headed for the French Quarter. There she embarked on a fabulous sandwich-making career at the Decatur Street Deli. Her safe house was Julie's home in New Orleans. In addition to her deli duties, Lian baby-sat for Julie's two children. It is entirely appropriate for the way-station sibling to receive some kind of services in exchange for rent and food. Lian happily chipped in with childcare. She built on this at her next stop. Older brother Jim was her next way-station sibling. In exchange for the occupancy of his attic (inexplicably named the Penguin Penthouse) in Westport, Connecticut, Lian helped Jim and his wife, Mary, care for their daughter.

Let me say a word or two here about the critical role siblings-in-law play in making the whole sibling way-station system function smoothly. Over the years, Julie's husband, Trem, and Jim's wife, Mary, have harbored all kinds of siblings to whom they are not related by blood. Of course, every one of my brothers and sisters believe they have a God-given right to camp out with any other brother or sister, but for an in-law to embrace this repeatedly shows great generosity of spirit. If Mary or Trem were ever worried that behind this sibling-in-transition there were two or three others on their way, they never let it show. I salute such siblings-in-law!

As an older single sister, I have harbored all of my younger brothers and sisters: Sheila, Monica, Brendan, and Lian. Sheila shared my hovel in Brooklyn. Monica lived in my house in Portland. Brendan and Lian enjoyed the aforementioned Manhattan couch. A few years later Lian came to visit Monica and me in Portland for a couple of weeks and ended up staying for three years—one of them in my basement.

The benefits of the way-station sibling are many. First of all, you get to enjoy the company of your brothers and sisters outside of the usual action-packed holidays. As semi-grown-ups, you can really enjoy each other's company as long as you deal directly with irritants such as smelly running shoes or clashing musical tastes. It is important to bear in mind, however, that the same sister who stole your clothes at thirteen (Sheila) will do the same if she moves in with you at twenty-three (Sheila).

Another benefit to being the way-station sibling is that you may actually need some of the services your siblings can provide. I have never had any need for baby-sitting, but I would be the first to admit that Monica cared much more about cleaning my kitchen floor than I ever did. She also purchased and operated the lawn mower. What a deal for me, the way-station sibling! Brendan still reminds me that I managed to blame him every time my phone got cut off because I did not pay the bills on time. Having a sibling for a scapegoat is useful, too.

The sibling in need of a safe house gets housing, food, and phone (up to a point). The best sibling safe houses also provide cable and occasionally have a spare car. Most important, the sibling safe house provides the transition step, the halfway house between a college dorm or parent's home and the dingy, dangerous, over-priced first apartment that is the inevitable next step. The way-station sibling usually does not care what time you get up or what time you get home, as long as the stack of pizza boxes does not get too high or the supply of Diet Coke too low. In a large family, the big kids are often the way-station siblings for the little kids because they have gotten a head start out into the world. However, this is not an absolute. Any sibling with an open couch and an open mind can be called upon. Way-station siblings have been there, done that, and don't care. In other words, they may be parents, but they aren't your parents.

Having singled out siblings-in-law, let me salute the entire extended family way-station support system. My first safe house was actually provided by my cousins Joe and Beth Morningstar. They could see that I was a cousin-in-need. I had recently finished college, started my first job in New York, and was living with my parents. As great as the setup was (walk to train, my own room, nice family dinners, and lots of Yankee baseball), my cousins provided the way station they knew would aid in my personal development: a bedroom in Brooklyn with a bodega on the nearest corner and the F train on the next.

A map of my family's movements during the last three decades reveals an interesting pattern of clustering. The way-station siblings have established safe houses in New York, New Orleans, and Portland that have attracted multiple other siblings to those cities. As the baby, Lian has probably made the most extensive use of the way-station system, but we've all benefited. There's nothing like a good stint on a family member's couch to put life into perspective.

Hello, My Name Is _____

by Julie

I have been married for more than twenty years and still haven't made up my mind about my last name. I married at a time when people didn't automatically take their husband's name. There were no rules for me to follow. For two decades, I have tried on a variety of surnames as a way to fit into my different career and life situations. Some people change jobs, partners, locations, or hair color to find their way in the world; I change my last name.

We were pretty casual about names growing up. My parents selected unique names for us, but once that was done, they didn't dwell on the various nuances and meanings of our names. They were usually busy trying to come up with another name for the next baby on the way. The sheer volume of names often led to confusion. When my mother would be angry with me, for example, she would spit out several of my brothers' and sisters' names before she landed on mine. Further complicating matters, we also all had nicknames, most of which were just plain mean, and alternative names from foreign-language class. Sheila and Monica, for example, were transformed into the exotic Solange and Monique. In addition, my parents had a tendency to call all boyfriends and girlfriends "Dear" until there was an official engagement.

With the exception of a brief period in sixth grade when I wanted to be called Christy, I like all my names—first, middle, maiden, and married. I wasn't given a name loaded with expectations, although my fifth-grade CCD teacher thought Julie St. James would be a lovely name for a nun. Allegedly my father wrote a short story in college titled "Julie." That is all I ever knew about the inspiration for my name. No namesakes to guide me, just my intuition and imagination.

It's surprising to me that some aspect of my sense of identity was bound up in my last name, rather than a place. I had always thought that who you were and where you were going in life were grounded in a place. You become a place. You are reminded of your life's purpose by the familiar landmarks around you—family, community, profession. But as an adult, I have moved from place to place. Each time I move, I have to begin the process of defining who I am and where I am going all over again. Each time, I draw on the reserve of who I've been—wife, mother, daughter, sister, coworker, friend, and neighbor. Each time, I come up with a slightly different conclusion resulting in the need to make an adjustment to my name.

As a newlywed, I marched off to graduate school with the hyphenated name Dolan-Smith. I think I was one of the first hyphenators to hit Central Pennsylvania. Several of my classmates inquired if I was British. The registrar was unclear about whether to file me with the D's or the S's and a representative from the Department of Motor Vehicles strongly advised me against attempting to put a hyphen on my Pennsylvania driver's license. I was insistent that I was going to make this curiosity of a last name work because it was symbolic of my newly formed and very modern married partnership.

Later, when I moved to New Orleans, pregnant and with an eighteen-month-old in tow, a real-estate agent required my signature, and I just wrote Smith. Maybe I was exhausted from four years of defending why I had a funny name and the thought of having to explain my two-part name to this overly made-up realtor, who I knew wouldn't get it anyway, was more than I could handle. It may have been the heat or morning sickness or maybe I simply faced the reality that it was going to be difficult to play the part of a hard-charging MBA, pregnant, with a toddler wrapped around my knees. The real-estate agent didn't notice my internal struggle, but I remember it well. My life was moving in a different direction. For a time it was simple. I had a husband, two sons, and a last name that matched theirs.

It is surprising how few repercussions there are from a name change. Unlike most people who change names to signify a change in marital status, for me it signaled a change in focus. My brothers and sisters understood. They would ask, "How do you want me to address the Christmas package to you?" or "What name are you registered under?" It is important to have people around who understand that you are not crazy, even if your actions suggest otherwise.

When I resurrected my career after several years at home, I had to choose a name to put on my résumé. Which way was I going to go? There was no way I was going to retreat to hyphenation. Like the tiny bow ties that matched my career-woman suits, my hyphenated-name stage was over. I didn't want to stop being Smith, but Smith didn't quite express where I had been before I was a wife and mother or where I was headed. I opted for a stripped-down version with no reference to my marital status, not even a middle initial. I put Dolan, plain and simple, on the résumé. It was an overreaction, an attempt to go back to some earlier life form and extract my singular self. It was as if I needed to reach back and remind myself where I came from in order to figure out where I wanted to go.

I lived with two names, sometimes Dolan and sometimes Smith. It really wasn't a problem because the elementary school (where my children went) and graduate business school (where I worked) crowds don't usually intersect. I told a few key people, like my baby-sitter, the office receptionist, and my husband and sons, that I had this name thing. There were only a few awkward moments, like when I would run into a faculty member at a Little League game, that my dual identity was revealed. The two-name system was a lot like my life at this point—a workable but complicated dual course of action. Like my surname, I was constantly flipping back and forth from Dolan to Smith, from career professional to mother.

I was presented with another opportunity to address the issue when we moved to California, the land of made-up names. If ever I was going to take liberties with what I wanted to call myself, this was the moment. For the first month, I tried Julie Dolan Smith. In this new location, I was determined to achieve a better balance of a family and professional life. I wanted a last name that reflected my resolve. Well, maybe Mary Tyler Moore or Pamela Anderson Lee have enough poise to pull off three names, but I didn't get the respect or the balance that I was hoping for. My mother was the only one who really seemed to make the effort. She would dutifully send me cards with all three names. Even if she didn't fully understand what I was doing, she was supportive.

Honestly, it is a lot of work to say and write three names, and somewhat of an imposition on others. Why should others be taxed just because of my quest for balance? Within a short period of time, I replicated my New Orleans never-enough-time-skimping-on-work-shortchanging-my-kids-and-husband lifestyle in California with one name for work and one for home and a brutal commute on the Santa Monica Freeway during which I transformed from one into the other.

Believe it or not, Thailand is an ideal spot for someone with my dilemma. Because of the impossibly long Thai last names, it is common practice to use only your first name when leaving a message or booking a reservation. Most days I am relieved of having to mention my last name. When forced, by day I am Julie Smith but late at night when I get to the radio station to link up with my sisters around the world, I start each show with "This is Julie Dolan in Bangkok."

My multiple personalities have made me more understanding of others' seemingly irrational life moves. I cheered my sister Liz's decision to leave her job of a lifetime to find another way to live her life. I understood when my brother Brendan dropped out of business school to go to law school, or when my friend Linda, long before it was fashionable, left her perfectly good job to move to France to study French cooking. One's path in life is not a straight line. Detours, dead ends, and delays are what life is all about.

Finally, after twenty years of struggle, I really don't care what I am called and apparently nobody else is too worried about it, either. I've got it straight with the IRS, my family, and my friends. I realized that no matter what I call myself or what others call me, my life is never going to move in an orderly, linear fashion. I have learned that forward is not the only direction. In some cases, moving backward or sideways makes a lot of sense.

I may never settle on just one course or one name, and that's fine. I have found that it is not so much where you are going but what you take with you. To me, a guiding principle is always to carry with you something that reminds you of where you've come from. My direction is shaped by the rich set of experiences from the places I've lived, the people I love, and those who love me, with or without a hyphen.

It's the Thought That Counts

by *Monica*

We are not a family of gift givers or card writers. You would think having eight brothers and sisters every birthday would mean an automatic windfall of cards and presents. Not so. I confess I have never sent my brothers a birthday card in thirty years. And I have not received one, either. It's not that we don't like each other, it's just that those sorts of gestures have lost their meaning. When we were little, gift giving was as much about the process as the gift. Now, without the ritual, we're a little lost.

When we were young, on the eve of our birthday my mother would tuck us into bed, read us a story, and, once we were fast asleep, lay out our birthday presents at the foot of the bed. Despite the excitement and anticipation of presents, I never was able to wake up in time to catch the birthday fairy in the act. In the morning my brothers and sisters would rush into the room to see what I had gotten. I remember the year of the pink gingham bathrobe and the book of Robert Louis Stevenson poems. My biggest haul was a record player that came in a blue carrier case and a copy of the first Monkees LP. I also remember being surprised to find out that other kids didn't receive their birthday presents by the same mode of delivery.

Christmas presents in our house were dispensed via magical ritual, too. When you are ten years old, there is no chance that you're going to be able to buy eight Christmas presents with the five-dollar bill Grampa gave you at Thanksgiving, so my parents devised a clever and equitable plan. Every child would give and receive two sibling presents. The month before Christmas, every child's name was written on two slips of paper and put into an old top hat of my grandfather's. Every child drew out two names. You gave two presents and you got two presents.

There were many ground rules. The name drawing was conducted in birth order, from Jimmy to Lian. The cycle was repeated twice. If you drew your own name or the same name twice, that earned an automatic do-over. If, however, you drew a name of a brother or sister who was tough to please, you were stuck with it. No trading names, and, in the spirit of the Christmas season, no cheating. The names of the brother and sister you drew and who had drawn your name were to be kept an absolute secret. My father made a great ceremony of having us memorize the names on the slips of paper before he burned the evidence in the fire. Let the games begin.

Gift giving became a competitive sport. But how competitive can you be on five dollars? What's more, our shopping venues were limited to the one store we could reach by bike, the Greenfield Hill Pharmacy. Christmas presents for the girls were easy—Lemon-Up shampoo or Love's Baby Soft cologne were sure bets, because those were the presents you really wanted for yourself. Sometimes I opted for giving pre-read Archie and Veronica comic books carefully selected (and screened) from the pharmacy's library. The sibling who posed the biggest challenge was Jimmy, because he had the most sophisticated taste. You could always get him a forty-five of a recent Beatles hit, but unfortunately the Greenfield Hill Pharmacy did not sell records. So, for the boys, it really came down to two choices: tube socks or the classic hockey puck. A challenge to wrap, but in our family, the feeling was a boy could never have too many hockey pucks. One year I made an embarrassing faux pas and gave Jimmy a stick of Mennen deodorant. In my defense, I didn't know what deodorant was. And, lest you think it's the thought that counts, homemade gifts were out, because everyone would suspect you'd kept the five-dollar bill for yourself.

One year Dick shattered all the rules by announcing he had presents for everyone. He had bought a Bic ballpoint eight-pack and wrapped all the pens individually in enormous decoy boxes. He probably still had a couple of dollars left over from the Grampa five-spot. This stunt earned Dick the reputation of being a cheapskate, though he insists he was merely being clever and thrifty. No matter—he has spent the last thirty years trying to improve his image.

These days, we have no clear plan for gift giving. Take eight brothers and sisters, six in-laws, and eleven nieces and nephews, then factor in geography, and it's clear that the hat trick is not going to work. We've tried and failed several times to establish a loose set of rules. For instance, if you have to travel a long distance to get home for the holidays, you have no obligation to bring gifts, the effort is enough. If you are local, you have to buy gifts, but don't expect any from the travelers. Or, you can buy gifts for the people who show up, but don't bother putting anything in the mail. Small children are the exception in all cases. And, every year, no matter what the agreed-on policy, some spoiler always comes along bearing beautiful gifts for everyone. Usually it's Dick, still trying to make up for those pens. The process is in chaos.

What I have discovered is that it's not the gifts I miss, it's the ritual. The suspense, the top hat, the five-dollar limit. The whole magical delivery system that gave meaning to a bottle of Lemon-Up shampoo. I wish that I could take one more stroll through the

Greenfield Hill Pharmacy, looking for the perfect present. I think now I might even find it. Because, after all, even if it turns out that there is such a thing as too many hockey pucks, it's the thought that counts.

Litmus Sister

by Lian

In our family, we do a lot of preliminary investigations—testing the waters, so to speak—before we float an idea out to the general family population. For these sorts of investigations, you need a Litmus Sister—a sister in good standing who can correctly predict how the family might react to an idea such as skipping the family Thanksgiving to be with friends or naming your child Bliss. Based on common sense and early polling, the Litmus Sister might predict that no one really wants to get together this Thanksgiving, so you're giving everybody an out to stay home, bless you. Or that Mom has always loved the name Bliss, so go for it. Then again, your Litmus Sister is just as likely to tell you that this is a big Thanksgiving, so don't miss it, or that Bliss won't go over well with the grandparents because they think it's a street name for heroin. A good Litmus Sister can spot a bad idea or, at least, a controversial idea. And that is invaluable in any family—big or little.

Once the initial consultation is over, a really astute Litmus Sister can assist in strategizing and executing any idea that may go against the family grain. In general, that plan would be to tell your siblings, gain support, and then face the family elders. This works with your lesser family controversies—skipping your niece's baptism for a spa vacation, blowing off your brother's thirty-seventh birthday, wearing pants to your cousin's wedding. But for larger affronts to family sensibilities, your Litmus Sister really has to work it.

Say, for instance, that you decide to drop out of your residency program in neurosurgery to become a textile artist while your parents are still paying off your loans for med school. Here's a case where you clearly need a Litmus Sister. "The best way to tell Mom and Dad" is Job One for the Litmus Sister.

The Litmus Sister becomes a consensus builder who will help you roll out the information in a manner that will be most supportive and beneficial to your cause. It may be necessary for the Litmus Sister to do some in-the-field polling on your behalf, anonymously surveying other siblings, friends, coworkers. For the next step, the Litmus Sister may leak information to those in the family who will be sympathetic and champion your cause if need be. Finally, the Litmus Sister may hint at the news to your parents, bear the initial blows of their anger and frustration, then report back with a new action plan for your revelation. This three-pronged strategy is a noble effort on the part of the Litmus Sister. Then it's up to you to take it from there.

The need for a Litmus Sister doesn't begin and end with family matters, especially if your friends are like family, meaning that they, too, can be touchy about the smallest things. In any group of Satellite Sisters, you might have to call in a Litmus Sister to gauge reaction on your plan to invite So-and-so's old boyfriend to dinner because he happens to be in town and you're old college friends and you always thought he was a good guy. The job of your Litmus Sister is to evaluate your actions and their effect on So-and-so. Your Litmus Sister might advise you to A) go ahead and invite Old Boyfriend but don't tell So-and-so, B) invite Old Boyfriend, but let the Litmus Sister pave the way with So-and-so, or C) abort the idea or risk the silent treatment from So-and-so for several weeks. A

Litmus Sister, whether by blood or proximity, is a valuable asset in avoiding controversy with loved ones.

The key is to pick the right Litmus Sister for each situation. Do not pick a sister with shaky communication skills, certain family biases, or alternate viewpoints on everything from religion to the proper melon-balling technique. Their views are likely to get you in trouble. (N.B.: The black sheep is *not* a good Litmus Sister.) The most useful Litmus Sister is well respected, on speaking terms with most family members, and has a point of view on matters. She does not always have to agree with you—you need someone with judgment, not just unconditional support—but she does need to understand your willingness to strike out on a different path. The best Litmus Sister will be able to balance your needs with the conventional wisdom of the rest of the family.

Every situation has special requirements. "One size fits all" does not work with a Litmus Sister. Your Litmus Sister for family holidays may be different from your Litmus Sister for family gift giving or for the appropriate attire for anniversary parties. Everyone specializes these days. Choose your Litmus Sister wisely, then heed her advice. Think of her as a cross between a Gallup Pollster, Ann Landers, and a spin doctor.

The next time you are about to announce your upcoming sex change operation at your nephew's high-school graduation or your intention to move in with your boyfriend at Grandma's seventy-fifth birthday party, stop and think. How would my Litmus Sister react? Then, before you make the announcement, call your Litmus Sister.

Classic Bad Advice

In the process of developing one's sense of direction, one ought to solicit and filter advice. These are excellent skills. The difficulty lies in knowing who to solicit and what to filter. While we have no definitive answer, we have a few hard-won suggestions in this area. All sorts of people are willing to give advice. For some people, it's a mission. Giving advice makes people feel more useful and together than they really are. Solving your problems means they can put their own on the back burner for a while. The advice they give can be skewed by their own agendas and not at all helpful to your situation. We all know this, and yet, at moments of great personal vulnerability, a woman in the frozen-food aisle becomes an expert on breastfeeding and the guy behind you in line at the post office seems like a reliable career counselor. Why not stop and consider the source?

Here's our best advice on advice: When you're at a crossroads, turn to your Satellite Sisters, get their opinions, sleep on it, then act on roughly 50 percent of their suggestions. And always be wary of advice from the following people.

- Radio talk-show hosts.
- People who know it all.
- People who know nothing.
- People at the opposite end of the political spectrum from you.
- Real-estate agents.
- Ex-romantic anythings.
- The black sheep.

- The person who used to have your job.
- The person who wants your job.
- The weird guy in accounts receivable.
- Doctors who smoke.
- Anyone, other than a bride, wearing white pumps.
- The busybody room mother.
- The neighbor who never leaves his or her house.
- The office suck-up.
- The town gossip.
- The clothing saleswoman with a visible pantyline.

There is also a category of classic bad advice, most of which we've actually heard and followed at some point in our lives. Should you hear anyone utter the following phrases, proceed with caution.

Don't miss Graceland!

Wear a snappy hat to the interview.

Everybody parks here.

Order the oysters.

Just tell him the way you really feel.

Take astronomy. It's easy.

All this house needs is a little TLC.

You don't have to declare that as income.

Put your picture on your résumé!

Kilts are back in.

A perm would look great on you.

You don't need air-conditioning in that car!

Marry him. He'll change.

Doctor, It Hurts When I Do This:

OUR POSITIONS ON FREE ADVICE

Monica: Here's a story I wanted to share with you. I was at a party a few weeks ago, when a woman I had just met learned that I was a nurse and that I worked with pacemaker patients. She then proceeded to tell me about every friend and family member she's ever known who had a pacemaker "installed"—as she put it. Then she held out a wrist, and she asked me to take her pulse and tell her if she had any skipped beats.

Sheila: What did you do?

Monica: Of course, after juggling the drinks, I obliged, even though I really think it's inappropriate in a social setting to ask a doctor, lawyer, or really anyone for professional advice. And I am not alone. When we posted this question on our website, 55 percent of the people who responded agreed that it's just wrong. So sisters, what's your position on this—if you met a lawyer or doctor at a cocktail party, would you ask them for free advice? Lian?

Lian: It's a *party*. You should be talking about things that are a little more entertaining than Uncle Norm's pacemaker installation. As a matter of fact, I once had a doctor give me an unsolicited diagnosis at a party. We were in the middle of a conversation, and she said, "Your eyes are yellow. Do you have hepatitis?" which was a little jarring to hear, actually.

Monica: Especially at a cocktail party.

Liz: It saves an office visit. I think that's really very nice of her.

Monica: Sheila, how about you? I'm sure you have a position.

Sheila: As a former New York City school principal, sometimes I just like to remain anonymous at a party. I see a whole room full of parents and I just clam up, because I know the first question is going to be something about education or this teacher or that test. Once a woman who was just a few months pregnant started grilling me about where she should send her child to school—he/she/it wasn't even born yet! Anyway, I do not ask for advice at parties. As for medical information, I have a mainline to a nurse. Monica, you know if I have any medical questions, I go right to you. At a party, I just like to relax.

Monica: OK, Liz?

Liz: Never. I would never ask a professional for advice. It just seems totally inappropriate.

Julie: In any setting?

Lian: Liz knows it all; she doesn't need advice.

Liz: Well, there's that, and also ... I think, unless it's someone who really wants to offer advice, but people in that category would be life insurance salesmen, and why would you want to open up that whole conversation at a cocktail party?

Monica: Julie?

Julie: Well, I don't do it with lawyers, but with doctors I can't help myself. I don't know what it is! I really just see it as engaging in a topic of conversation that's of interest to them: healthcare. Now, it happens to be *my* healthcare, but I like to start at broad-trend level and then work it down to the specifics of my case.

Sheila: And then she makes a little paper dress from cocktail napkins, and proceeds to remove her clothes.

Monica: Has it ever involved a physical exam of some sort?

Julie: No, I haven't gone that far. Yet.

I've Already Been to College

by Liz

The college tour is a rite of passage for many teenagers. We've all seen the tense family units moving around campus, lead by a student who may or may not know why that building is named Big Bridges or New North or Alfred D. List. These are the questions that parents ask on the tour. This is why most kids would prefer not to be on them. Watching these tours always made me extremely grateful for a gift my parents gave us. They rarely accompanied us on the college tour. Had we asked, I am sure they would have obliged, but we didn't. They cared where we went to college and supported us in our search, but they let us decide for ourselves where we would go and what we would study. "I've already been to college" was their refrain.

"I've already been to college" has become a classic family line we still use with each other to cover a wide range of circumstances. It is a cross between "Figure it out yourself" and "Go ask someone else." It is a loving brushoff, a hard-to-argue-with fact that shifts the responsibility back to whomever it belongs. Making life decisions for ourselves is an important skill to learn. Figuring out where to go to college is a good place to start.

From my parents' perspective, one can certainly understand that while their children's college education was a priority, the actual college tour was not. Eight children looking at a dozen colleges each would have resulted in my parents taking ninety-six campus tours lead by ninety-six underinformed undergraduate tour guides finishing up at ninety-six admissions offices where they didn't want to talk to the parents anyway. Many of these tours would have been repeats, such as the whole Jesuit circuit of Holy Cross–Boston College–Georgetown, and most of our potential choices were perfectly respectable educational institutions that my parents felt no need to prescreen. They had already been to college. This admirable hands-off, we-trust-your-judgment approach reached its peak with Lian, the youngest. Not only hadn't my parents checked out Pomona College in Claremont, California, with her, but Lian herself had never been there. The word was that Pomona was "the Williams of the West" with better weather. Being the youngest of eight, the "West" part appealed to Lian. Maintaining high educational standards, the "Williams" part appealed to my parents. Everyone was happy. No one needed a tour.

Those of us who did bother to visit potential choices went in pairs or trios in my mother's station wagon, usually heading north on I-95 to the land of colleges, the state of Massachusetts. Julie and I took the first sisters tour at the start of her senior year in high school. I was a sophomore, so just being on a college campus was a thrill for me. We started with Boston because of its high college density and because we had cousins in the suburbs who would put us up overnight and lead the tour. Our older cousin Patty Kirshner did not attend any Boston-area colleges herself, of course, but her brothers did and she grew up in the area. More important, she was cool. Being three years older than Julie and five years older than me, we could count on her to know the right hangouts and direct our attention to the important things we needed to ask ourselves while visiting places we might have to spend four years. How many Frisbee-playing dogs are around? Are there posters up for parties that look fun? What's playing at the midnight movie theater? Would you want to dress like these people? I suspect if we had taken the tour with our parents, these are not the issues we would have focused on, but they are, in fact, key quality-of-life issues that should enter into any kind of decision-making.

From Boston, we headed west toward Northampton. The frequent stops at Friendly's were as key to this adventure as any actual information we were gathering, but I did enjoy collecting all the catalogs, brochures, and stickers that were dispensed. I read aloud from them while Julie drove west on the Mass Pike. College looked really fun and I liked the idea of trading in high school biology for the history of French cinema. Every school catalog seemed to list that course in 1972. College was going to be great! My father has always been a big believer in studying the great works: Euripedes, Shakespeare, Joyce. It seemed that most colleges now included Truffaut on that list. Cool.

Julie loved Smith College, and went on to love the four years she spent there. We were both at an all-girls high school and she believed in the value of women's-only education. I took one look at Smith and knew that my future would definitely be coeducational. It saved me a whole leg of my own college tour, eliminating dozens of potential choices in one fell swoop. By the time we headed that station wagon south, Julie and I had each made big decisions, and they were completely opposite.

Several years later, Sheila and I headed north again. I was a senior and she was a junior. Another overnight with our Boston cousins, another stroll up Brattle Street, and another drive down Commonwealth Avenue, and we got the feel for the places on our list. The rest of my college visits involved spending a weekend with a relative or friend at other schools I was interested in. My brother Dick was at Holy Cross. A friend from my high school was at Brown. My cousin Joe was at Wesleyan. The visit with Joe was the most memorable because we spent the afternoon stapling bags of live goldfish to the ceiling and firing up a fog machine for a party he was having that night. I feel certain I would not have gotten this glimpse of college life on the official admissions tour or if I had been accompanied by cousin Joe's parents, Uncle Jim and Aunt Edna.

Ultimately, we all graduated from college—some of us in four years from the same institution where we started, others after a longer period of time that included several stops and starts. Monica knew from the beginning that she wanted to be a nurse. I changed majors four times. Sheila had her eight-year-old daughter and her then-husband at her graduation. Julie's graduation was a lovely affair under the trees. Lian's was nice, too, but she was throwing up in the bushes. All three of my brothers graduated from my father's alma mater. We all found our way through and now we can all say "I have already been to college." But it is the spirit of the statement, not the fact, that matters and that spirit is the recognition that any good decision mixes equal parts adventure and direction, independence and support.

We've all got to make the occasional leap of faith. It's up to us to make the leap. The people around us provide the faith.

Insufficient Credits

by Sheila

No one was more surprised than I when I graduated from college. I started my journey in 1976 and came to the end of the road fourteen years later. When it was finally time to graduate from Hunter College in the winter of 1990, I kept thinking that someone would discover that I was missing two credits and hold me back. I wouldn't be able to graduate with my class of hundreds in the rowdy ceremony on the 68th Street campus. I would miss the purple-balloon drop and Donna Shalala's commencement address. I'd be required to go back for the spring semester because I didn't have sufficient credits and that's all it really boils down to, sufficient credits. I struggled with those words all my life, and this time they were going to get me. I would be exposed to the world as the woman without sufficient credits.

It all began back in grade school when I embarked upon a clumsy courtship with Brian "Bad Boy" Roberts. He was in my sixth-grade class at Pequot School, along with Martha, my best friend. Martha warned me about him, but I didn't listen. I was the new girl in town and spent all year thinking Brian was nothing more than the class clown. Our field trip to the Bridgeport Museum in June kind of changed how I felt about Brian. Little did I know that my entire academic future would hang in the balance.

On the last day of sixth grade, the janitors decided to make some repairs in the old coatroom in our class. They covered over a hole in the floor with fresh cement. The coatrooms in Pequot School were legendary places for innocent mischief of all kinds. You could go in the coatroom with a friend and just stand there, without the teacher's knowledge that you were missing. Sometimes kids would hop up when the teacher's back was turned, and hide in the coatroom for a few minutes. The best part of the coatroom was the small window that you could peer through while hiding. Kids made funny faces in the window, which would cause the rest of the class to lose control. Mr. Manelli, our sixth-grade teacher, was new, like me, and had no authority over the class. He was desperately trying to teach, but we were so distracted by coatroom activity that we'd always be cracking up during lessons. I felt sorry for him, but I also wanted to be popular, so I succumbed to the lures of the coatroom.

On the last day of school, Brian Roberts asked me to go in the coatroom with him. I turned bright red and said, "OK." We walked to the spot with the fresh cement. He pointed down at the floor and said, "There, that's where we'll write it." I had no idea what he was talking about but watched as he bent down and made a big heart with his finger in the fresh cement. *My god,* I thought, *he's going to write our initials!* He then told me flatly, "Write S.D." I didn't think about it, and Brian seemed so manly at that moment, it was hard to say no. I wrote my initials. He then made a plus sign and inscribed his initials, B.R. We returned to our seats without a word. The next thing I knew, we were on our way to see the principal, Miss Lindsay. A formidable woman of few words, Miss Lindsay was the only person in the school I feared. On the short walk to her office, my nice, friendly school took on the atmosphere of a scary, dark prison. It was Brian's fault. That's what I'd say.

We were taken in together and not allowed to speak. We were found guilty of "defacing school property" and were going to be fined five dollars. If we didn't pay the fine, we would not be permitted to graduate. Five dollars? Not graduate? I was terrified but knew there was absolutely no way that I would be held back from graduating. My parents would die, my life would be over, and I wouldn't be able to go to the graduation party at Southport Beach. It was all Brian's fault. But where would I get five dollars?

Brian told me to go home and get the five dollars. Our house was down the street from the school; since I often went home for lunch, my mother wouldn't suspect anything. *I'll go home,* I thought. But this time, it was going to be because I wanted to, not because he told me to do it. I would hand over the money and set us free. I had to steal the money, which made me even angrier with Brian. I ran back to school and went to the principal's office with the ransom. The secretary looked at me with a disappointed grin as I sat and waited for Miss Lindsay. When she came out, I stood up and showed her the five dollars. She took the money from my hand and said, "You're a nice girl, Sheila. What are you doing with him?" No adult had ever spoken to me like that, and I still think about her words today, words that seemed so sensitive coming from a woman who had just bribed a twelve-year-old for five dollars.

We graduated, thanks to me, but under duress. I had officially stopped talking to Brian that afternoon. I was breathless the whole day, waiting for the ceremony, which was to be held at night in the yard in the front of the school. It was extremely hot, and I wore my blue-and-white polka-dot dress. I looked like any other child, not a potential holdover or a thief, which I was.

Brian and I didn't see each other again until my junior year in high school, when I switched from Catholic boarding school to the local public high school. It was amazing to see him after all that time, riding around in a big car with his friends in the school parking lot. We looked at each other with a knowing glance, nothing more.

Who knows if Miss Lindsay meant what she said, but the threat of not graduating stayed with me until I got my second master's degree three years ago. I was always waiting for that tiny pink slip in the mail that read "Insufficient credits" or "See the bursar." I learned from that experience that basically it's up to you: You have to make sure your papers are in order, the credits are there, and the bursar is paid. Of course, I paid them with my Visa card, repeated classes endlessly until I got them right, and even cried to a few deans along the way. I got it done, though, and I now hold more higher degrees than anyone else in my family. Go figure.

After the Hunter graduation, my parents, my ex-husband, and my daughter, Ruth, went to the old David K's restaurant on Third Avenue uptown. We ate from a giant lazy Susan in the center of the table that held Chinese delicacies of all kinds. At a quiet point in the meal, my father stood up, quite unexpectedly, to make a toast. He has a big, booming voice when he needs to talk to large numbers of people, and this night, he chose to toast me in front of the whole restaurant. "To my daughter Sheila, the graduate, and the only child of eight to graduate summa cum laude." Everyone in the restaurant raised their glasses, as did my eight-year-old daughter, Ruth, who thought this was the best party ever. So it was official: I made it, I graduated, and, thanks to my father, most of the Upper East Side of Manhattan knew it, too.

Say It Out Loud

by Liz

I have never been particularly goal-oriented, at least not in the traditional sense. I do not dream of climbing Mount Everest or running a Fortune 500 company, though I might sign up for either under the right circumstances. I do not have a five-year plan. I do not write to-do lists. I don't even like advance-purchase plane tickets. Too much pressure.

Achievement does not motivate me. Embarrassment does. That's why occasionally it is important to just blurt out your goals. Whatever it is, say it out loud. Once you have announced to your Satellite Sisters that you are giving up sweets, you can't say yes to the dessert menu. It would be too embarrassing. To say it out loud is a commitment far more powerful than a secret scribbled in a journal. To say it out loud is to paint yourself into a corner. If you are like me, this is good.

Saying things out loud to friends sets a goal they can hold you to. Saying it out loud also allows you to gauge how hard the task will be. Guffaws are an indicator. If your usually supportive Satellite Sisters express skepticism, strap yourself in. They may know you better that you do.

In the summer of 1996, my four sisters and I met for a long weekend in the mudbaths of Calistoga, California. Our goal was to spend some time alone together. Some families sing around the campfire together. Our planned activity, other than the actual mudbaths of course, was to develop an idea for a radio show. We had an idea we could launch our own radio show with each sister living her life in a different city, connecting on the radio just the way we connected on the telephone. Women actually *like* talking to each other, we reasoned, but there is not much on the radio that captures that sound and that spirit. Couldn't we build on that idea? It seemed like a good thing to ruminate about while we soaked. Does this qualify as the long-range planning I just swore I did not do? Oh, well. This was different because it was so . . . so *outlandish*. We might as well have been planning our own mission to Mars. At the time, Julie was living in Northern California working in business-school admissions. Sheila was principal of a public school in New York City, Monica was an R.N. doing clinical research at a pacemaker company, Lian was an at-home mother, writing at nap-time, and I was vice president of marketing at Nike. Oh, and none of us had ever worked in radio.

Anyway, at lunch that Friday in August, I asked each of my sisters what their goal was for the coming year. Lian vowed to wean her first-born son and get at least one decent night's sleep. Monica decided to begin her lifelong mission to visit all of America's national parks. Sheila was making some big changes in her life, including getting a divorce. Her aim was to get on her own two feet emotionally and financially. Julie wanted to stay closer to home; her job was taking her away from her teenage boys and husband too much. She also wanted to rid herself of a gourmet dinner club she had foolishly joined, thinking it would help her make new friends. Instead, it was just one more obligation that was driving her crazy. She just did not care that much about stuffing goat cheese and pignoli nuts into anything.

When it was my turn, I said, "I want to quit my job before I turn forty." That gave me a little more than one year. A long silence ensued, followed by raucous laughter. I think Sheila's Diet Coke came out of her nose. Monica upended the chips and salsa. My sisters were skeptical that their workaholic, type-A, fly-to-Berlin-for-an-hour-then-come-right-back, never-had-a-Christmas-tree-or-a-day-off sister could leave her corporate cocoon. Actually, is there a stronger word than skeptical? Apparently, the mission to Mars sounded more likely. Not only didn't they believe me, they didn't believe that *I* believed me. Sure, Liz is going to quit her job. Yuk, yuk, yuk—that's a good one.

This was a galvanizing moment. How dare they not believe me? I may have just blurted it out on a whim, but now I *had* to do it. Otherwise, I would be too embarrassed.

The only vote of support I got was from Julie. Her comment was something along the lines of "Right, that job is killing you. Get a life." True Satellite Sisters provide perspective. She reminded my sisters that I was now traveling with a personal sphygmomanometer, taking my own blood pressure three times a day. I am not a hypochondriac. I had begun doing this because my BP at my physical two months ear-

lier had been 180/120. Not only had this been a big wake-up call that changes were needed, but I began to worry about how embarrassing it would be to collapse at work one day. Rock stars can get away with this "hospitalized for exhaustion" ruse, but your average corporate executive cannot. Passing out during a presentation is very bad for your career. And hugely embarrassing.

There may be professionals in the psychoanalytic field or self-help gurus who say that letting embarrassment, or the fear of embarrassment, motivate one's behavior is wrong. I am not an expert, but these people are wrong. Guilt, embarrassment, fear—these are natural human emotions that I can get in touch with. Success and achievement are not emotions. They are just plain old nouns. We try to make sure we do not trail toilet paper on our shoe as we leave the bathroom, not because it is an achievement to be toilet paper-free, but because we don't want to humiliate ourselves. Simple.

Having said that, it is important to investigate where the desire to quit came from in the first place. Did I really think it or did I just think I thought it? This much I knew: I wanted to end one chapter of my life and begin fresh. It was not just about my health. I could get healthier and still keep my job. I wasn't tired of my line of work; I liked it a lot. I was just done. It was time to turn the page. I kept asking myself: What's next?

After that weekend in August 1996, I did not rush back and change my life. I rushed right back into the same rut. I began taking blood-pressure medication and visiting an acupuncturist, but otherwise changed nothing. Months went by. I would chat with my sisters on the phone, careful not to complain too much about work because I knew what they were thinking. (Note to the reader: They weren't making much progress on their goals, either, so we could all share in the guilt and embarrassment. This is why it is important to have these conversations out loud. Everyone has something to hold over the others. That's what friendship is all about.)

By early 1997, I came to two important realizations. Number one: The desire to move on was not a whim. Number two: If I waited until I knew what I wanted to do next before I left what I was doing now, I would never make the leap. From inside my work world, I would not see other possibilities. I would only see the options that were most like my current job. I had a great job. If I thought I was looking for a better job, I would never find it. I was looking for a different life, not just a different place to report each day at 8 A.M. The new chapter needed to be truly different.

I thought the hardest thing to say out loud would be "I quit."

This was not the case. Apparently, everyone wants to quit—or at least say the words. We all have the quitting fantasy. In September 1997, I went in and said it.

People had one of two reactions. Some said, "Good for you," then immediately began to share the list of books they would read, sports they would take up, or languages they would learn if only they had the time. They also had lots of new business ideas or public-service projects they would take on, making it clear that the goal was not to not work. The goal was to work more creatively.

Others said, "What are you going to do now?" That's when I learned that the hardest thing to say out loud is not "I quit." The hardest thing to say out loud is "I don't know."

*T*hree Things I Learned by Starting Over at Forty *by Liz*

1. *Just because your job changes doesn't mean your personality does.*

Sure, once you don't have to sit around in meetings all day trying to figure out when you'll have time to do your actual work, you do relax a little, but your basic instincts don't change. Before I quit my corporate job, I drove myself crazy with self-imposed pressure. After I quit my job? Same pressure, different list. I squeeze in a few more novels now, and I have the luxury of spending more time with friends and family, but I still find myself e-mailing at midnight. I guess I just like to work. I think that's true of many people. The key is to work on something that's worth it. Which leads me to lesson #2.

2. *Making the decision to work on something that is worth it is completely worth it.*

I loved my job, but when I quit, I knew I wanted to work on things that were mission-driven. My first project was the marketing of the Women's World Cup Soccer Tournament. What a thrill! It introduced some great female athletes to the world and inspired a whole generation of girls and boys. My other big project has been Satellite Sisters. I love public radio and its ability to reach a curious audience with ideas that provoke and entertain. It's also a great gig when you can work with your sisters. And if we can start conversations that both mean something to people and make them laugh, then that's a mission I'm proud to be part of. We try every week. Writing this book together has also been a pleasure.

3. Sometimes we can't know what's next until we put what's now behind us.

We'll figure out what to do next in our spare time, right? Well, I looked but I just couldn't find the spare time. I had to manufacture it. Some people can work all day at a job and then go home and write their big novel. I admire those people, but I realize now that I'm not like that. I need to remove the safety net in order to get going. Having no answer to the question "What do you do?" provides great motivation to figure it out.

No Carping Day

by Lian

Every January for the last ten years, I have made the same New Year's resolution: Be nicer. I realize I have very little hope of ever achieving "nice." I am willing to settle for "nicer."

I spent most of my late teens and early twenties being fashionably cynical, opinionated, and, frankly, not very nice. Though I enjoyed the power of being mean, I found it tiring to be so jaded all the time. In my mid-twenties, I attempted to cross over to the sunny side of the street. I had moved to Portland, Oregon, and found that prolonged exposure to Oregonians does that to people. Being around pleasant, considerate human beings has a domino effect.

But now that I've moved from the Pacific Northwest, I am subject to more unpleasantness. Southern California may be sunny, but I am not always warm. The traffic, the smog, the vast number of thin women with breast implants talking on cellular phones while driving SUVs to the mall—it all adds up to one big headache, and some bad behavior. So every year, I am forced to renew my goal to be nicer. Then I develop a game plan. Now I see that in the past my plan has been too broad and, therefore, not entirely successful.

I can usually sustain an open, willing demeanor until March. A smile for a stranger, patience under pressure, even the occasional "Have a nice day!" By mid-April, I'm the person in line behind you at the post office harrumphing at the slow service. July rolls around and I'm taking out all my travel rage on the rental-car agent. By Halloween, I've spiraled downward and I'm laying on the car horn for the slightest traffic infraction. December comes and it's time to re-up my commitment to be nicer or fall even deeper into the well of negativity.

This year, I stole a strategy from one of our listeners, Diane Zitek. Diane e-mailed us that she has designated one day a week as "No Carping Day"—No complaints voiced to others, no complaints muttered to herself, just positive thoughts. Diane does not even entertain carping from others. When coworkers start down a negative road, Diane fends them off with, "Sorry, today is my no-complaining day," and that stops the whiners in their tracks.

Diane's idea has much merit. It is simple, self-administered, and sustainable. This idea of no carping one specific day a week seemed like something I could maintain over the course of a year. By thinking only positive things, I believed positive behavior would follow. If I stopped complaining, I would start being nicer—at least one day a week.

It is much harder than it sounds. I've discovered that sometimes I start carping internally before I even get out of bed! I can't brush my teeth without a few negative thoughts popping into my head or muttering a snide comment to my husband about his refusal to make coffee for me. And by the time my children wake up, it's all over. Carp, carp, carp. Such a simple idea that is so hard to execute because the negative grooves in my brain are so deeply entrenched.

Still, I try to catch myself and turn it around. Some days, I'm all carped out by 9 A.M., so I call a do-over and start fresh. I have a couple of techniques that work in situations that have a high carp factor. Waiting in a line is tough for me, so on No Carping Day, I bring catalogues if I know that any line waiting is in the offing. At the grocery store, I make free use of the magazine rack to distract me from the fact that the man ahead of me has seventy-two cans of dog food in the express line. Hey buddy, just because it's the same item doesn't mean that volume doesn't count. See the sign? Fifteen items. No checks. Whoops, that was a carp.

With my children, I avoid anything that has the potential to be contentious, especially late in the afternoon, a period of high carping for me. No haircuts, no dentist appointments, no trips to Target. Let's just stay at home and Slip 'N' Slide on No Carping Day.

Socially, I try to avoid gossips on No Carping Day. I don't like gossips any day of the week, but even more so on No Carping Day, because I have not yet summoned up the guts to proclaim, as No Carping Queen Diane does, "Today is my no-complaining day."

Little by little, I am getting there. But I can see that rechanneling all the negative grooves may be a lifetime project. I have found that the nicer I am on the inside, the nicer I am on the outside. There are a lot of mean people in the world, and six days week I may be one of them. But for a couple of hours on No Carping Day, I am one of the nice ones.

So far, the longest I've made it without carping is to my midmorning coffee break, when I usually find myself cursing the fact that there's no more milk. The breakthrough for me will come when I learn to drink my coffee black.

Regrets, We've Had a Few . . .

JULIE

Regrets undervaluing the rigors of commuting from one coast to the other. Living on West Coast with teenage sons, two dogs, and a husband who travels, while working on the East Coast was a bad idea.

LIZ

Regrets taking a job that involved completely transforming not only her wardrobe but also her personality. Took a full year to come to her senses.

SHEILA

Regrets leaving the supportive, esteem-building environment of a girls' summer camp early to go home for cheerleading tryouts, an environment that promoted backbiting and peer-pressure-induced smoking.

MONICA

Regrets not studying the map a little more closely before she moved to Sacramento. Discovered too late that Sacramento is not really the San Francisco Bay Area at all, but a dry, flat town in the middle of nowhere.

LIAN

Regrets her Linda Evangelista short haircut in the early '90s, which left her looking nothing like Linda Evangelista. Took almost a full decade to get back to her classic pageboy.

People, Not Props

by Lian

The other night my husband, my children, and I had a perfect night. It wasn't orchestrated or expensive. It was just a Saturday night at home, free from the pressures of work or school the next day. My husband and the boys were wrestling on the bedroom carpet and I was the kiss monster. Simple, perfect fun. As I put my son to bed, he declared, "This was the best night."

Then the next evening, he tried to re-create it all. "Come upstairs and wrestle, Daddy. Mommy, you be the kiss monster!" But it wasn't the same. There were dishes to be done and homework to finish. Laundry needed to be folded. We tried to duplicate the fun for my son's sake, but it didn't work. There are moments in life so perfect that you would pay to have them back. If my son had had a million dollars, he would have handed them over. I could see that in his disappointment. But even a million dollars can't buy back a moment.

I learned that when I was little. I spent a lot of my childhood watching the comings and goings of my older brothers and sisters. Back from school, off to work. Moving here, moving there. Home for Thanksgiving, but not for Christmas. A new job or work over the holidays meant that I could go months, even years, without seeing a certain brother or sister. I came to understand that their presence was something special. Their comings and goings made for an endless number of combinations of people and possibilities, but a finite number of moments. This group of people at this dinner table, playing thumper and eating Hamburger Helper was not going to happen again for a very long time, if ever. This is the moment. Enjoy it.

There are many factors that go into making something memorable. The occasion, the setting, the food, the music—all the checklist items that can be found in some event planner's notebook. My mother made a big effort to ensure that those sorts of tangible items were in place, maximizing the possibility of any occasion. Even a simple picnic dinner at the beach came with a tablecloth, candles, and garden flowers. I have inherited her ability to stage things, to produce events with a little flare. But the moments that I would re-create from my past are not the ones with the great centerpieces. They are the ones that happened because the right people were in the right place at the right time. Those people were my parents and sisters and brothers, first. Then cousins and aunts and uncles. As I grew older, friends from school or work or other associations filled in. Now, I can add my husband and children to the roster. Maybe I can orchestrate the right place and the right time, but the people are always a variable. I've learned that people, not props, create the best memories.

I've learned, too, that those people come and go.

When I was little, it was easy to put myself in the way of the people I wanted to be with. I would rush home from school, skipping after-school activities, to wait for my brothers and sisters to straggle in for holidays or for big events like a wedding or a graduation. I probably spent weeks of my life at the Amtrak station in Bridgeport, waiting for the train, hours late from Washington or Boston or Providence, that would bring my siblings home. I liked to be in the kitchen when Liz would burst through the door on a Friday night, home for the weekend from her big-city life in Manhattan. I'd run to the driveway to welcome Julie and Trem after an eight-hour drive from Pennsylvania. I'd even be glad to see Brendan, my nemesis, arrive home safely after hitching a ride from college in Worcester. I had a lot going on when my brothers and sisters weren't around. But when they were, I knew life would be a little more special. I knew, also, that they wouldn't be there for long.

As I've made my way in the world, I've gathered friends at many stops. I have tried to keep in touch, as the yearbook saying goes, but I haven't always. People drift in and out of your life. I think that's OK. Everybody needs a context. Some relationships have a definite beginning and end. Some friends don't carry over from one part of life to another, but that doesn't mean that their presence was any less magical, just fleeting. The moments endure and that's what matters. Watching a meteor shower and listening to *Some Girls* with Liz Csapo and Alyssa Burger, days before we all departed for college. Going to midnight mass at the Vatican on Christmas Eve with roommates Ann Bortz and Tricia Duffy, using tickets we had scored from the Swiss Guard. Attending a staff meeting with Michael Doherty and Bob McIrvin, two of the funniest men I have ever met, featuring laughter so gut-wrenching that my muscles hurt the next day. The right people in the right place at the right time.

Now, I have to make a dedicated effort to be with my people. My family is spread around the world. My friends from high school and college are scattered, too. I have to orchestrate putting myself in the right place and time. I show up for weddings, reunions, and the like because I think those things matter. Nothing is ever perfect, and sometimes the effort doesn't pay off. But usually it does. And, every day, I try to remind myself to look around for something that I can hold on to—to take a breath and enjoy and remember. This group of people, in this place, at this time.

I never get blue when something is over. Things have to end, people have to go. A moment happens. That's just the way it is.

Unlike my son, I don't want to re-create perfect days. I am not one for prolonged good-byes or false promises of "Same time next year."

"Good-bye," I say. "Thank you. It's been great."

And it has. And it is.

Who Do I Want to Be When I Grow Up?

by Liz

I think people get the direction thing all wrong. I have wrestled with this during my adult life, questioning when exactly it is that I will figure out what I want to be when I grow up. Finally I have realized that's not the right question. The right question is, *who* do I want to be when I grow up?

If I am lucky and work hard, I can be many things. I may have run out of time to live out my rock-star fantasy, and a gold medal in anything seems out of reach, but I do still have time to start a new business or go back to school. I have loved something about every job I've ever had, from telephone operator to corporate executive, so I feel no need to pick one thing and stick with it.

No, the key thing to think about is who I want to be when I grow up. It's not a choice of firefighter vs. figure skater. It is learning how to be a friend and a family member, a contributor to my community and an explorer of the world. Doing all those things is hard, and that's where a keen sense of direction comes into play—it helps you figure out the hard stuff.

Most of my life I have been surrounded by friends and family members who have had their own very highly developed senses of self, connection, humor, and adventure. I have learned much about my own from them. If the fifth sense is a sense of direction, then lately I have pointed myself in the direction of appreciating those fine things in the people around me and trying to be more like them in little ways.

Patience is a virtue, or so our mother always said. I could use a little more of it. I think of the patience my mother must have summoned while dressing eight kids in eight snowsuits and eight pairs of boots and mittens so we could go outside in Connecticut in January, and I know who I want to be. I want to be my mother and have her patience. I watch Lian with her two boys now and am reminded of the virtue of not being in such a hurry all the time. They live in Southern California, so there are no snowsuits involved, but she does stop at any firehouse they pass on their way anywhere so her sons can collect the special Engine Company Whatever stickers the firefighters have for members of the community. Could they get to the store and back more quickly if they didn't stop? Sure, but why?

I'd like to be more openhearted. When I watch my sister Sheila with the students at her elementary school or with her teenage daughter, Ruthie, or with the community of friends she has built around her home in Greenwich Village, I see how they are drawn to her gentle and trusting nature. I want to be Sheila. I can see the same in Monica, who is a very conscientious and caring nurse because she has such empathy for both her patients and their families. She is a good friend to her Satellite Sisters for the same reason. I want to be Monica.

This openheartedness I see in my sisters was much in evidence in the adults around us when we were young. The very definition of our family was open. Of course, there were ten of us—two parents, three boys, five girls—but that was just the beginning. My mother's identical twin sister, Eleanor, had nine children and was widowed at thirty-eight. Every holiday I can remember included all of the Morningstars. It was like having a fantastic second set of brothers and sisters. Sometimes it was even better, because I never had the fights with my cousin Beth that I had with my sister Sheila. The time was too special.

On Christmas, we'd open one set of presents at our house, go to mass, then drive to New York for a second Christmas at the Morningstars, complete with more presents, more food, and some kind of Christmas show we would develop upstairs in the bedroom that cousins Beth, Mary, and Martha shared. Thinking back to the openheartedness that my father, my mother, and my aunt Eleanor showed at those moments, I am struck by how little we were aware of how hard or sad it must have been for them that my uncle was not there. For us, it was just more family and more fun. I want to be my father. I want to be my Aunt Eleanor.

Christmas vacations also usually included a few special outings into New York City. My mother and aunt would take the girls to see *The Nutcracker*, all of us in our matching bunny-fur hats we'd gotten under the tree. My father would organize the boys in both families for a Rangers hockey game. Or there would be pairs of outings—the big kids going to a play one day and the little kids going to a museum in a second shift. When we went out as a combined group of one father, identical-twin mothers, and seventeen children, we'd get odd stares and strange questions. Were we a day camp? A religion? A traveling circus? If it appeared somewhat cult-like, I guess it was.

The logistics of those outings were mind-boggling. We rarely ate in restaurants, tables for twenty not being easy to come by. A hot dog in our seat was great and there'd always be snacks in the station wagon. With cabs being limited to four passengers, we would take the subway around New York. One adult plus three kids times three cabs still would have meant five kids left stranded on the sidewalk.

When the Dolans and Morningstars would drive to Massachusetts to see our other cousins, we'd pack two station wagons full and head up I-95. Those were the days before child safety seats, so four kids in the back with another three in the way back and one in the little space in between was perfectly acceptable. I can still recall what a kick those of us in the trailing car would get at the New Haven tollbooth when the toll collector would say that the car ahead of us with my father at the wheel had already paid for our toll. Why was this so cool? I don't know, but it was.

Our family clustered, not in pairs or trios, but in big clumps. In Sudbury, Massachusetts, our two aunts lived directly across the street from each other, with five Lockerys and our grandfather on one side of Moore Road and seven Kirshners on the other. When we pulled up, interchangeable Dolans and Morningstars would pour out of the station wagons, disappearing randomly into either house with cousins of matching ages. All of my aunts and uncles shared the same openheartedness I could see in my parents and admire in others to this day. Only now that I am older can I fully appreciate the commitment they made to loving all of us, not just their own. I want to be Aunt Patty, Uncle Harry, Aunt Virginia, and Uncle Dick.

Patient. Openhearted. I'd also like to be more fun. To my mind, there are two kinds of fun. The spontaneous dancing-in-the-Trevi-fountain-with-a-lover kind of fun that we all saw in the movies. I could definitely use more of that. Then there is planned fun. We had loads of that as kids. Putting us to bed at night (no fun) required great bedtime stories from my father (much fun). Having the measles at the same time as Sheila meant being quarantined in our room for a week (no fun) but giving us the brand-new *Meet the Beatles* album to entertain us in there (much fun).

The kind of fun that you have with eight kids or seventeen cousins or thirty-five family members requires a plan. Otherwise, it's just not fun. You don't need to plot the actual fun (i.e., Noon–12:30 P.M.: Hilarity ensues). You do need to plan other stuff so the conditions for fun exist (i.e., Noon–12:30 P.M.: Feed the kids so they don't get tired and cranky and start throwing rocks at each other). The grown-ups in our lives were good at creating the environment for fun.

Enough has been written here about the complex logistics of an average Thanksgiving dinner at our house, but the real moments of fun were the football game (which could happen because the table had already been set), the post-dinner slide show (made possible because my cousin Tom always brought the projector and the screen), and the small moments after dinner when clusters of cousins could break away from the big group. The teen boys would be upstairs listening to music, the younger girls would be downstairs teaching each other dance steps, and the little kids would be in the TV room playing with the toys Uncle Dick brought. These were the most memorable moments, and they were made possible because our parents, aunts, and uncles had made the effort to get us together in the first place.

Not long ago, Tour de France winner and cancer survivor Lance Armstrong wrote a memoir titled *It's Not About the Bike*. When I think of our family holidays, I think the story should be titled *It's Not About the Turkey*.

Be patient. Be openhearted. Make room for fun. What other direction would I set for myself? Be brave. My father is brave, taking chances as an inventor in midlife and as a writer later in life. My mother is brave. Who else would take a gang of little kids to a ticker-tape parade for the Gemini astronauts so we didn't miss a moment in history? My aunt Eleanor is brave, creating a household of joy and love not only for her nine children but for all her nieces and nephews as well. I watched my older cousins build their own glider in their yard and my aunt Virginia stage a production of *Our Town* in the local cemetery. All brave. I have also seen members of my family break away to do the things they needed to do for themselves: live in a monastery, quit drinking, rediscover their creative souls, carry on after loss. Braver acts still.

My sister Julie has shown serial bravery, moving to new cities and new countries, plunging into new jobs, and getting her sons settled into new schools each time. I want to be Julie. She's also got the patience, openheartedness, and sense of fun to make the most of it all.

One final attribute I admire in those around me is conviction. My parents, aunts, and uncles all believe that their lives have some larger meaning and responsibility. Some of this is religious conviction. Some of it is social responsibility. Some of it is simply trying to do a good job at work every day or at home every night. We grew up in an era of great social change, living through everything from Vatican II to Vietnam. We got the local version of these massive changes. One day, the priest turned the altar around and spoke to us in English instead of Latin. Another day we got out of seventh grade early so we could participate in the Moratorium march through town. We watched the women around us taking jobs for the first time and saw the men around us being laid off from theirs. During the summer of 1973 when I was fifteen, I had a great summer job. I worked mornings and evenings, but had the middle of the day off. I spent every moment watching the Watergate hearings. The heroes and villains of my adolescence were not animated characters or cinematic fictions. They were Sam Ervin and G. Gordon Liddy. Ideas were examined and tested at our dinner table and, while it wasn't always pretty, it certainly made us understand that it was important to have a point of view about what you believed, and then it was important to act on that point of view.

A sense of direction is not an answer to a specific question. Should I move? Should I marry? Should I make cranberry relish for Thanksgiving dinner? There's no right answer. There is only a series of questions to ask and choices to make that turn us into who we are going to be when we grow up.

Who do I want to be when I grow up? I want to be elements of the many people I have grown up around—my parents, my brothers and sisters, my aunts, uncles, and friends. I want to be patient, openhearted, and fun. I also want to be brave and live according to my convictions. That's where I am headed in this part of my life. It's enough direction for now.

To-Do Lists

We're not done yet. The book is, but we're not. So we offer our UnCommon Senses To-Do Lists, a Satellite Sister tradition.

Lian Dolan

SENSE OF CONNECTION
Send holiday letters every year, even to people who profess not to like holiday letters.

SENSE OF SELF
Embrace the notion of pacing myself. As one radio listener wrote in, "You *can* do it all. Just not all at the same time."

SENSE OF HUMOR

Be a good audience for my sons. Laugh at their knock-knock jokes, give them time at the dinner table to tell their stories, and teach them the value of a good punch line, like, "Orange you glad I didn't say banana?"

SENSE OF ADVENTURE

Pack up the kids, my husband, the dog, and the Rand McNally road atlas and get lost in America for one year.

SENSE OF DIRECTION

Find my way back home.

Monica Dolan

SENSE OF CONNECTION

Call my Satellite Sisters more than once a year.

SENSE OF SELF

Speak up.

SENSE OF HUMOR

Learn to laugh when the only way from Portland to a business meeting in Philadelphia is a red-eye that goes through Dallas.

SENSE OF ADVENTURE

Put air in my bicycle tires.

SENSE OF DIRECTION

Cherish the times when I have no direction, like when I'm on the other end of the leash.

Sheila Dolan

SENSE OF CONNECTION

Get another phone line in my apartment so I can write the next book while talking on the phone to my friends everywhere.

SENSE OF SELF

Wipe out all credit card debt by Thanksgiving 2002 and give thanks.

SENSE OF HUMOR

Research the whole stand-up scene in New York and see if I can turn any of this material into a solo act.

SENSE OF ADVENTURE

Take my first adult vacation for which I make all the necessary arrangements by myself, pay for the entire trip by myself, and get to and from the airport by myself.

SENSE OF DIRECTION

Stay on this path because it seems to be working out just fine, thank you.

Liz Dolan

SENSE OF CONNECTION

Find pleasure in the fact that I can now measure many of my friendships in decades. This is the upside of middle age.

SENSE OF SELF

Decide once and for all if it is a bad thing that I have had pretty much the same hairstyle since I was seven except for that long-hair-parted-in-the-middle phase in high school and that curly perm in my early twenties. Am I in a rut or have I just found my look?

SENSE OF HUMOR
Laugh out loud more.

SENSE OF ADVENTURE
Stay home. See what happens.

SENSE OF DIRECTION
Let other people decide for a change.

Julie Dolan

SENSE OF CONNECTION
Make it to my annual women's weekend this year, no matter what.

SENSE OF SELF
Nag less.

SENSE OF HUMOR
Remember the beginning, the middle, and the punch line of at least one good joke.

SENSE OF ADVENTURE
See the Taj Mahal.

SENSE OF DIRECTION
Pray more and see where that leads me.

Acknowledgments

We are five sisters in four cities on two continents. Between us we have two parents, three brothers, thirty-five cousins, five kids, six nieces and nephews, three current and former husbands, ten in-laws, twenty-nine current and former employers, seventeen former baby-sitters, several business partners, many coworkers at our day jobs and on Satellite Sisters radio and web production, lots of friends, hundreds of former elementary-school teachers, high-school advisers, drivers-ed instructors, and pizza delivery personnel, and hundreds of thousands of public radio listeners, all of whom shaped us and this book in some way. So if you don't see your name listed here, please don't take it personally. It was hard enough to get all five sisters to agree on what should go into the actual book.

So, with that disclaimer in place, we would like to present some individuals with special Sassie Awards. A Sassie is the highest honor the Academy of Satellite Sisters can bestow upon individuals, teams, or really great local coffee shops and newsstands that have contributed to our lives and to our book. Former boyfriends and/or cosmetic-counter salespeople who stopped us from buying that awful shade of lipstick may have been important to us in the past, but this is not their moment. Sassie winners, this is your moment.

The Super Sassie must, of course, go to our parents, James and Edna Dolan, and our brothers Jim, Dick, and Brendan Dolan, who have very gamely accepted the notion that if they want equal time, they will have to write their own books. Thank you for your love, support, and sense of humor. Our Satellite Sisters-in-law Mary McGuire, Susan Arnold, and Laura Leibesman, and brothers-in-law Trem Smith and Berick Treidler get special "Good Sport" Sassies because they have to put up with all of this no matter what.

The "Please Sign This Release" Sassie goes to all of our other friends, kindergarten playmates, former coworkers, and bank officers whose lives have intersected ours in important and trivial ways. Luckily, you were nice to us long before you ever knew we would write a book that mentioned you.

The "If It Wasn't So Dorky, We Would Call You the Wind Beneath Our Wings" Sassie goes to our partners, who took the original leap of faith on Satellite Sisters. Laura Walker of WNYC Radio has been our sassiest advocate from the start, supporting the birth of the idea even while on maternity leave herself. Laura shares this Sassie with Dean Cappello, Mitch Heskell, Betsy Gardella, and everyone at WNYC Radio; Virginia Breen, Maynard Orme, and everyone at Oregon Public Broadcasting; and Steve Salyer, Melinda Ward, and everyone at Public Radio International. This team rallied around Satellite Sisters when it was a notion on a single piece of paper and five voices on a single piece of tape.

The "Go to Your Rooms and Write" Sassie goes to Rosemary

St. Clair of Mudbath Productions. As boss and backbone, she is the sixth sister any group of five could want. Whenever we needed her to say "It will be fine," she did. Convincingly.

The "Big Sister" Sassie goes to our sisters who created the original spirit and sound of Satellite Sisters: Mary Beth Kirchner, who got us on our feet, and Marjorie Kalins, who got us on the air. They can each whisper direction in the sisters' ears any time. And Marge Ostroushko? You'll always be one of us.

"Sister of the World" Marjorie Kalins gets a Double Sassie for her invaluable contributions to creating the whole team and leading us to this book project. If not for Marjorie, Lian might still have that echo in her ears and Sheila would not have accomplished her lifelong dream of paying homage in writing to her favorite bell-bottoms.

The "Sense of Adventure" Sassie goes to all the patient and funny professionals who have helped invent the radio aspects of Satellite Sisters: Susan Sperling, Loretta Williams, Brad Klein, Marty Goldensohn, John Keefe, Jennifer Morrow, Czerina Patel, Megan Ryan, Sarah Lemanczyk, Rosha Forman, Sarah Cattan, Jessica Brock, Steve Nelson, Curtis Fox, Rob Weisberg, Dean Western, Steve Syarto, Leo DelAguila, Marcia Caldwell, John Frazee, David Switzer, Mikel Ellcessor, Emma Dunch, Brenda Williams, Carol Leister, Ken DuBois, Eleanor Harris, Dale Spear, Julia Mears, Sue Winking, and our friends at the BBC. The web team of Jean Railla, Ethan Lipton, Valentina Powers, Dana Barnes, Kerrigan Kessler, and Virginia Prescott at WNYC, plus Bob Kernen, Kristin Milotich, and Lisa Kinne at Women.com also get accolades. More thanks to the many public radio program directors who introduced us to their listeners, and to the public radio listeners who responded with so many of their own Satellite Sister stories. To all who jumped on the Satellite Sisters bandwagon early, your sense of adventure is appreciated.

Elyse Cheney, our literary agent at Sanford J. Greenburger Asso-

ciates, has been voted a special "Sense of Direction" Sassie for finding us in the first place and then for finding a wonderful publishing
home for us at Riverhead Books. She qualifies for Lifetime Charter Membership in the Satellite Sisterhood for her ability to laugh
through it all and remind us to do the same. She also nominated
herself, in that bossy way that agents have, for the "Sense of Cents"
Sassie, which makes sense to us.

The "Trust Your Tarot" Sassie goes to Susan Petersen Kennedy
and Julie Grau at Riverhead Books. They followed their instincts
throughout this whole project and we followed theirs. They are
both also charter members of the Satellite Sisterhood and have the
bathrobes to prove it. Others at Riverhead and Penguin Putnam,
including Phyllis Grann, Catharine Lynch, Marilyn Ducksworth,
and Mih-Ho Cha made us feel that we were in the right hands
right from the beginning.

Our editor, Julie Grau (Big Julie to us), gets a second shout-out
with a "Wow, Five Sisters, Five Really Different Personalities" Sassie. Working with five first-time authors on one book demands an
unusual level of talent, humor, and diplomacy. Lindsay Sagnette at
Riverhead provided more of same. They are both invited to manage any Dolan Thanksgiving planning session they wish. Sheila
would like to give Big Julie a separate Sally Field "You Really Like
Me" Sassie because . . . well, because Sheila always likes to do
things her own way.

Other business advisers Lisa Davis at Frankfurt Garbus, Julianne
Davis at Chernoff Vilhauer, Bert Wells at Covington & Burling, and
Donna Fazzari, Chris Coelen, Al Hassas, and everyone else at UTA
share the "Yours, Mine & Ours" Sassie for their good work with all
the sisters and all the business partners. And Valerie Taylor-Smith,
you didn't ask the obvious question three years ago when we asked
you to design a logo for us, so you get the "Who Is Going to See It
on the Radio?" Sassie.

A one-time-only "If Irving Thalberg Had a Sister It Would Be You" Humanitarian Award is voted by special subcommittee to Lian Dolan. Making the leap from baby sister to senior sister editor/writer called upon all of her wit, talent, organizational skills, and baby-sitting hours. Without Lian at the head of the book team, the other contributors might not have made the transition from sisters to coauthors.

Julie would like to award a "See What Happens When You Encourage Us" Sassie to her husband, Trem, for his suggestion that she and her sisters ought to think up something to do together and his unwavering support and love when they actually did. To her son Nick, who taught her everything she knows about radio engineering, she awards the "You Can Do It, Mom" Sassie. The "It's Better Than a Summer Job at McDonald's" Sassie goes to her son Will, who stepped in to help her with rewrites and to teach her three new functions of Microsoft Office. A "Deuce Is Coming" Sassie goes to the International Women's Tennis League of Bangkok for their enthusiasm and interest in the show and book, her life, and her backhand. And the "Say It Out Loud" Sassie goes to her Women's Weekend Group, friends at UCLA, Tulane, and GMAC, and others near and far who listened when she finally had the nerve to tell them about the radio show. Never mind the book. Finally, a "Taste of Home" Sassie goes to the baristas at the Bangkok Starbucks, Sukhumvit Soi 33. They make a nice beverage.

Liz would like to award the "Spill All for the Sisters" Sassie to her many friends who, against their better judgments, have been strong-armed into sharing their lives on the radio and who are nice enough not to mention that this whole Satellite Sisters experiment has not exactly resulted in her slowing down and getting a life. A "You Told Me So" Sassie is locked away in a special place for the family of Claire Grossman, because she believed that listening and being listened to give meaning and purpose to each of us, a fundamental Satellite Sister principle. Automatic charter memberships into the Satellite Sisterhood are voted for any Rumbledoll or founding fellow of the Allbright Institute. And a "Let's Fire Up Old Stormy" Sassie goes to the Satellite Sisters, male and female, in her life who remind her every day that friendship is worth the effort.

Sheila's "Shining Star" Sassie goes to her daughter, Ruth, because, even if she can't physically track her down, she knows Ruth is always there brightly lighting up her world. The "Keep Me Grounded and Going" Sassie goes to her soulmate Kenji who had no idea how this thing would take off when he bought Sheila her first home computer. The "Keep Coming Back" Sassie goes to her long-lost cousin Karl, who edited her first writing sample and told her to quit that @#*#? day job. A "Live Wire" Sassie goes to her switchboard operator Lisa and a big batch of "We Can Do It" Sassies go to Joan, Leslie, Devonne, Young Sarah, Laura, Lisa, Catherine, Amy, Janet, Mary, Lynnie, Sarah (aka Lisa), Red Hair Pat, Giselle, Nancy, Jennifer, Skinny Sarah, Little Sarah, Pat, Gaige, Savannah, Stacey, Dayna, Maria, Candace, Jean, Pat, Leda, and sweet Victoria somewhere in the U.K. And to her sisters, Julie, Liz, Monica, and Lian, Sheila awards the "This Is Even More Fun Than Playing Dress-Up" Sassie.

Monica breaks new ground by awarding the first ever Sassie to a nonhuman. The "Always by My Side and Usually in My Lap" Sassie goes to her puppy dog, Quin. Her "Forever Friend" Sassie goes to Anne Hardy, who is herself an expert in big-family dynamics. Monica's charter memberships in the Satellite Sisterhood are awarded to the many nurses she has worked alongside over the years, anyone who has ever worked a night shift anywhere in any kind of job, and the Benton Street crew.

Lian would like to award the "Don't Call Me, I'll Call You"

Sassie to her Satellite Sisters, near and far, who have called in with support and encouragement only to be told, "I can't talk now. I am writing a book." Thank you. She will call you soon. The "Please Don't Leave Me" Sassie goes to her gracious and good-tempered baby-sitter Lorena Ayala, who is the wife her husband thought he was getting. Her great in-laws Judy and Brookes Treidler win the "In a Pinch" Sassie for never failing to say yes and mean it. Her sons Colin and Brookes don't want a Sassie. They want a trip to Legoland for being troupers. They'll get it now. And, finally, her husband, Berick Treidler, wins a Sassie for "Best Performance as a Rock" during the writing of this book, and for his unconditional support of her wacky ideas when they were still just wacky ideas.

One last Sassie voted by all of the sisters goes to our cousins, aunts, and uncles, who are part of many of our favorite stories in this book and the best memories of our early years. This is the "Let's Do Thanksgiving" Sassie. Julie will bring the turkey satay. What do you think?

Well, that's it for this year's awards. Congratulations to all the winners. If you believe you deserve a personal thank you and have not seen one here, please call our toll-free number, (877) 913-1122. We have a prerecorded message of thanks that we hope will make you feel better. After the beep, please leave the correct spelling of your name and we will immediately begin to amass a more comprehensive and thoughtful list of acknowledgments for our next book, which will be titled *Satellite Sisters: Common Sense Should Have Told Us Not to Thank Specific People in the Acknowledgments Because Important People Always Get Left Out.*

Or, if you would prefer a printed thank you note from the sisters, please go to our website at Satellitesisters.com, click on the "Be a Satellite Sister" icon, fill in your name, hit print, and presto, you'll have one suitable for framing.

In the meantime, we can only encourage you to embrace one of the key messages of this book: You are not the center of the whole damn universe. We mean that in a nice way.

Julie Dolan, Liz Dolan, Sheila Dolan,
Monica Dolan, and Lian Dolan

SATELLITE SISTERS was born when the five Dolan sisters set out to create some work they could do together that celebrated the importance of sisterhood and friendship. Singing and dancing were out of the question, but talking seemed like something they could pull off, and so a radio show hit the air on April Fool's Day 2000.

Satellite Sisters' UnCommon Senses is the Dolan sisters' first book, but Lian has several unsold screenplays in her drawer and Sheila still has her high school poetry.

Among them, the Satellite Sisters have two parents, three brothers, two husbands, five children, four dogs, and no cats.